Omar al-Mukhtar

ENZO SANTARELLI—GIORGIO ROCHAT
ROMAIN RAINERO—LUIGI GOGLIA

OMAR AL-MUKHTAR
The Italian Reconquest of Libya

Translated by John Gilbert

DARF PUBLISHERS LTD

FIRST PUBLISHED 1986

ISBN 1 85077 095 6 HARD COVER

ISBN 1 85077 135 9 FLEXI COVER

Printed in Great Britain by A. Wheaton & Co. Ltd, Exeter

Contents

TRANSLATOR'S NOTE

sottomessi—prisoners
sottomesso—prisoner
ailet—families
alala—three cheers

Omar al-Mukhtar in chains outside Benghazi prison (12 September 1931)

Enzo Santarelli

The ideology of the Libyan 'reconquest'
(1922–1931)

1. In Italy, very little research, and that in no great depth, has gone into the question of Fascist colonial policy, even though it is as important as Fascist domestic policy on the mainland, and inextricably bound up with all the other activities of the dictatorship and the regime.

On the other hand, in order to judge the phenomenon of European Fascist movements in the 1920s and 1930s on a broader, more objective scale, a distinction has to be made between Fascism in Italy—the only country possessing a number of colonies and hence able to engage continuously in 'colonial' ventures—and Fascism in Germany. Generally speaking, the Italian model of Fascism set the pattern for southern Europe during the 1920s, whereas the National Socialist model gained the upper hand once and for all in the ensuing decade, following the crisis of 1929, and in the very heartland of Europe. The interruption caused by the economic crisis also influenced the development of Mussolini's colonial policy, and indeed the entire evolution, strategically and ideologically, of Fascist colonialism. In Libya, the 'reconquest' or 'pacification' of 1930–1 was followed by 'mass' colonization which, in contrast to preceding trends, now assumed an overtly Mediterranean, imperialistic guise, culminating in the aggression against Ethiopia as part of an even more ambitious political design.

In this context, the deportation and confinement in concentration camps of the Gebel peoples of Cyrenaica, were not haphazard occurrences but represented a political, strategic and ideological escalation of 'colonial' Fascism, which in the meantime had recruited many personnel from the pre-Fascist era as well as new volunteers versed in the organization and methods of the Partito Nazionale Fascista (PNF). Finally, the consequences of this operation, climaxed by a brutal and indiscriminate programme of

11

extermination which exposed the wholly triumphant, extremist face of Fascist colonial imperialism, were more terrible and far-reaching than any comparable repressive measures by other European governments, whether in North Africa, the Middle East or anywhere else[1]. For this reason, too, it will be instructive to look more closely at the 1922–31 period, and to focus our inquiry, particularly, on the line of continuity that increasingly clearly links domestic and colonial policies, as first manifested, around 1926–7, in Libya. Even a limited survey of the methods and aims of Fascism, as publicly proclaimed, will at least make it possible to assess the historical background to the qualitative leap forward which occurred in 1930–1, and which still remains an open question.

What one writer has described as 'the almost general abandonment of critical viewing of our colonial past'[2] has, especially in recent years, been underlined in various ways by other historians; even a recently published, self-critical survey of national historiography, carried out by Ruggiero Romano, rightly drew attention to this trend, attaching some significance to it[3]. As late as 1967, Luigi Federzoni, former minister of the Colonies in the 1920s, was writing that 'one of the finest achievements after the March on Rome' was the reconquest of 1922–31, and in this context proceeded to whitewash 'the impetus given to the Italian population of Libya by virtue of the simultaneous transference of large numbers of rural families'[4]; an apologist's viewpoint, understandably, but until then not questioned or, at best, only half-heartedly challenged by native writers on colonial history. There always has been, and still is, a much more ample body of research on Ethiopia, probably in large measure due to the national traumas of 1896 and 1935–6[5].

The subject, it seems to us, is in some way connected with the popular myth about the Italian 'character', which became current after the downfall of the Fascist regime, in contrast to the people with whom the Italians came in contact during the colonial and European wars, and particularly in comparison with the 'legendary image of the *italiano brava gente*'[6]. Broadly

---

[1] Enzo SANTARELLI, *Storia del movimento e del regime fascista*, Rome, 1967, Vol. I, where mention is made of the 'genocide' of the Cyrenaican people in relation to the 'colonial and Mediterranean resurgence' after 1926 (cap. VI, 'La costruzione del regime').

[2] Giorgio ROCHAT, *Preface* to Claudio G. Segrè, *L'Italia in Libia dall'età giolittiana a Gjeddafi*, Milan 1978, p. VII.

[3] Ruggiero ROMANO, *La storiografica italiana d'oggi*, Milan, 1978, pp. 90–102.

[4] Luigi FEDERZONI, *Italia di ieri per la storia di domani*, Milan, 1967, pp. 137–8 and 154–5.

[5] See Roberto BATTAGLIA, *La prima guerra d'Africa*, Turin, 1958, Angelo DEL BOCA, *La guerra d'Abissinia 1935–1941*, Milan, 1965, and the same author's *Gli italiani in Africa orientale*, Vols. I and II, Bari, 1976 and 1979.

[6] Cf. the review by Luigi GOGLIA of the afore-mentioned work by Segrè, in 'Storia contemporanea', a. VI, no. 2, June 1975, p. 365. After the war, a critical judgment of the Italian character, going beyond the colonial experience, was given by Fabio CUSIN, *L'Italiano, Realtà e illusioni*, Rome, 1945.

speaking, when bringing moral and historical judgments to bear on the origins, significance and nature of Fascism in Europe, a difference of emphasis tends to be placed on the moderate Italian form and the totalitarian form of Nazism. In our view, however, the former differed from the latter simply in being more backward in structure and capable of developing and gaining ascendancy in an area, and during a period, that was earmarked, in the main, by colonial ventures and repressive measures. Nevertheless, within such an orbit, these activities took on a 'total' character that was typical of Fascism; and these repressive exercises are indistinguishable from the savage anti-guerilla campaigns that were subsequently conducted in the Balkans. Further-more, this colonial programme was explicitly patterned on the model, in one form or another, of virtually all the most notable and classic examples of European Fascism, from the German to the Spanish, and even Quisling's Scandinavian version. As far as the Italian situation is concerned, these facts present serious problems in the specialized field of historiography, both in terms of interpretation and documentation.

One of these problems goes beyond the subjective and objective bounds of anti-Fascist resistance, as conventionally understood, and merges with the theme of anti-colonialism in popular Italian tradition, where, in confrontation with the ruling or dominant classes, internal economic and social motives have tended to prevail over the less widespread but nonetheless cogent political and cultural motives of international socialism[7]. We should also bear in mind the 'missionary' or 'crusading' spirit, Catholic in origin, which at the time of the Libyan war sustained Italian nationalism and colonialism, strongly influenced lower and middle class attitudes, and was orchestrated, then as later, by a part of the press[8]. Another question, perhaps the most topical, concerns the distinction that some have attempted to trace between the colonialism of the Liberal years and that of the Fascist era. This question, in its turn, tends to be approached in different ways even by historiographers of democratic leanings, their conclusions diverging on at least two fundamental points: (a) the contribution and methods of the colonial personnel of Liberal persuasion; (b) the points of difference, over a period of time, between pre-Fascist and Fascist colonial policies. It is evident, however, that both Marxist and middle-of-the-road historians are united, though with varying emphasis, in criticizing what Rochat has called 'national-patriotic colonial historiography'[9]. And because of this general consensus, a collaborative study of the Omar al-Mukhtar episode affords a stimulating opportunity for rethinking and reassessment.

[7] Romain RAINERO, L'anticolonialismo italiano da Assab ad Adua, 1869–1896, Milan, 1971.
[8] Luigi GANAPINI, Il nazionalismo cattolico, Bari, 1970, cap. IV.
[9] Giorgio ROCHAT, Il colonialismo italiano, Turin, 1973, p. 30.

2. It is generally agreed that the Libyan war against Turkey, the so-called Tripoli episode (1911–12), unified the Italian nation. Gioacchino Volpe has stressed the manner in which middle-class nationalistic fervour, both in and outside Italy, reached unprecedented levels. It would be more precise to say that the crisis caused by Giolitti's reformist policies, as well as the economic crisis of 1907, created a favourable climate for the resumption, on a lesser scale, of the imperialistic policy that had collapsed so dismally under Crispi. In 1910–11 three new factors had emerged. The Bank of Rome, which was established in Libya as well as in the Near East, needed outside help from the Italian government in order to consolidate and improve plans that had reached a critical juncture; a movement initiated by public opinion, eroding Liberal values, had led to the formation of the Nationalist Association; and the higher echelons of Italian nationalism were joining forces, especially through the influence of *L'Idea nazionale*, with the barons of heavy industry, who now formed an iron and steel trust. Recent historical writing on the Labour and Socialist movement has reflected not only the changing policies but also the uncertain attitudes within the Socialist camp[10], which found new momentum only in the aftermath of the Libyan war, culminating in the insurrectionary events of 'Red Week'. As the political axis of the nation shifted towards the right, the rising tide of colonialist feeling found expression in the opposite extremes of Nationalism and revolutionary Syndicalism. There is nothing new in all this, and the sole reason for dwelling on the point here is to focus attention on what can be seen as the most radical and most equivocal departure from democratic Italian anti-colonial traditions. What now emerged was a political and ideological alliance between capitalism, the middle classes and a marginal fringe of the working class, whose converging attitudes were summed up in the pronouncements of *Italia proletaria*, the indirect, literary precursor to Fascist colonial policy up to the Ethiopian war. This phenomenon of Italian colonial imperialism, described by Michels as 'poor man's imperialism', was discussed by Lenin, revived by Gramsci in his essay on the southern question in 1926, and has more recently been analyzed, both at home and abroad, by historians such as Miège and Webster, with differing conclusions[11].

We are not so much concerned here to attempt a theoretical definition of Italian colonial imperialism, its particular features and its social implications,

---

[10] Maurizio DEGL'INNOCENTI, *Il socialismo italiano e la guerra di Libia*, Rome, 1976. Prior to that, it is worth recalling, there had been a theoretical undermining of socialist anti-colonialism, with the famous interview of Antonio Labriola on *Tripoli, il socialismo e l'espansione coloniale* (1902).

[11] J. L. MIÈGE, *L'imperialismo coloniale italiano dal 1870 ai giorni nostri*, Milan, 1976, and Richard A. WEBSTER, *L'imperialismo industriale italiano 1908–1915. Studio sul prefascismo*, Turin, 1974, rather more concerned, however, with its penetration in the Balkans.

14

which vary with the passage of time, as to establish—or recognize—the leading role that came to be played increasingly from 1911 onwards by Nationalist intellectuals, so much so that the message, the attitudes and the ideology of Nationalism subsequently penetrated the core of the Fascist movement and regime. It was they who traced the continuity of thought and feeling—accelerated by the upheavals of the Great War—in the transition from Liberal to Fascist policies. After the war the beginnings appeared of a new phase in the development of that aspect of Italian colonialism which concentrated especially on Libya, its role in the Mediterranean, and its reconquest and exploitation. With the return of peace to Europe, whereby the colonial ambitions of Italy and its allies in the Entente were frustrated, the conditions arose (though not immediately) for relaunching the coalition between capitalism and the middle classes, and attempts were made, though with more difficulty than in 1911, to win over the support of the urban working classes. During this entire period a body of colonial literature and propaganda reflected very accurately the sense of a long and arduous process of transition. In 1927–8, by which time much of the work had already been achieved, there was talk of Italy's 'double delay' in Africa, firstly at the beginning of the modern era and secondly during the Congress of Berlin period; but there was a tendency to conceal the structural limitations of the government and of Italian capitalism, which were again demonstrated very clearly in 1918–19 when the whole colonial system and its relationships with mainland Europe underwent a far-reaching revolutionary crisis all over the world. Once again Nationalist intellectuals fanned the flames of a new form of imperialism, Fascist in inspiration, which endeavoured to explain away these historical and structural 'delays' by blaming them on the greed of rival imperial powers, the self-interested structure of the post-war international community, and the blunders of Liberal governments.

Italy had emerged from the war with a manifold awareness of its structural limitations: shortage of coal and iron for heavy industry and manufacturing, which led to the use of electrical power, especially in the transport field; a surplus of manpower, accentuated by the ban on overseas emigration; weaknesses in agriculture, which was incapable of satisfying the growing food demands; and the poor productivity of the colonial territories, which were not an integral part of the national trade scheme, and incomparably poorer and more expensive to support than their French and British counterparts. The more moderate and traditional element of Liberalism, considering the colonies in the context of general post-war problems, had been compelled to observe that public opinion had 'as a rule shown little interest' in colonial matters; it proposed, nevertheless, (a) 'to consolidate our rule wherever present-day circumstances have rendered it somewhat insecure'; (b) 'to extend our influence gradually over neighbouring peoples'; and (c) 'to bring improvements to the colonies, whose wretched conditions can cause us serious moral and material harm', so getting embroiled in the vicious circle of post-war colonialism, perpetuating the aforesaid contradictions. In practical terms, Senator Scialoja, president of the Royal Commission for the post-war period, put forward a plan for a 'large-scale programme of public works, harbours, railways, roads, water supplies, etc.'. He recognized (in accordance with traditional practice) that 'in Libya, particularly, the religious question is of fundamental importance', and warned that 'we shall not be able to get a just, sound settlement of our relations with the inhabitants of the colonies unless we first take account of their moral requirements'[12].

Soon afterwards Mussolini wrote in the *Popolo d'Italia*: 'As for Libya, it is obvious that we cannot withdraw the garrisons that are needed for our security'; this was early in 1919 and a short time later came the meeting at which the *fasci di combattimento* were formed[13]. It is worth pointing out that Mussolini, in his exchanges with Scialoja, emphasized the military facts, but it should also be noted that during those weeks the *Popolo d'Italia* committed itself to the support of the economic claims of heavy industry and capital outside the national frontiers, and especially in the Orient, using language designed to spur the imagination and stir up romantic images among the activist elements of the lower middle classes of the post-war era. The task of ministers of the colonies during the final Liberal phase, from 1918 to 1922, was to set in motion the reconquest of Libya and to stimulate broad discussion on the colonial theme. Gaspare Colosimo, a politician of southern origin and radical tendencies, who was responsible for the colonies from 1916 to 1919 in a secondary governmental position, was unquestionably influenced by Nationalist pronouncements which proudly compared the solidity—in terms both of territory and population—of Italian rule with that of other colonial empires. At the beginning of 1922 it fell to Giovanni Amendola, another, very different type of southern politician, subsequently the founder of the anti-Fascist National Democratic Union, to consolidate the reconquest of Tripolitania with the occupation, already under way, of Misurata. At this point the first Mussolini government came to power, and, most significantly, the colonial ministry was given to the Nationalist Luigi Federzoni, who held the post for a couple of years (from July 1924 to November 1926 he was replaced by the ex-Nationalist and Agrarian Lanza di Scalea) and resumed office for the whole of 1928. Federzoni was then replaced by Mussolini in person and, from September 1929 to January 1935, by the quadrumvir General Emilio De Bono.

[12] Vittorio SCIALOJA, *I problemi dello stato italiano dopa la guerra*, Bologna, 1918, pp. 296 and 299.

[13] Benito MUSSOLINI, *Il solito ricatto*, in 'Il Popolo d'Italia', 22 March 1919.

During the post-war years the emphasis, for various reasons, was placed on Libya: it was the country most immediately associated with the overall pattern of Italian ambitions in the Mediterranean sphere, a territory to be regained by political and/or military methods, and, finally, an area ripe for economic exploitation, springboard for a more vigorous and up-to-date colonial policy. The platform for the new Italian political programme in Libya, as well as in Tripolitania, was established and tested by Count Giuseppe Volpi in the course of his govenorship[14]. The report of his four years of administration (1921–5) may be regarded as a basic text both on Italian colonial ideology and strategy, in the transition phase from Liberalism to Fascism; it demonstrated the continuity between both movements and provided evidence of a fundamental choice, i.e. an agricultural form of colonization, carried out by capitalist methods, and entrusted to big city investors, supported by the state. This was the basis on which the second phase of the reconquest of the 'fourth shore', Cyrenaica, now proceeded. But here there was still a need to clear the ground, for by and large matters had been delayed for about a decade because of popular resistance to Italian rule. The operations, initially carried out between the 29th parallel and the Gulf of Sirte, during the period when Federzoni had gone back to the Colonial Ministry and following Mussolini's visit to Tripoli, assumed the character of a huge mopping-up process, the objective being to re-establish the links that had been broken between western and eastern Libya. In addition, this was to be a preliminary to the first offensive against Fezzan and then against Cyrenaica, as well as setting the seal on the stability of Italian rule in Tripolitania[15]. The second phase of the 'reconquest' would commence as soon as the dictatorial regime was consolidated in Italy, and after the government in Rome had obtained from Paris and London possession of Gadames and of Giarabub, at the two extremes of the colony.

3. Before turning to the political and social background to the colonial thrust which in 1926–7 was to lead to the repression of the Cyrenaican

[14] See the collected volume *La rinascita della Tripolitania. Memorie studi sui quattro anni di governo del conte Volpi di Misurata*, Milan, 1926, with a letter from Mussolini (23 April) which describes it as 'classic', a preface by Di Scalea and an introduction by Volpi himself. Soon afterwards, Volpi, already in Giolitti's time a member of the 'Venetian imperialist group' (R. A. WEBSTER), was hailed as 'the only politician of the old regime who had fully understood the greatness of Fascism': cf. Edoardo SAVINO, *La nazione operante*, Milan, 1928, p. 27.

[15] Odorico RALZ, *Le operazioni libiche sul 29° parallelo nord*, Rome, s.d. ('summary and critical essay', published by the Colonial Ministry). On the situation in the Benghazi area during the 'liberal' period, there is an interesting accusation in *Africano* ('La Cirenaica nell'ora presente') in 'La Tribuna coloniale', 24 July 1920: 'Civilizing does not mean killing . . . , it does not mean destroying . . . and these principles, in the past and up to a short time ago, have been completely upheld. The military occupation has been a constant process of demolition, etc, etc.' On the last pre-Fascist ministry, cf. Renzo DE FELICE, 'Amendola ministro delle colonie', in AA. VV., *Giovanni Amendola nel cinquantenario della morte, 1926–1976*, Rome, pp. 161–75.

resistance movement, it is worth saying something about the trends of literature and propaganda during this period of transition from Liberalism to Nationalism and Fascism, through which Italian colonial ideology was expressed. Libya was proving to be, or had become, the pupil in an ultra-nationalist political classroom run by a band of journalists who, as a result of the Great War and the advent of Fascism, had notably increased their power in the cities. It was brought about partly by gradual evolution and partly by reason of the actual state of affairs: Eritrea and Somalia were far away and decentralized, so that there were no other reliable power props in the Mediterranean. There were still broad gaps in ideology, and objectives did not yet appear to be completely settled. Journalists dealing with colonial matters could find no common ground, often voicing individual opinions, shying away from any serious discussion on the difficulties that faced the Fascist government, right through 1924, on the domestic front and then in getting to grips with economic and financial problems. Salvemini drew attention to the manner in which, from the very start, Fascist approaches to foreign policy swung from one objective to another[16], merely settling from time to time on a more immediately realizable programme. Something similar happened with regard to colonial expansionist aims, and this tendency had its origins both in the extravagant and vociferous claims of the Nationalists during the war and in the chaos created by the colonial agreements' or, to put it more bluntly, disagreements at the Peace Conference. From all this emerged a body of journalism which, in a belated bibliographical review of the Fascist era, was schematically subdivided into three different 'tendencies', according to the countries and regions being earmarked for subsequent expansion; (a) Eastern (centred upon Asia Minor and thus interested in the partition of the former Turkish empire); (b) Libyan (access to Chad, Giarubub and Sollum); and (c) Ethiopian (protectorate over Addis Ababa and considerable adjustments to the frontiers of Somalia and Eritrea)[17]. Actually there were many points of agreement among these currents of opinion, and the subject deserves investigating in more detail. Already during the war Liberals and Nationalists agreed that the best and most profitable plan would be to press the Turkish claims; these, in fact, were realized under the treaty of St Jean de Maurienne, only to be dissolved in the light of Mustafa Kemal's revolution. All that remained, therefore, was the Libyan solution, as the most readily attainable; and this now became the focus of all manner of claims from African and Mediterranean sources, variously articulated in the

[16] Gaetano SALVEMINI, *Mussolini diplomatico*, Bari, 1952, *passim*.
[17] Alberto GIACCARDI, *Sintesi della storiografia coloniale italiana fino al 1939*, in *Bibliografia del'Italia d'oltremare, Anno 1939*, Rome, 1940, p. XXX. A timely analysis (and challenge) of Italian aspirations, with particular regard to the Nationalist literature of 1914–18, can be found in the pamphlet by Ernest LÉMON, *La politique coloniale de l'Italie*, Paris, 1919, pp. 36–74.

vaguest, most ambitious terms. This 'modest' programme, entailing the reoccupation of the territory and the subjection of its people, was exploited, in much variety and colourful detail, for propaganda purposes by a select advance guard of mainland Italians or colonials, and by a horde of mediocre journalists and authors popular with the middle class, who took it upon themselves to remind the government and other influential persons of the existence of the 'fourth shore'.

In fact, it was widely recognized, though never openly admitted, that Italy hardly knew where to start in trying to assess properly the economic and geopolitical potentialities of Africa and, in particular, North Africa. In many respects, given that Mediterranean or Near Eastern objectives were originally predominant or still continued to receive priority in long-term planning, Libya and its peoples were relegated to the position of scapegoat or sounding-board for undirected, unfulfilled imperialist policies. At the beginning of this cycle a generally formulated programme of overseas policy was put out in 1917 by the Nationalist publishing house[18], concluding with statements in which the African, Middle Eastern and Mediterranean themes and trends were variously interlinked[19]. The Romanizing rhetoric, already evident in 1911 and even when the agreements with the Senusi order were being hailed, was now intensified[20], and from it stemmed less noble, crueller attitudes towards the Arab populations. In her essay of 1924 to the Italians of Tunisia, Margherita Sarfatti, who worked on *Gerarchia* and was Mussolini's confidante, smoothed over the ugly aspects[21]; and rousing phrases such as a 'colonial epic', conducted in an 'atmosphere of masculinity and war-like passion', were employed by Mario dei Gaslini in a book dealing with the 'memorable raid led by General Cantore south of Benghazi in the hunt for the Grand Senusi', the author receiving praise from Badoglio, who said that 'the memory of it should convince officers and soldiers that without a spirit of aggression the army is a machine with no fuel'[22].

[18] Giovanni Alessandro ROSSO, *I diritti d'Italia oltremare*, Rome, 1916.

[19] Paolo D'AGOSTINO ORSINI, *L'Italia nella politica africana*, Bologna, 1926; Ferdinando NOBILI ASSUERO, *Ombre e luci di due continenti*, Milan, 1926; Gaspare AMBROSINI, *L'Italia nel Mediterraneo*, Foligno, 1928.

[20] Aldo CHIERICI, *Italiani e arabi in Libia. Note di viaggio*, Rome, 1919, p. 63.

[21] Margherita SARFATTI, *Tunisiaca*, Milan-Rome, 1924, prefaced by *Latinus* (a short essay by Mussolini, perhaps not all his own work, omitted from *Opera omnia*). Sarfatti spoke of the beginning of a 'large, continuous flow of Italian-Tunisian people' into Libya, compensated by 'the introduction of new blood' from Italy into Tunisia (pp. 102–3).

[22] Mario DEI GASLINI, *Col generale Cantore alla caccia del Gran Senusso*, Milan, s.d. but 1926. The quotation by Badoglio is in catalogue no. 2 of the Libreria Nanni, Bologna, 1979, and is contained in a letter of 19 February 1927. The operations of the Cantore column took place in the summer of 1914.

Broadly speaking, all this literature was of minor importance, and highly subjective, ranging widely over North Africa from Tangier to Tunisia, Libya and Ethiopia, often touching on matters that were totally unrealistic, such as Trans-Sahara railways. The political thinking behind it was unsophisticated, frequently giving the appearance of being improvised, but every pronouncement was given out and received as if it were official ruling and, taken together with all the others, wholly practicable. Around 1926–7 a more serious note crept in, dealing with organizational and political matters. Prior to this, periodicals had been expressing new opinions with regard to the pre-war years. Francesco Coppola, in *Politica*, had discussed 'Italy's world expansion' without adopting the accents of petty colonialism, and connecting it with the problems of peace; but even his views tended to dwell too much on theory and were little concerned to propose concrete solutions and objectives for a nation such as Italy, so poorly equipped in terms of economic organization and initiatives. It is worth adding that the collected writings of Giuseppe Volpi, which appeared under the title *La rinascita della Tripolitania*, summed up the various ideological trends of post-war Italian colonialism; but in this instance emphasis was at least placed on the agricultural possibilities of the territory, while other side-issues (including the archaeological imperialism of one Roberto Paribeni) were simply mentioned in passing. Yet Nationalist ideology, as expressed by theorists such as Coppola or journalists like Pedrazzi, focusing attention on questions of leadership and strategy, needed the active cooperation of personnel brought up in the Liberal camp; since Fascism, even after the assumption of power, lacked autonomous agencies, because the best qualified organizations were for some time run along more or less traditional lines, and because direction of the government's colonial policy was almost continuously in the hands of ex-Nationalists, there was a tacit alliance between the two. During the administration of Lanza di Scalea, from July 1924 to November 1926, the colonial under-secretary was the young Roberto Cantalupo, who had gained some international experience at the Conference of Paris and who toed the Nationalist line.

From Milan, Arnaldo Mussolini, editor of the *Popolo d'Italia*, only concerned himself with the colonies, at least until 1926, in occasional marginal notes (his first important articles date from 1930)[23]. But the Duce's brother was very circumspect, voicing and repeating general principles, waiting for

[23] Arnaldo MUSSOLINI, *La lotta per la produzione*, Milan, 1937, which includes, among other items, 'Egoismi d'oltre mare', 'Attività e colonie' and 'I fittavoli del mondo', all from 1930. Shortly before this L'Associazione fascista dell'industria laniera had given attention to the products of Cyrenaica (Armando Maugini and others, *Le pecore e le lane del'Africa settentrionale*, Biella, 1929, the account of an inquiry conducted by the Italian society for studies into the raising of sheep in the colonies).

problems to take shape and counselling mediation and equilibrium; nevertheless it was he who aired, in plain and simple terms, many problems relating to the development and control of the nation's economy. Thus in the early years, the main impetus for a new colonial initiative came from what appeared to be secondary sectors and not from the higher echelons of the party, and were of an activist nature, emanating from an essentially political pressure group; yet these stimuli were tempered by tradition, combining with the impulse to prepare the ground, to take into account public opinion, thus creating, as it were, the prerequisites of a mass ideology, which chiefly distinguished the Fascist school from all other groups. The Fascists, in fact, appeared to be mainly interested not so much in colonialism for its own sake as in the spirit of imperialism; and in making this choice, and so not having to depend on formulating policy at any given moment, they succeeded in creating a feeling of continuity, of orientation and of integration, admittedly somewhat belated and vague, but grafted on to previous experience[24]. Mussolini himself, while regarding colonialism as a traditional and independent theme, always seemed to place it in a broader, frankly imperialist, perspective, as, for example, in the speech of October 1922 in Naples, on the eve of the March on Rome, when he revived the myth of the Mediterranean, of *Mare nostrum*. The vision of Africa exerted a powerful hold on the South, and Mussolini used it cleverly to play upon a succession of themes echoing the conflicting thoughts and impulses of both the middle and the lower classes, not least in rural areas; and in this he proved himself a master in persuading those of different viewpoints to agree. As he spoke in Naples about the Mediterranean, he was probably mindful of all the controversy that had surrounded the Tripoli episode, and which he had witnessed, in another capacity, during his youth.

4. Between the summer of 1924 and the end of 1926, following the Matteotti crisis and the speech of 3 January 1925, Leftist elements were finally driven out of the cities, putting an effective end to the working class movement and to all organized democratic opposition in the nation's public life. In respect of freedom of choice and method in the field of foreign policy and of colonial action itself, this entailed a change of structure, the consequences of which appeared both in the reconstitution of organs of government, in Rome and in the colonies, and the fascistization of bodies such as the Italian Colonial

---

[24] Franco CIARLANTINI, *Africa romana*, Milan, 1928, prefaced by Emilio De Bono. The author, who argued a confused 'spiritual imperialism', reprinted articles and letters on Tunisia and Tripolitania which had already appeared in 'Popolo d'Italia'. De Bono called it a 'patriotic, Fascist and salutory work', but dissented on one point ('Ciarlantini: let's concentrate for the time being on an *Africa Italiana*'). For a contribution of classical studies to the 'Roman' cult in Italian colonial imperialism, see, in general, Mariella CAGNETTA, *Antichisti e impero fascista*, Bari, 1979.

Institute[25]. This is not the place to go into a detailed examination of the connecting links between the progressive defeat of the working class Left and, more generally, Italian democracy in 1925–6, nor to outline and expand upon a Libyan policy ever more imbued with Fascist ideology and strategy, loyal to the ideals of Mussolini and to the directions indicated by nationalism, now officially sponsored by the regime. Whereas class dictatorship had been a reality in the country ever since the autumn of 1922, the repercussions of the end of the democratic system were only felt in the colonial field after a delay of several years, corresponding with the period of domestic crisis and a series of related events in the nearest overseas possession (notably the agricultural programme and confiscation of land initiated in Tripolitania). It was at this point that Mussolini made the journey, in April 1926, to Tripoli, from which can be dated the launching, in grandiose style, of Fascism's programme of colonial action in the Mediterranean and in Africa, beginning in North Africa itself. This was the first time a head of state had gone to inspect a colony, and it represented a turning point in Italian politics. The visit had been requested, some months previously, by the new governor De Bono; and the propaganda value of the exercise, in true Mussolini style, with leaders of the National Council of the PNF in attendance, was, for its time, considerable, in a sense outweighing in importance what was actually said in Tripoli. The prologue, on board the *Cavour* ('We are people of the Mediterranean and our destiny is on the sea'), might appear a 'commonplace event reminiscent of D'Annunzio', but it focused attention on the 'problem of outlets'[26], turning the occasion into a spectacular naval demonstration.

Just before this, the *Popolo d'Italia* had published some letters from an agricultural 'technician' who, on instructions received from Arnaldo, extended his mission into 1926. These reflected the theme of 'development of the new colonial consciousness', a rallying cry taken up by the daily press in a campaign based on the belief that 'the colonial idea must be expounded and circulated through its practical programme of economic development'[27]. The plan of battle had, during that same period, been laid down by Volpi. Now, however, orders from on high were to reconstruct the image of a popular

[25] At the end of 1927 the Council of the Institute was dissolved and its president, Count Pier Gaetano Venini, ex under-secretary of the colonies, was appointed officer for its reorganization. With contacts in Lombard capitalist circles, Venini had in 1922 organized the first colonial fair at Milan's Fiera campionaria. He came from a Liberal background and was accepted by the National Fascists. Under his aegis the Colonial Fascist Institute was established: in 1930 he took over the editorship of 'L'Oltremare'.

[26] Fabio CUSIN, *Antistoria d'Italia*, Turin, 1948, p. 434.

[27] Andrea CRAVINO, *Vedute economiche della Tripolitania* (*L'avvenire agricolo delle colonie*), Milan, 1927, with a preamble by Arnaldo Mussolini, pp. 3–12. Cravino then became the first chairman of the agricultural conference at Tripoli.

colonialism, continuing uninterruptedly, the tradition of 1911; it was a task that the Nationalists, with their elitist structures, had been incapable of achieving, but were now in a position to tackle with the assistance of the regime's own organizations and periodicals. Mussolini, in Tripoli, confined himself to a brief address to local dignitaries, some exhortations to his officials and the colonists, and the customary pronouncements to the men of the Fascist militia. There were, however, two significant short passages. The first affirmed that 'destiny drives us towards this land. No one can halt destiny and, above all, no one can break our indomitable will.' The second expressed his wish 'to concentrate the attention of Italians overseas'. Meanwhile, at the First Colonial Agricultural Conference, with which the visit ended, all the ingredients of Fascist colonialism made an appearance, from the usual theme of Italian and Roman 'destiny' to the emphasis on land hunger ('because we are prolific and intend to continue so'), from a plea to practice 'modern farming techniques, capable of virtually any miracle', to the exaltation of 'the Italian race, a singular prodigy of human history'[28]. On 21 April the first Italian Colonial Day was celebrated in the cities, with rallies and speeches; in the forefront were the ex-Nationalists, clearly representing an element of continuity and authority in this area of imperialistic propaganda[29].

Colonial Day was organized by Cantalupo and was also repeated the following year. In the autumn of 1927 it was Cantalupo who founded the review *L'Oltremare*, in which the Mediterranean and African themes were united, and which, during its first years, paid special attention to the problems and events in Libya. Four previous publications were merged under the new title: *La Rivista coloniale italiana*, founded by Roberto Forges Davanzati and later published as *La Tribuna coloniale; La Rivista delle Colonie e d'Oriente*, of Bologna; and Milan's *Esotica*, edited by a 'colonial man of letters', Mario dei Gaslini. The policy of *Oltremare*, which published the acts of the Colonial Institute and reflected the official trend of the government, was founded on the likely emergence of a 'colonial policy based on the economy' and was formulated under five headings, which provide a complete summary of the National-Fascist 'plan' at that time. The following is an extract:

(1) To exploit as rapidly and as thoroughly as possible the Colonies that we already possess, and the Dodecanese, so as to make them the real,

[28] The complete texts of these passages are in Benito MUSSOLINI, *Opera omnia*, Vol. XXII, Florence, 1957, pp. 112–18.

[29] Mario dei Gaslini established that year a 'Gruppo artisti imperialisti coloniali', whose statutes are in 'Esotica', a. II, no. 1, 15 January 1927. An important testimony to the euphoria of that period is a speech by the former minister of finance, given in Milan on 24 May 1927 ('the lack of raw materials, the increase in population, the poverty of the soil and the preconstituted positions are purely material facts which we cannot, on their own, regard as decisive'). Cf. Alberto DE STEFANI, 'L'Impero', in *Colpi di vaglio*, Milan, 1928, pp. 1–9.

independent base for our . . . economic expansion in surrounding seas and neighbouring lands;

(2) To give support to commerce, capital and labour . . . in other parts of Africa and in the Near East . . . with a view to expanding, unceasingly, Italian influence in the (Mediterranean) Basin; politically, the Red Sea is included in this system; . . . producers must collaborate in the transition from the *colonial* phase to the *African and Mediterranean* phases;

(3) To investigate and establish . . . the economic, technical, harbour, commercial, agricultural, banking and land-owning structures of our colonial possessions; this point is of maximum and decisive importance;

(4) To develop an Islamic policy throughout the Basin;

(5) To encourage the growth of a body of 'foreign' literature . . . ; a colonial policy which does not envisage a flourishing literature alongside its own will always remain incomplete[30].

The programme was thus outlined but there were various opinions as to how best to strike a satisfactory balance between development and population in the course of colonization. The most acceptable were the arguments expressed in a widely successful book, *L'Italia musulmana*, published by the *Voce* in 1928[31]. But in dealing with this subject, part political and part sociological, the author-editor, in fact, failed to touch upon some of the policy issues implicit in the unified programme outlined in the four previous paragraphs, and sponsored by minister Federzoni. The 'political committee' of the *Oltremare* included leading representatives of the financial and economic world, such as Giuseppe Bianchini, De Stefani, Guido Jung, Gino Olivetti, Alberto Pirelli, etc. However, the appeal to 'producers' for a direct contribution to the programme of Mediterranean and African expansion very soon proved an illusion; it was precisely in these areas, in coordinating policies and rationalizing the apparatus of propaganda set up in 1927, that the first setbacks occurred[32].

5. In *Italia musulmana*, Libya is envisaged as a bridge to the Levant ('without the backing of the easterners we cannot organize the infiltration of the East'), and thus there is no alteration in the Nationalist outlook, with Libya as the strategic objective. 'Colonial policy', 'military policy' and

[30] *Le idee per l'azione*, in 'L'Oltremare', a. 1, no. 1, November 1927, editorial initialled by Roberto Cantalupo.

[31] Roberto CANTALUPO, *L'Italia musulmana*, Rome, 1928; two editions followed in 1929 and 1932. 'This is the book,' wrote the author, 'of Italy's colonial policy in Africa, the Orient and the Mediterranean, from Vittorio Veneto and under Fascism. Thus it is a book of foreign policy . . . of what should be the foreign policy par excellence of our country.'

[32] However, in August 1928 the 'Esplorazione commerciale', established in 1877, was also absorbed in 'L'Oltremare'.

'foreign policy', as applied to Libya, are therefore seen in a tactical context, the call being 'to carry out to the finish the occupation and unification' of the colony so as to make it 'a broad, secure and autonomous Mediterranean base'[33]. The Italian hinterland ('a government that does not change, a parliament that does not provoke interference, a press that can be counted upon to collaborate and not stir up outside factions, a bureaucracy that is part and parcel of the state') must be secured, and the fascistization of departments dependent on the foreign ministry is presented as a further prerequisite, seeing that the Fascist government has 'greatly perfected the military instrument'[34]. Cantalupo warns, nevertheless, of the intrinsic difficulty and contradiction of a 'policy towards the Moslems'; if 'nine-tenths of our African subjects are Moslems', if long-term plans concern an Islam which professes to be 'impoverished and declining' yet endowed with a 'fine, immediate sensibility', which has been awakened and is on the increase in the post-war period, there is the danger of exacerbating relations with the Senusi in the religious field[35]. In these pages, which reflect and help to form and influence domestic public opinion, there is too much emphasis on the Islamic element and a notable under-estimation, verging on silence, of the nationalist and/or popular aspects of Arab resistance. This would explain the oscillations of Italian journalism within this period, which visibly retreats from the more positive and confident assertions of the Liberal period. The ideology, contradictions and all, which is reflected in *Italia musulmana*, is nevertheless firmly rooted in Italian culture and politics, and worth dwelling upon.

The most distinguished of Italian scholars on Islam and the Orient, Leone Caetani, declared himself opposed to the Tripoli operation back in 1911, before the war broke out; and Gaetano Salvemini had persisted for years in his opposition to the venture, conscious, among other things, of 'the harm that this wave of nationalism might cause Italy'[36]. In Liberal and Democratic circles of Italian society critical self-awareness had never been more acute, although the signs were evident throughout the country, and especially among the middle classes, of support for the views circulated by the majority of authors and journalists, summed up by the term 'primavera italica'[37]. The Libyan war led journalists of different persuasions to examine and discuss the

[33] Roberto CANTALUPO, *op. cit.*, 1929 ed., pp. 145, 154 and 157, particularly the chapter 'A programme for Libya'.

[34] Roberto CANTALUPO, *op. cit.*, pp. 154, 267, 271.

[35] Roberto CANTALUPO, *op. cit.*, pp. 242–5. Cantalupo devoted pp. 104–127 to 'The origins, development and decadence of Senusiya', 'Our relations with the Brotherhood', the politico-military situation in Cyrenaica and the 'limits of indigenous colonization'.

[36] Francesco MALGERI, *La guerra libica, 1911–1912*, Rome, 1970, p. 95.

[37] Emilio SCAGLIONE, *Primavera italica. La guerra italo-turca* (an anthology of the finest pages in the Libyan enterprise), Naples, 1913. This is a very detailed and little known work, interesting, in our opinion, for the light it throws on the whole range of colonial propaganda and ideology in those years.

links between Islam, the Senusi and Italy, from a viewpoint that was inevitably coloured by colonialist ideology. It was no accident that among the first to broach the subject was a colonial official, who concluded his brief informative survey on an optimistic note, recommending a government based on 'religious freedom'. However, he drew attention to the 'intimate relations between the Grand Senusi and the principal Arab religious leaders', and still regarded the Turkish caliphate as the main source of difficulty. Finally he proposed a 'firm and constant attitude', yet with an eye to 'conciliatory expedients' in the Liberal tradition[38].

Other advisers to the newly formed Colonial Ministry sounded a warning, in much sharper tones, being quick to point out—not predicting yet not excluding—certain alternatives that in due course came to be realized. One of them even emphasized that Italy alone, 'the third great Moslem power', had a choice 'between a policy of extermination or elimination of the indigenous populations who would, *ipso facto*, be replaced by our colonists' and a line of conduct based on respect for local traditions, defined, by reason of a predominantly religious content, as 'truly Islamic'. The choice of one or the other policy would depend exclusively on the 'greater or lesser resistance' of the people on the spot, while the Italians themselves were bound by the 'ethical conduct required of any civil colonizing power'[39]. Others wondered whether it would be possible 'to avoid a long guerilla war by some political means', but the answer ('a Moslem policy of broad horizons') was ambiguous, ranging from a drastic military solution ('fight guerillas with guerillas!', resorting 'if need be to hostages') to the suggestion of an unlikely 'divide and rule' programme[40]. From the very start, Italian colonial thinking on Libya, weak and irresolute yet with authoritarian overtones, fluctuated between these two equivocal extremes.

Broadly speaking, the views to emerge from this small but symptomatic journalistic output reflected both the inflexible attitudes of Italians at home and the scarce room for manoeuvre or for new initiatives on the part of the colonists. Liberal entreaties on religious grounds were almost always out-

[38] BOURBON DEL MONTE SANTA MARIA, *L'islamismo e la Confraternita dei Senussi*, Città di Castello, 1912. The book was published by the Corps Command of the General Staff, Colonial Office.

[39] Giuliano BONACCI, *Il califfato, l'Islam e la Libia*, Rome, 1913, pp. 23-4. The work bears the date of 1 October 1912. See also Aldobrandino MALVEZZI, *L'Italia e l'Islam in Libia*, Florence-Milan, 1913, the first book licensed for printing at the end of the previous year by the Italian Society for Libyan Studies, which, however, has a more balanced point of view.

[40] Guido SABETTA, *Politica di penetrazione in Africa. L'Islam e l'Italia*, Rome, 1913, pp. 72-3, 83-5, 90. It is worth observing that the investigation of local Arab powers was later entrusted very largely to the politico-military office of the Tripolitanian government. See the 'memoir' of Emilio CANEVARI, *Záuie ed Ichuan senussiti della Tripolitania*, Tripoli, May 1917, with a preamble by Major Mario Sani.

weighed by considerations of the 'fourth shore' in its role of demographic reservoir. The propagandists were, however, taken aback by the resistance offered by the local population, both for reasons of pride and national frustration, and it was then that they yielded to the call for a *coup de grâce* against the enemy. In general, this view was aired by the provincial press and it stemmed from earlier studies, classic examples being the much-quoted work of Depont and Coppolani, dating from 1897, or of Douveyrier, reprinted by the Colonial Ministry as late as 1918[41]. Opinions that urged caution and reflection carried little authority and were of brief duration; as nationalist thinking gradually gained the upper hand, so progressively illiberal and anti-democratic arguments began to prevail. A clearer and more realistic viewpoint was contained in the proposal put forward in 1917 for a 'protectorate', based on the rejection of the concept of demographic colonization and on a more balanced appraisal of the strength and economic-social reasons behind the Arab-Senusi movement for self-government. But the formula of the protectorate was explicitly derived from the British model adopted in Egypt in 1914 and developed in the context of 'splitting Islamic unity', which, from the European point of view, was seen as a priority; Italy, on the other hand, was only concerned with the benefits accruing from trade between the coast and the interior, and between North Africa and the Mediterranean basin[42].

From 1919–22 onwards, as a result of a new wave of nationalism and force of circumstances, the argument in favour of an agreement with Islam, the so-called 'Islamic sanction', lost ground and conviction, revealing a comparative absence of realism in continuing to place as much reliance on public opinion at home as on conditions in the colony itself. The options presented after the turning-point of 1926–7 were somewhat more radical, but, on the basis of prior tradition, the 1928–9 alternative—'either conditional surrender or slow and fatal attrition by armed force'[43]—was in a sense a false one, in that it persisted in giving more weight to Islamic pressures than to the

---

[41] It was a tradition that continued up to the time of the early work of Carlo GIGLIO, *La confraternita senussita dalle sue origini ad oggi*, Padua, 1932, with a preface by General Graziani: the defeated Arabs were frequently described as 'fanatics', 'traitors' and 'shammers'. Perhaps the highpoint in Italian Arabist policy was reached in the 'secret' collection of documents published by the Colonial Ministry, *Arabia*, Rome, 1919 (with an appendix on the question of the caliphate by A. C. Nallino). Giacomo Agnesa denounced the tight English 'ring of iron' around the Arabian peninsula; however, claim was made to the Farsan islands in the Red Sea. Despite the monumental size of the volume, the customary poverty of means and ideas, so typical of Italian eastern policy, is all too evident.

[42] Savino ACQUAVIVA, *Il problema libico e il senussismo*, Rome, 1917. The author was determined not to concede to Great Britain, as 'the power with Moslem colonies', any pre-eminence, remaining steadfast to the strategic objective of preventing 'any solidarity, even if only ideal, among the Moslem peoples' (*op. cit.*, p. 136).

[43] Roberto CANTALUPO, *op. cit.*, p. 271.

27

developing Arab resistance movement, relying upon distorted interpretations of events that had their epicentre elsewhere[44] and being guided in its preparations by a wholly self-deluding analysis of the political and military situation:

'In Cyrenaica we have not yet struck on a grand scale; and we must do this if we are to cut things short. Only then shall we be able gradually to satisfy the essential needs of all the powers in North Africa, namely to create a state of affairs that does not entail continual warfare. The mark of a great colonial power in Africa is not to lay down arms but to use them as little as possible'[45].

This was obviously a contradiction, and for the time being intransigence won the day as the decision was taken for a course of action—blatantly in contrast to the burgeoning reform policy of the British Commonwealth—based on the 'grand-scale strike'. This is what took place in 1930–1. Furthermore, there was now little if any mention of confraternity. On the one hand there was the Italian interest in colonizing the lands of Cyrenaica (apart from the experimental scheme in Tripolitania), and on the other the resolve not to permit the native populations of the Gebel and the desert to leave; hence it was decided to crush them. This was the commencement of what might be called the culminating phase of the 'second wave' of colonialism[46]. The Nationalists now embarked on their proclaimed role, exacerbating by every means the conflict between Italians and Arabs in a Libya regarded as a zone simply to be subjected and fortified by the 'dominant power'[47].

6. When General Graziani was transferred to the command of operations in Cyrenaica, the battle, from the Italian point of view, was largely won. Civil and military representatives from the homeland and the colony had gradually established themselves in different positions, united in their determination to make a show of force and utilize their technical superiority in such a manner as to leave the enemy minimal room for manoeuvre. Even so, resistance and open rebellion continued throughout 1931. Graziani was undoubtedly the

[44] Italo ZINGARELLI, *Il risveglio dell'Islam*, Milan, 1928: the book appeared as the second volume of the 'Biblioteca di cultura politica', of the National Institute of Fascist Culture and was subtitled 'La Turchia senza Corano—Russi e inglesi in Oriente'.

[45] Roberto CANTALUPO, *op. cit.*, p. 122.

[46] Biagio Pace, in the parliamentary report on the colonial budget for 1932–3, furnished the relative facts on the cost of reconquering Sirte, Fezzan and Cyrenaica; a total of 199 million lire, of which 20 million was spent on the barbed wire along the Egyptian border and 13 million on the concentration camps. He then said that 'without these three measures—concentration camps, barbed wire and occupation of Cufra—the guerilla war might perhaps have gone on for another fifty years'. Cf. Alberto GIACCARDI, *Dieci anni di fascismo nelle colonie italiane*, Milan, 1934, pp. 34–5.

[47] Roberto CANTALUPO, *op. cit.*, p. 155.

most experienced but also the most implacable of all the commanders who had been trained in the colonies. Since 1921 his operations had all been of a repressive nature; he was therefore hailed as 'a man of action par excellence', though at the same time with some measure of reserve in more enlightened colonial circles[48]. Nevertheless, the government, the Colonial Ministry, Badoglio in his role of govenor of Libya, and Fascist opinion itself, pressurized by the colonial press, all bore a measure of responsibility in the development of a plan and operative mechanism that would very shortly lead to mass slaughter. The 'man of action par excellence' was, in practical terms, responsible for carrying out the genocide policy against the Arabs of Cyrenaica, and was to become its symbol. His rough, uncompromising nature is manifest in an autobiographical article of spring 1930, in which he declares himself the nation's man of colonial destiny:

'I was born on 11 August 1882 in the Valle dell'Aniene, of a Latin father and a Roman mother. . . . Right from childhood I embraced the royalist feelings that my father taught me . . . I never managed to understand the Socialist movement, which was spreading during those years. . . . I have never been a freemason. . . . I believe I was a Fascist from birth. So it seems to me when I look back on my life. . . . I scorn any type of base action and all those that may have been attributed to me. . . . Sentimental and romantic by birth, I have managed not to become sceptical or cynical, but to make myself an absolute realist. . . . After two years of garrison life, Africa attracted and enthralled me. I rid myself of every weakness and took on the marks of character'[49].

Graziani's state of social frustration and 'colonial passion'—dating from his voluntary service in Eritrea from 1907 to 1912—was closely related to Fascism in the post-war years:

'In 1919, in Macedonia. . . . In 1920, fighting Bolshevism in Parma. . . . At the end of 1920, at my own request, exiled to the East and travelling in the Balkans, in Turkey, in Asia Minor and in the Caucasus at the time of the Bolshevik invasion—which ruined the economic and commercial activities that I had already so splendidly begun. I returned home in the summer of 1921. I was offered the post in Tripolitania that I had been asking for since 1918 . . . and I reached Tripoli in September'[50].

It was to be Graziani himself who would speak of disarming the people, of 'concentrating' them, of confiscating their goods and of adopting the policy

---

[48] *Graziani in Cirenaica*, in 'L'Oltremare', a. IV, no. 4, April 1930; see also the article *La pulizia del Gebel cirenaico*, ibid., a. IV, no. 12, December 1930.

[49] Rodolfo GRAZIANI, *L'autobiografia di un soldato d'Africa*, in 'L'Oltremare', a. IV, no. 4, April 1930.

[50] Rodolfo GRAZIANI, *op. cit., loc. sit.*

that led, in 1931, to the occupation of Cufra, to the capture and execution of Omar al-Mukhtar, and to the 'pacification' of the colony entrusted to him. But he was not the only one[51]. *Cirenaica pacificata*, with its wide circulation, remains the most explicit public document of the 'Reconquest of Libya in which Fascist ideology is most fully reflected'[52]. Reading the reports of the Italian general, it is not difficult to regard the personality of the rebel leader with 'a very complicated feeling in which hatred mingles with admiration, and contempt for the "Bedouin" with envy for the martyr venerated throughout the Islamic world'[53]. Of Omar al-Mukhtar, for whose death he was the most directly responsible, he leaves a portrait drawn by the executioner himself: 'He was endowed with a ready, lively intelligence; he was well instructed in religious matters and he revealed a nature that was energetic, impetuous, unselfish and intransigent. He remained very religious and poor, in spite of being one of the most important of the Senusi people.' 'He was always hostile to us, and had it not been for his peace-making attempt, which he himself betrayed with a stupid act of retaliation, he would today certainly have appeared a far more respectable figure, and perhaps would have saved his own life'[54]. This, however, is an ungenerous, self-justifying judgment and so distorts the known facts. The first passage seems to be lifted from some police record file, and the second echoes the sentences of the special tribunals, until now not investigated, which in 1930 decreed summary punishments for colonial subjects, for the most part humble farmers and shepherds, found guilty of supporting Arab resistance[55].

The most blatant and extremist Fascist propaganda of that time praised Graziani's avenging 'Romanism'. Paolo Orano, the former Syndicalist revolutionary who had written *Cristo e Quirino*, and would shortly help to solve the Jewish question in Italy, had something to say about it[56]. Mussolini spoke

[51] Guglielmo NASI-Enrico DE AGOSTINI, *Ossatura geografica della Cirenaica. La guerriglia e l'impiego delle truppe in Cirenaica*, Benghazi, 1931.

[52] Rodolfo GRAZIANI, *Cirenaica pacificata*, Milan, 1932. In the next volume, *Pace romana in Libia*, Milan, 1937, the chapter 'The agony of the rebellion' was drastically reduced and the pages devoted to the 'campaign of the press and the pan-Islamic committees' were eliminated.

[53] Arminio SAVIOLI, *Storia di un eroe arabo e di italici 'cacciatori'*, in 'L'Unità', 5 August 1979.

[54] Rodolfo GRAZIANI, *Cirenaica pacificata*, cit., pp. 263, 265. For Graziani, Omar was 'the heart and mind of the Cyrenaican rebellion' (p. 235), a 'perfect barbarian chief' (p. 263), a 'bigot' (p. 271) and 'merely a brigand' (p. 273).

[55] Adriano DAL PONT, Alfonso LEONETTI, Pasquale MAIELLO, Lino ZOCCHI, *Aula IV*, Rome, 1961, pp. 152-3, in which mention is made of trials for armed uprisings, for belonging to rebel bands, for desertion, for stealing arms, for assisting rebels, etc. and of a particular inquiry on the special colonial tribunal.

[56] Paolo ORANO, *Graziani generale scipionico*, Rome, 1936.

of 'Cyrenaica, green with plants, red with blood'[57]: metaphors and mystic pronouncements that underlined the weight of pressure brought to bear from on high upon Italian public opinion. Badoglio, for his part, after the execution of 16 September, addressed the troops and stressed the need 'not to relax our strength'. 'Continue to strike. *And go on striking hard until there is not a single rebel on his feet. . . .* In short, the rebellion is to be completely subdued'[58]. In Italy, anti-Fascists, workers and even simple soldiers had very few opportunities to express their disagreement, although they were undoubtedly in the great minority[59]. *Gerarchia*, in answer to accusations that had appeared abroad in Arab and western papers, maintained that the 'Kabyle encampments in the Gebel-el-Akhdar had been formed solely for the purpose of preventing dangerous contacts between the natives and the now-vanished Omar al-Mukhtar, who had become a tyrant'[60]. The regime's principal organs of communication, on the other hand, had not concealed the harshness of the operations 'against rebel manoeuvres'. They had, nevertheless, belittled and disguised, with extreme subtlety, the true facts and the methods whereby an entire section of the population had been, or was in process of being, destroyed; the curtain of silence and the evasions, typical of a post-colonial regime, relating to this question, were to continue into the early post-war years and even beyond[61]. With the 'biblical transmigration' of 1930, the way lay open to a colonizing programme which was to bring the military and political solutions into closer accord and to combine economic development with repopulation endeavours, particularly as mainland Italy was then hit by unemployment. The destruction of the Arabs also caused an immense ecological upheaval, as traditional animal breeding activities were disrupted.

[57] See the preface to Attilio TERUZZI, *Cirenaica verde*, Milan, 1931 (Mussolini's contribution dates from December 1930).
[58] The text of the proclamation was given in Paolo MALTESE, *La terra promessa*, Milan, 1968, p. 366. The italics are Badoglio's.
[59] The article by Luigi GALLO (Luigi LONGO), *Due anni di guerra coloniale fascista*, in 'Lo Stato operaio', a. III, no. 8, November 1929, was followed by other works; under the pseudonym of Etienne Gamalier, Leda RAFANELLI published *L'oasi. Romanzo arabo*, Milan, 1929, which serves as popular anti-colonialist reading; Ernesto MELZI, *Volontario in Cirenaica*, Milan, 1971, contains the private correspondence of a twenty-year-old recruit, valuable for conveying the contrasting feelings of an ordinary soldier and as an indirect testimony of the repression.
[60] *Cronache di politica coloniale*, edited by Francesco Geraci in 'Gerarchia', a. XI, no. 11, November 1931.
[61] Two books published in the same year were E. E. EVANS-PRITCHARD, *The Sanusi of Cyrenaica*, Oxford, 1949, which documented and denounced the operations of 'war' and the destruction of 1923–32 (pp. 157–90), and Corrado ZOLI, *Espansione coloniale italiana, 1922-1937*, Rome, 1949, which was a Neo-Fascist publishing house's justification of the former regime, ignoring or even disguising the cost to the Arabs of the final phase of the Italian reconquest (pp. 181–91).

On this point, too, there was silence, in spite of the potential interest shown some time previously by wool producers in the north of the colony.

The violent upheavals in Cyrenaica were inevitably linked, in Italian colonial circles, with the social question of repopulation. Journalists such as Dario Lischi and former 'rural' Syndicalists like Luigi Razza now campaigned loudly for the 'agricultural colonization' of a Cyrenaica finally at Italian disposal, and declared that the 'box of sand', as Salvemini had termed it, was now finally opened, its water-bearing capacities ready to be tapped anew[62]. Bringing this plan to fruition was made all the more urgent by the economic crisis, ten years after the Fascist rise to power. In a farming area like Ferrara, Nello Quilici, editor of the *Corriere Padano*, middle-class by background and Balbo's spokesman and adviser, harped on the colonial theme around 1932. It all heralded a decisive new period. The earliest investments of the Banco di Roma had been followed by limited capital outlays in Tripolitanian colonial farming ventures[63], and then by a heavy-handed, imperialistic programme of public works and land reclamation during the 1920s, which to some extent attracted private capital investment. Now, however, the state stepped in on a more massive scale, with what was virtually a compulsory resettlement programme. Fascism had, on the one hand, crushed the 'nomads' by reasserting 'direct' and 'absolute' (to use Graziani's term) rule over the colony, and, on the other, evolved an overall plan for the territory[64].

Disagreements, however, soon surfaced on the question of links with the homeland, when it became acutely evident that there was a lack of funds for a colonial resettlement programme, given its high cost, while imports continued at a much higher level than exports[65]. The Nationalist dream of a self-sufficient, well populated 'Overseas Italy', complementing the national economy, rapidly faded. As the years passed, the government could only look back wistfully to the time when it had not been committed to the colonization of Libya[66], particularly when, after the outbreak of the Second World War, defensive arrangements and military preparations on the Cyrenaican front

[62] Dario LISCHI ('Darioski'), *Viaggio di un cronista fascista in Cirenaica*, Pisa, 1934 and Marco POMILIO, *Apriamo lo scatolone di sabbia*, Rome, 1935, with a preface by Luigi Razza, minister of public works.

[63] G. LEONE, *La colonizzazione agraria della Tripolitania settentrionale nel suo primo ventennio*, Rome, 1933.

[64] Giorgio ROCHAT, *La repressione della resistenza araba in Cirenaica nel 1930–31 nei documenti dell'Archivio Graziani*, in 'Il Movimento di liberazione in Italia', a. XXV, no. 110, January–March 1973, pp. 36–9. Cf. also Enzo SANTARELLI, *Omar al-Mukhtar partigiano*, in 'l'Unità', 16 September 1971.

[65] For the budget in economic terms of the Italian colonization of Libya, see the data supplied by Miège and Segrè.

[66] Luigi FEDERZONI, *op. cit.*, p. 138: 'In order to hold on to Libya, we should not have gone to war in 1940.'

proved to be wholly inadequate. Furthermore, from 1931 onwards, Rome was already beginning to set its eye on other goals, Libya being regarded as merely one step towards a far greater Mediterranean and African colonial project. The direction of colonial expansionism now shifted quite rapidly towards East Africa; and the 'fourth shore' adventure was now clearly seen as the first stage to Empire[67].

7. From the time of its origin, Italian colonialism in Libya, both in its ideology and strategy, though wavering in its aims, fixing its sights at one moment upon gradual demographic saturation and at the next on geopolitical expansion in *Mare nostrum*, had been a reflection of late 19th-century Imperialism; and from the very start it was predictable that the result could only be a resounding failure, as men such as Salvemini had foreseen. Fascism, which had emerged during the post-war period in order to provide solutions to the new problems of strengthening the state and also modernizing Italian society, had clung to the second horn of the dilemma, opting, decisively and with the maximum brutality, for the demographic saturation of overseas territories. It cannot be proved that there was a pre-determined, totalitarian intention right from the start; but we believe we have shown that there was a powerful process of ideological conditioning to bring this about. This conditioning was, in its turn, carried to extremes by Fascist policy, with its strongly contrasted behaviour at home and in the colonies, by the demographic doctrine or myth systematically expounded by Mussolini in his speech of Ascension Day 1927, subsequently stimulated by the economic crisis of 1927, which lent urgency to the 'problem of outlets', and by the imperialistic plans of the ruling party[68]. Those most responsible for the plans and methods of anti-guerilla warfare and for the repression in Libya are the head of the Fascist state and his government, and, as direct executors of the policy, men like Badoglio and Graziani, in their double role as soldiers and politicians, and their subordinates. It is true, however, that during the process of 'defascistization' of the Italian republic by the Resistance, even generals like Graziani, who organized the massacres of 1937 in Ethiopia and was head of the armed forces of the Salò Republic, slipped virtually unscathed through the net of justice, pleading 'defence of the fatherland'[69].

---

[67] These opinions, of a general nature, were expressed in the journal 'Gerarchia' in its special number (a. XII, No. 7–8, July–August 1932) dealing with *Problemi africani* (see the opening article by DE BONO, *Ieri e oggi in colonia*), from the collection edited by Asvero GRAVELLI, *Africa. Espansionismo fascista e revisionismo*, Rome, 1933, as well as the opening academic address by Nello QUILICI, *L'enigma di Adua*, Ferrara, 1932.

[68] In 1939 transfer requests to Libya of some 40,000 rural families were pending or outstanding. Cf. Claudio G. SEGRÈ, *op. cit.*, p. 161.

[69] Zara ALGARDI, *Processi ai fascisti*, Florence, 1958, prefaced by Ferruccio Parri.

Relying on the decisive and preponderant support of the state, for reasons of social and domestic policy, and on a showy but fragile apparatus of popular agitation—an offshoot, especially on the Libyan problem, of the Nationalist school—Fascist imperialism had abused its power in tackling national questions which, in any event, were wholly insoluble. The mass sacrifice demanded of the Arab populations was thus all the more pitiful, sad and useless. There is no single cause for the consequences, and the responsibility of Fascism itself stems from propositions and trends which came to a climax in the 1930s but which were as much rooted in the 'Italian spring' of 1911–12, or even prior to that, as in the class dictatorship imposed on Italians at home in 1919–22. Above all, Italy's colonial ideology and strategy, particularly in Libya, were intellectually barren, the mythical allusions to history and archaeology empty devices. During the thirty years or more of rule over the 'fourth shore', Italian culture gave and received next to nothing. Nor did it leave much behind. This is due, among other things, to the manner in which the Arab peoples, even prior to Fascism, were denied a national personality and identity, and to the way in which the guerilla movement was demolished.

Giorgio Rochat

The repression of resistance in Cyrenaica
(1927–1931)

I. Sources and terms of this study.

Italian colonialism between the two World Wars is one of the most neglected areas of contemporary historiography, despite the increasing number of works on Fascism and the importance that the dictatorship attributed, in terms of propaganda and prestige, to the African conquests[1]. Clearly for political reasons, the institutes, committees and individual scholars who ought to be professionally interested in these problems prefer to spend their time and energy on the more distant and forgotten aspects of 19th-century Italian colonialism. The archives of the now defunct Ministry of Italian Africa (placed in the historical archive of the Ministry of Foreign Affairs) can now be consulted only on a severely restricted basis, while the official Committee responsible for the documentation of Italian activities in Africa (set up in January 1952 by the Italian government, with the most eminent representatives of the ex-colonial scene) has decided to give the Fascist period a painfully inadequate measure of attention; this has resulted in a spate of uncritical biographies and specialized studies which defend, unquestioningly, the propagandist versions of the Fascist regime, without making any attempt at critical historic assessment or documentation[2].

---

[1] For general bibliographical information cf. Carlo GIGLIO, *Gli studi storici italiani relativi all'Africa dal 1945 al 1967*, in AA. VV., *La storiografia italiana negli ultimi vent'anni. Atti del primo congresso nazionale di scienze storiche*, Vol. II, pp. 1311–28, Milan, Marzorati, 1970; and Giorgio ROCHAT, *Colonialismo*, in AA. VV., *Il mondo contemporaneo*, Vol. I, *Storia d'Italia*, Vol. I, pp. 107–20, Florence, La Nuova Italia, 1978. See also Ruggero ROMANO, *La storiografia italiana oggi*, Rome, Espresso-libri, 1978.

[2] It is worth mentioning the books in the military historical collected series *L'Italia in Africa*, issued by the said committee, which deal with the Italian operations in Libya between the two World Wars, i.e.: Massimo Adolfo VITALE, *L'opera dell'esercito*, Vol. I, *Ordinamenti militari*

The consequence of this political and cultural trend is that the available works on the Italian conquest of Libya (except for the period of the war with Turkey, 1911–12, which continues to provide scope for useful studies unconnected with colonialism in the traditional sense[3]) emanate chiefly from the National-Fascist journalism of the 1930s and the post-war years[4]. So even the best of these works display a total incomprehension of, and often a deep contempt for, Cyrenaican society and its long resistance to the Italian occupation, openly distorting the documentary sources for purposes of propaganda. Among the books not guilty of such dishonesty are the excellent volume by Evans-Pritchard on the Senusi, the more generalized works of Miège and Rochat, the book by Segré on Italian colonization, and several biographical studies on individual aspects of the Italian conquest[5]. The first work dealing specifically with the repressive operations in Cyrenaica was an article by the author in 1973, based principally on the personal files of General

e reclutamento, Rome, Poligrafico dello stato, 1960, and Vol. III, *Avvenimenti militari e impiego, Africa settentrionale*, ibid, 1964; Vincenzo LIOY, *L'opera del'aeronautica*, Vol. I, *Eritrea. Libia*, ibid, 1964. These books wholly justify the Italian operation, quoting excerpts from Fascist propaganda without substantial reserves, and utilizing only a small portion of the documentation drawn upon, providing a reconstruction that is sometimes detailed (especially Lioy) but generally evasive and unreliable.

[3] Paolo MALTESE, *La terra promessa. La guerra italo-turca e la conquista della Libia 1911–12*, Milan, Sugar, 1968; Francesco MALGERI, *La guerra libica 1911–12*, Rome, Ediz. di storia e letteratura, 1970; Sergio ROMANO, *La quarta sponda. La guerra di Libia 1911–12*, Milan, Bompiani, 1977.

[4] We would mention particularly Rodolfo GRAZIANI, *Cirenaica pacificata*, Milan, Mondadori, 1933 (largely drawn upon in the later *Pace romana in Libia*, ibid, 1937, and *Libia redenta*, Naples, Torella, 1948): Attilio TERUZZI, *Cirenaica verde. Due anni di governo* (December 1926–January 1929), preface by Benito Mussolini, Milan, Mondadori, 1931; Ottorino MEZZETTI, *Guerra in Libia. Esperienze e ricordi*, Rome, Cremonese, 1933; Carlo GIGLIO, *La confraternita senussita dalle sue origini a oggi*, preface by Rodolfo Graziani, Padua, Cedam, 1932; Agostino GAIBI, *Storia delle colonie italiane*, Turin, Schioppo, 1934; Touring Club Italiano, *Libia*, Milan, 1937; Raffaele CIASCA, *Storia coloniale dell'Italia contemporanea*, Milan, Hoepli, 1938 (2nd ed. 1940); Alessandro AUSIELLO, *La politica italiana in Libia*, Rome, L'Arnia, 1939; Emilio CANEVARI, *La guerra italiana. Retroscena della disfatta*, Rome, Tosi, 1948; Enrico DE LEONE, *La colonizzazione dell'Africa del nord*, Padua, Cedam, 1960; Francesco VALORI, *Storia della Cirenaica*, Florence, Sansoni, 1961.

[5] E. E. EVANS-PRITCHARD, *The Sanusi of Cyrenaica*, Oxford, Clarendon Press, 1948 (Italian translation *Colonialismo e resistenza religiosa nell'Africa settentrionale. I Senussi di Cirenaica*, introduction by Vittorio Lanternari, Catania, Edizioni del prisma, 1979); J. L. MIÈGE, *L'impérialisme colonial italien de 1870 à nos jours*, Paris, Sèdes, 1968 (Italian translation Milan, Rizzoli, 1976); Giorgio ROCHAT, *Il colonialismo italiano*, Turin, Loescher, 1973; Claudio SEGRÈ, *Fourth Shore. The Italian Colonization of Libya*, Chicago, The University of Chicago Press, 1974 (Italian translation *L'Italia in Libia dall'età giolittiana a Gheddafi*, preface by Giorgio Rochat, Milan, Feltrinelli, 1978); Piero PIERI-Giorgio ROCHAT, *Pietro Badoglio*, Turin, Utet, 1974; Sergio ROMANO, *Giuseppe Volpi*, Milan, Bompiani, 1979. Particular mention should also be made to the articles on 'Lo stato operaio' by Luigi LONGO, *Due anni di guerra coloniale fascista*, 1929, no. 11, pp. 678–83, and by Egidio GENNARI, *Per una coscienza coloniale proletaria*, 1935, nos. 1 and 3, pp. 24–33 and 205–9, which show how clearly Communist anti-Fascism condemned Italian colonialism and its massacres.

Graziani; these, being kept in the central Roman State Archives, were available to students even during the period when access to the archives of the defunct Ministry of Italian Africa was permitted only to students associated with former colonial affairs[6].

In recent years there has been much freer access to ministerial archives. This study differs, in fact, from our 1973 article (on which, nevertheless, it is largely modelled, including, verbatim, the conclusions) in that it is based on three different archives, in addition to the afore-mentioned bibliography. The first is the personal archive, already noted, of Graziani, composed of seven envelopes of documents selected by the general himself, which mainly demonstrate his preoccupation to claim principal merit for having crushed Cyrenaican resistance, along the lines already clearly explained in his book dating from 1932, *Cirenaica pacificata*[7]. Secondly, there is the archive of the army's Historical Office, whose *Fondo Libia* has been open to inspection without hindrance. This is an excellently arranged archive, with much material relating to the Italo-Turkish war of 1911–12, compiled under the direct supervision of the army high command, but less comprehensive for the successive years, when the Colonial Ministry assumed direction of operations. Nevertheless, it is still of interest because the army General Staff was kept informed about the military aspects of the repression[8].

Thirdly, there is the archive of the discontinued Ministry of Italian Africa, kept in the Foreign Ministry, which might be expected to constitute the principal source of information and research on Italian colonialism. This archive, however, is of less significance because the Committee for the documentation of Italian activities in Africa (which included distinguished historians such as Ciasca, Giglio and Toscano), during the 1950s authorized those engaged in the drafting of the volumes in the collection to remove and take home the most interesting papers, so violating the traditional rules for keeping documented files. Thus the files which have finally been made available to independent researchers in recent years have been skimmed of documents considered to be of major importance, yet not used, even so, in

---

[6] Giorgio ROCHAT, *La repressione della resistenza araba in Cirenaica nel 1930–31, nei documenti dell'archivio Graziani*, in 'Il movimento di liberazione in Italia', 1973, no. 110, pp. 3–39 (from here on termed simply ROCHAT, without further specifications).

[7] The Fondo Graziani of the central state archive will from here on be termed ACS-FG, followed by two or three numbers which indicate respectively the envelope, the fascicle and (where there is one) the sub-fascicle. Also of some use are the fascicles of Mussolini's private secretariat, kept in the central state archive, and from here on termed ACS-SPD/cr (carteggio riservato), followed by the fascicle number.

[8] The Fondo Libia in the archive of the army's Historical Office will from now on be referred to as AUSE-FL, followed by two numbers, indicating respectively the file and the fascicle. We thank General Rinaldo Cruccu, head of the Historical Office, and his colleagues, who have assisted our research in every way.

the compilation of the volumes in the collection entitled *L'Italia in Africa*[9]. Even when these documents were returned to the archive, it proved impossible to put them back into the files from which they had been lifted, nor for the time being to make them available to students[10]. The irregular procedure condoned by the Committee has made it impossible to determine exactly how much harm was done to the archive; our investigations, and comparison with the other archives, leave us with the impression that the removal of the documents in question, by reason of the wealth of material and the poor way in which it was prepared by the Committee's experts, reduced but did not destroy the value of the archive, which suffered mainly in the sense of being incomplete but not in terms of the interest value of the documents that survived[11].

Finally, it has to be pointed out that in all the archives we consulted, Cyrenaica is afforded far less space than Tripolitania, the area on which general interest was focused throughout the 1920s, and that there is every evidence that a collective censorship was brought to bear on the more brutal aspects of the Italian repression, as is shown by the sparseness of documentation that has been kept on the subject of the concentration camps in which the peoples of the Cyrenaican Gebel were confined in 1930.

Our reconstruction of events can therefore not be regarded as definitive, although it is the fullest and best documented account so far undertaken. For reasons of space as well as availability of sources, we have chosen to examine only the military operations conducted by Italy in the Cyrenaican Gebel during 1927–31; consequently, there is no emphasis on the operations in Tripolitania and those for the recovery of the semi-desert regions south of the

---

[9] It is worth mentioning Vitale's books on army events, for the compiling of which a large number of documents were drawn upon (as far as can be judged from the gaps in the files currently available), but only a small part of which were used.

[10] The short-sighted policy of the Committee for documenting Italian activities in Africa has been aggravated by the refusal of the Foreign Ministry, depository of the archives of the dissolved Ministry of Italian Africa, to put their facilities and staff at our disposal. We thank Dr Mario Gazzini, who did all he could to make available to us the documents withdrawn by the said Committee, even though his painstaking efforts were not sufficient to trace the files removed by Vitale.

[11] We will refer to this archive as ASMAI, followed by three numbers which indicate respectively the position, the file and the fascicle. We would also have liked to quote the archive of the Foreign Ministry, secondary but not irrelevant to our enquiries. After many decades of being closed to independent historians, this archive (together with the afore-mentioned archive of the Ministry of Italian Africa) has recently been opened for wider consultation, but on conditions which seem designed .to discourage an influx of outside scholars; it is worth mentioning the lack of equipment for photographic reproduction and even the small number of chairs and tables provided, which enables the very small staff to forbid visitors, who may have travelled long distances (as I personally discovered), to consult the files. The opening of this extremely important archive has thus been severely limited by lack of the most elementary facilities, so much so that we were compelled to give up using it.

Gebel (the so-called oases of the 29th parallel), nor have we analyzed the deep causes of the Senusi resistance and the internal events of the Cyrenaican tribes.

The transcription of Arabic names posed some problems, and we have therefore followed the modern styles for names of individuals and those most frequently used in contemporary Italian documents for place and tribal names, thus giving them uniformity.

II. *The operations in the Gebel 1928.*

1. *Operations 1923–6*

Until the beginning of 1923 relations between the Italian government and the Senusi were dictated by a compromise, formally approved by the agreements of Acroma, er-Regima and Bu Mariam, which, in fact, left to the Italians (as to the Turks previously) the harbours and adjacent strips of plain, and the hinterland to the Senusi. The Fascist rise to power brought about an immediate reversal of direction: on 6 March 1923 General Bongiovanni, the new governor of Cyrenaica, launched a surprise attack on the Senusi forces, so initiating the operations for the conquest of Cyrenaica[12]. Bongiovanni had at his disposal four Italian battalions, destined for garrison duties, five Eritrean battalions and two Libyan battalions, with an overall infantry strength of 8000–8500 men; in addition he had two Savari (Libyan cavalry) squadrons, two mountain batteries drawn by pack-animals, two gunnery companies for fortifications, two companies of engineers, two squadrons of aircraft including four Caproni Ca 3 bombers and eight Sva spotter planes, and finally a motorized unit divided into twelve sections. The Senusi were able to call upon some 2000 regular soldiers, concentrated in the so-called mixed camps, and 3500–4000 irregular fighting men among the Gebel tribes[13].

[12] Fascist propaganda spoke of 'reconquest', and actually the term had some basis as far as Tripolitania was concerned, for in 1913–14 Italian troops occupied Fezzan, but not in relation to Cyrenaica, the hinterland of which had always remained under the control of Senusiya, the political-religious organization that represented state power in the Gebel and in the semi-desert regions of Cyrenaica.

[13] These facts, like all the successive ones, come from the typewritten account, *Dieci anni di storia cirenaica*, compiled by Captain Clemente Menzio for the command of the royal corps of colonial troops in Cyrenaica; this consists of about 200 pages, dated 25.12.1931, kept in ACS-FG, 3/5, and from now on referred to only by its title. The same facts are contained in EVANS-PRITCHARD, *op. cit.*, p. 159, which does not quote the source (presumably Menzio's report), while using it extensively for successive years. It should be noted that all the figures given by the Italian high command relating to the numbers of Senusi soldiers and their losses have to be accepted for what they are worth, and that the Eritrean and Libyan battalions, with an average strength of 750 men, were composed of volunteers recruited respectively in Eritrea (with a large contribution by so-called Ethiopians) and in Cyrenaica, organized by Italian officers.

41

Bongiovanni's offensive registered a few initial but hardly decisive successes, such as the breaking up of the mixed camps[14] and the temporary occupation of Agedabia. In June Italian troops managed to gain control of the part of the Gebel closest to Barce, obtaining the first mass submissions (about 20,000 people), but were soundly defeated by the Mogarba in two successive engagements in Sirtica, losing 13 officers, 40 Italian soldiers and 279 *ascari*[15]. In the course of that year a division of Cyrenaica was sketched out, which saw Italian rule established over the more stable tribes located in the neighbourhood of towns (the northern Auaghir, the Orfa, the Hasa, and a part of the Dorsa and of the Abeidat), and the open resistance of the tribes of the Gebel and of the semi-desert southern regions (the Mogarba, the southern Auaghir, the Brahasa, the Abid, the Faied, and some of the Dorsa and Abeidat)[16]. It is impossible, however, to stake out this division territorially, because Senusi control extended even to peoples who had officially submitted to the Italians.

In the spring of 1924 Italian forces resumed the offensive in the Gebel with a series of operations which mainly affected the ordinary people but did not really harm the *duar* of Omar al-Mukhtar (according to official Italian figures, some 600 men and 25,000 animals were killed, but only 97 rifles were seized). The Italian occupation was reinforced with a string of fixed garrisons, which, however, did not seriously impede the movements of the rebels. In spring 1925 the Italian offensive was directed mainly towards the southern slopes of the Gebel, leading to a total of 250 men killed as well as 5000 camels and over 10,000 sheep slaughtered; the fact, nevertheless, that only 50 rifles were collected from the battlefield leads one to believe that once again the Italian forces had come down more heavily on the native population than on Omar al-Mukhtar's *duar*. The year 1926 saw Italian occupation cemented in the oases of Giarabub (an operation that showed the growing Italian mastery of the techniques of movement and fighting in desert zones, thanks to the use of modern means such as aircraft, radio and trucks) and a series of moppings-up in the Gebel, whereby the rebels lost 500 men, 100 horses, 2300 camels and more than 30,000 sheep (again according to official Italian statistics) and the Italians three officers, 25 of their own soldiers and 24 *ascari* killed[17].

During four years of war the Gebel tribes had lost around 1500 men and 90,000–100,000 domestic animals, according to Italian estimates, but retained control of the greater part of the tableland and the semi-desert regions to the

---

[14] Despite the surprise, Senusi losses were small: 12 dead, 168 prisoners and 198 rifles captured, indicating that almost all their soldiers managed to escape the Italians (*Dieci anni di storia cirenaica*, cit.).

[15] *Dieci anni di storia cirenaica*, cit.

[16] EVANS-PRITCHARD, *op. cit.*, pp. 159–60.

[17] All these figures come from the report *Dieci anni di storia cirenaica*, cit. The *duar* (singular *dor*) were the rebel formations, each several hundred men strong.

rear; their efficiency was demonstrated on 28 March 1927 when the Seventh Libyan Battalion, 750 strong, was routed in an ambush at er-Raheiba, leaving more than 300 dead. The situation was clearly described by General Mezzetti:

In March 1927 the rebels had chalked up a notable military success against us; three large *mehalle*, with an overall strength of over 1200 infantry and 400 cavalry, occupied the heart of the Gebel in immediate contact with our line Kaulan-Gerrari-Maraua-Gerdes Abid. This last redoubt, anyway, was held by few national (i.e. Italian) troops, seeing that the surrounding terrain was then, as now, only of limited value, so that, truth to tell, our line passed through Barce (the plain and not the brow of the plateau), based on el-Abiar.

Behind their line of outposts, made up of guard-houses and supports, protected by the main body of troops, the rebels lived with their families in their tents, with large numbers of livestock and huge herds of camels, sowing and reaping, with fairly convenient access to the north along the line of waterwells following the border of our occupation zone, and to the south along the line of waterwells running close to the Zavie line.

More serious was the fact that in the Kuf region and along the coast between Tolmetta and Hanis the rebel organization had concentrated its logistic reserves, in the form of provisions and livestock, and set up a convalescent hospital for the wounded, which was one of the busiest centres for the collection of tithes. A line of *caracols* crossed the Gebel, running through Bir Gandula, Sira, Gasr Benigdem and Gergerumma, linking the *mehalle* with the coast and splitting our occupation force in two.

Counting the men of the *caracols* and those operating independently in the Kuf region, there were more than 2000 active soldiers readily available to the rebels in the Gebel.

The Kuf zone was considered by the rebels to be safe because the troops (Italian) had never pushed beyond the line of castles, that is to say beyond the escarpment of the plateau which slopes down from the Kuf to the sea. They also felt fairly secure in other areas, knowing from experience that any forward thrust by the troops, by reason of the difficult terrain and logistical problems, generally did not exceed a day and a half's march. Their defensive system allowed them to withdraw swiftly in the event of a heavy attack. In fact, all we came away with were the tail-ends of some caravan and the occasional flock which had carelessly been left grazing too close to our lines[18].

[18] General Ottorino Mezzetti, commander of the troops in Cyrenaica, to the government of Cyrenaica, 1 December 1928. This is a very full report (kept in AUSE-FL, 175/6), in which Mezzetti summarizes the events of almost two years in command of the troops in Cyrenaica, defending his political and military decisions. It should be remembered, however, that this report, like the later ones of Badoglio and Graziani, tends in the first place to enhance the author's own actions, emphasizing the negative aspects of the situation at the time he took over the command and all the positive features when he was subsequently replaced, and naturally always from the Italian viewpoint. *Mehalla* is another name used for the armed Arab formations (though in the Gebel *dor* is more frequent). *Caracol* is a smaller unit.

2. The Italian offensive of summer 1927

The substantial failure of the Italian offensive operations in Cyrenaica was in strong contrast to the successes enjoyed during those same years by the Italian forces in Tripolitania, where advantage had been taken of the inability of the nomad and semi-nomad tribes of the region to settle their traditional disputes and to form a united defensive front. In November 1926 General Mombelli, who had succeeded Bongiovanni in May 1924 as governor of Cyrenaica, was replaced by Attilio Teruzzi, a fairly important member of the Fascist party; soon afterwards he was given the support of General Ottorino Mezzetti, who had been (after Graziani) principal commander of operations in Tripolitania. The first objective they were given was control of the Gebel, for which purpose they were provided with huge mobile forces: nine Eritrean battalions, two Libyan battalions, four Savari (Libyan cavalry) squadrons, one *meharist* squadron, one squadron of armoured cars, various bands of irregulars (totalling over 10,000 men, not counting the garrisons of the towns and pacified territories, usually entrusted to units of Italian soldiers), plus some twenty aircraft. Against these forces the rebels could marshal the Abid, Brahasa and Hasa-Abeidat *duar*, joined under the command of Omar al-Mukhtar in the Wadi Sammalus, comprising about 1500 men (400 of them on horseback), plus some 350 armed Dorsa in the Kuf zone[19].

There is a detailed account of the operations, from the Italian viewpoint, in the afore-mentioned book of Mezzetti. The first important point to underline is the greater operative capacity of the Italian forces: thanks to aircraft and radio, Mezzetti was able to coordinate the concentric activities of several columns (the Eritrean and Libyan battalions in the Gebel, and the units of *meharists*, trucks and armoured cars in the southern semi-desert region), each of which carried enough water for five days and food for seven days. This overwhelming superiority of mobile forces, a greater decisiveness in their employment, and the active presence of the Italian air force brought about a reversal of the military situation. Omar al-Mukhtar's *duar*, which had given battle, were dispersed, the impregnable Kuf stronghold was overrun, with relatively light losses, and the Gebel was continuously attacked from July to

[19] Cyrenaican High Command (General O. Mezzetti), *Operazioni estive nel Gebel cirenaico 8 luglio-13 settembre 1927. Relazione sommaria*, printed fascicle of 50 pages, without date (but autumn 1927), kept in AUSE-FL, 156/5, amply drawn upon in MEZZETTI, *op. cit.*, pp. 153 *et seq.*; cf. also LIOY, *op. cit.*, pp. 116–20. For the reconstruction of events of 1927–8 the afore-mentioned volumes of Teruzzi and Mezzetti are fundamental, but it must also be remembered that both authors were writing mainly to claim for themselves much of the merit for the successes subsequently recorded by Graziani in 1930–1 when the rebellion was finally crushed; reliability is therefore subordinated to the enhancement of their own actions, as is the case, too, with Graziani.

September by Mezzetti's mobile mopping-up groups. Rebel losses were heavy: 1300 men dead, 250 women and children taken prisoner[20], 3000 camels killed and 850 captured, 5000 sheep killed and 18,000 captured. Yet the Italians seized only 269 rifles and 26 horses, indicating (and this is the second important point to be emphasized) that the main body of Omar al-Mukhtar's army managed to escape every time and that yet again the greatest losses were suffered by the population at large[21]. The increasing efficiency of the Italian forces marked the end of the large concentrations of armed rebels, capable of carrying out large-scale offensives, but it in no way impaired their popular support and hence the power of the Senusi and the vitality of the guerilla operations[22].

In his conclusive account of the operations of summer 1927 General Mezzetti, while claiming by now to have quelled the revolt in the Gebel, showed that he did not underestimate the possibility of resumed rebel offensives. We quote below his 'politico-military conclusions', which analyze, with clarity and in some depth, the general situation. Mezzetti singled out the strengths of Cyrenaican resistance, notably the solidarity of the *sottomessi* ('subjected' non-combatants), the leadership capacity of Senusiya, and the restrictions placed upon a policy of repression by virtue of the need to justify the imperial and civilizing mission of Fascist Italy, which implied the impossibility of recognizing the popular mass basis of the Senusi rebellion and the dignity of the struggle for national independence by the peoples of the Gebel. Mezzetti and other exponents of Italian colonialism were compelled to fall back on racist ravings in order to explain the innate belligerence of the primitive peoples of Libya.

Today, after the operations in the Gebel, the rebellion has been broken and quelled. But certain considerations on the complicated situation in the colony and various factors based on past and recent experience give cause for thought

---

[20] In the war in the Gebel prisoners were seldom taken (even the capture of women and children was rare), because neither the *ascari* nor the rebels would show any mercy, unless circumstances were exceptional, as in the case of high-ranking officers or leaders, or for mass surrenders.

[21] Mezzetti observed that most of the rebel losses did not occur in battle but in the course of flight to avoid being encircled by the superior Italian forces. During the operations of summer 1927, the only occasion when the rebels fiercely defended their ground, in spite of being outnumbered by the Italians, was in the Kuf zone, when they lost 150 to 350 men as well as 70 rifles, whilst inflicting on the Italians their biggest losses in the campaign—one officer and 35 *ascari*. In the summer battles the Italians lost in all two officers, five airmen and 61 *ascari*; in the Italian mobile detachments the infantry and cavalry were by now composed only of Eritrean and Cyrenaican *ascari*, with Italian officers, while Italian soldiers were normally used only in the artillery, where greater technical training was necessary. For these facts cf. Cyrenaican High Command, *Operazioni estive nel Gebel, cit.*

[22] For all these statistics cf. Cyrenaican High Command, *Operazioni estivi nel Gebel, cit.*, MEZZETTI, *op. cit.*, and TERUZZI, *op. cit.*

and little reliance on the apparent situation. Rebellion is congenital, almost endemic in these lands, with ethnic origins going back to remote times. Beginning with the testimony of Latin authors who already accused the native tribes of Libya as being little more than marauders, rebels who defied all laws, continuing through the lapidary documents of Greek, Roman and Byzantine fortifications, the ruins of which attest to the enduring force required to keep the country quiet, down to the most recent campaigns, Turkish and our own—everything points to the fact that authority, law and order must always be imposed by force of arms.

Nor can the situation be said to have changed today, because there is not yet (or at any rate only a promising start has been made) any economic basis for setting up farming areas and towns to attract and absorb the population. And that population remains as it has been for centuries, nomadic and war-like by instinct and choice, always responding to the persuasive calls for adventure, loot and religious warfare. . . .

Above all, it is necessary that an energetic, intelligent political programme should prepare the way for, and accompany, the military operations in order to exploit the results, eliminating the principal source and strength of the rebellion: *Senusiya and the connivance of those who have submitted.*

The first of these problems, Senusiya, is of such political importance that it goes beyond this book's terms of reference. It is enough to point out that Senusiya has always directed and inspired rebellion, providing it with the means to live and to fight, and that through the exaction of tribute and the virtual imposition on the people of military conscription, it has set itself up as a state within a state on colonial territory.

The problem of the *sottomessi*, however, is so directly linked with the operations that it has to be taken into account by the military authorities, since this is not a matter of distant or reflected influence but an immediate, visible fact of daily life.

It may, for example, happen that having won a splendid victory after a hard battle, and relieved the rebels of 50 soldiers and 200 camels, the next day the *sottomessi* will refurnish the rebels with another 50 soldiers and 200 camels. It is hard to imagine conducting military actions under such conditions, yet this is what is happening. In effect, connivance of the *sottomessi* with the rebels is the normal state of affairs here in the colony, where it is very common for a family to have some of its men belonging to the *dor* and some working with the (Italian) government. . . .

This state of affairs must at any cost be brought to an end, otherwise our military activity must, in the long term, prove sadly sterile. . . . It is essential that the *sottomessi* should, as quickly as possible, be organized and supervised in such a way that not a man, not a rifle, not a camel and not a sheep escapes our day-to-day control, and that at the same time they should be guaranteed a decent, dignified standard of living, so that they are not tempted to prefer the adventures and risks of the *dor*[23].

3. *The resumption of the rebellion in 1928*

In order to control the Gebel, Mezzetti aimed at setting up a tight network of fortified points that would hamper the movements of the rebels and provide tactical and logistical support to the Italian mobile groups (usually composed of an Eritrean or Libyan battalion, a Savari squadron and some artillery pieces drawn by pack-animals) charged with preventing a resumed offensive by Omar al-Mukhtar's *duar* by carrying out frequent patrols. The Italian high command aimed, first of all, at control of the territory to the north of the so-called Gerdes Abid-Maraua-Gerrari-Kaulan garrison line, reinforced in the autumn of 1927 by the creation of new forts at Bir Grandula, Bu Cassal, Gsur Megiahir and in the Kuf zone. This line was intended to mark a clear demarcation between the non-combatant population and the rebels, so that any man and any animal south of the line would be a legitimate target for Italian planes and mobile units. Actually, there could be no clear demarcation of the two groups, as Mezzetti himself realized; and the garrison policy led only to their multiplication, eventually weakening the Italian occupation force without preventing the resumption of the Senusi rebellion[24].

In October 1927 Governor Teruzzi and Mezzetti assembled in Benghazi all responsible officials for the administrative districts into which Cyrenaica was divided, asking them 'to specify the number of rebels they believed still to be armed within their territory'. According to them, wrote Mezzetti, 'there were not more than a hundred or so armed rebels in the whole of Cyrenaica'[25]; but this was simply the umpteenth demonstration of the inability of the Italian political and military authorities to understand the situation, because the *duar* were in the process of reorganizing and in November went over to a new offensive with a large-scale raid in the neighbourhood of Slonta and a series of attacks on the Italian lines of communication[26]. According to our information sources, Omar al-Mukhtar

---

[23] Cyrenaican High Command, *Operazioni estive nel Gebel, cit.* These conclusions are partially repeated by MEZZETTI, *op. cit.*, pp. 191–3.

[24] According to Mezzetti, there were 62 garrisons in March 1927 and 68 in November 1928, covering a territory almost twice as big (Mezzetti to the governor, 9 November 1928, in AUSE-FL, 175/6). According to other sources, there were more than 70 garrisons; again, by Mezzetti's reckoning (in the said report of 1.12.1928), a dozen or so of these garrisons were not set up for military reasons but to defend a number of private farming concessions and to protect the Benghazi-Barce railway.

[25] MEZZETTI, *op. cit.*, p. 195.

[26] *Dieci anni di storia cirenaica, cit.*

had recognized that he could not withstand a frontal attack with forces that were so superior in manpower and materials; so he decided from now on to adopt guerilla tactics, avoiding open combat on the battlefield and aiming, by means of ambushes, raids and skirmishes, mainly to reassert Senusi control over the peoples of the Gebel, in opposition to the formal control by the Italian authorities (Omar al-Mukhtar's 'night government' was the evocative name bandied around).

The renewed rebellion appeared to be compromised at the end of 1927, when Mohammed er-Redà, younger brother of the Senusi leader Idris-es-Senusi, and his representative in Cyrenaica, gave himself up to the Italian authorities, underlining the internal disagreements among the Senusi as to what attitude to take in the face of the Italian offensive. This gesture, however, had no effect on Cyrenaican resistance because Colonial Minister Federzoni, against the advice of Teruzzi and Mezzetti, immediately imprisoned er-Redà on the island of Ustica, where the Fascist regime sent its enemies, and because Hassan, elder son of er-Redà, took his father's place alongside Omar al-Mukhtar and the rebels, the latter having been nominated, on this occasion, plenipotentiary representative of Idris es-Senusi in Cyrenaica. Resumption of guerilla warfare in the Gebel was encouraged by the Italian government's decision in 1928 to concentrate its forces in Tripolitania and in Cyrenaica on the conquest of the Sirtic region and the oases (the so-called oases of the 29th parallel) south of the Gebel. These operations ended with a major success, which demonstrated how the Italian forces, availing themselves both of all the most modern technical discoveries (radio, aircraft, armoured cars and columns of trucks) and traditional means (camel caravans for transporting supplies, but particularly Libyan mounted *mehara* units, which were as mobile as the rebels' *mehalle* but with a marked superiority in weapons, supplies and technical methods), had by this time decisively gained the upper hand in the desert and semi-desert plains. In fact, in January 1929, a *mehalla* of 400 men, which had left Cufra to attack the Italian occupation forces in Sirtica, was spotted, followed and bombed by aircraft, then attacked and destroyed by Italian mobile units at Bu Etla, with the loss of 226 men and 173 rifles, and the rout of the survivors.

The weekly *Notiziari* of the Cyrenaican government, a good number of which have been preserved for 1928[27], provide an interesting glimpse of the

---

[27] See in AUSE-FL, 174/7, the collection of 28 numbers from 1928 of the 'Notiziario del governo della Cirenaica'; these are typewritten 4–6-page fascicles, written (in a far from polished Italian) by the Benghazi office for civil and political affairs and signed by Teruzzi or his replacement, on a weekly basis. The collection that we examined contained two large gaps between August and September, and some minor ones as well.

situation in the Gebel, as seen by the Italian high command. In spite of noting a series of raids and some considerable movement of herds and flocks along the Egyptian border (proof, no doubt, that the Senusi organization continued to control the life of the Gebel populations and to carry on its vital trade with Egypt)[28], the January news-letters showed high optimism, because the surrender of Mohammed er-Redà was interpreted as confirmation of the very serious crisis confronting the rebels. In February concordant information reported the reorganization of Omar al-Mukhtar's *duar* (250–300 Brahasa, 150 Hasa, 200 Abid, 70 Abeidat—making a total of around 700 armed men, 150 of them mounted)[29]. Furthermore, the successful outcome of the operations in Sirtica warranted great optimism:

The advance of our troops and the consequent occupation of the oases (of Gialo) have upset the vacillating Senusi organization. The people are displaying their delight for the ensuing liberation from a pseudo-government compelled to oppress them in order to milk from them the means of continuing the revolt, which by now is flagging[30].

Nevertheless, guerilla activities broke out again in the Gebel and in Marmarica, with a series of lightning attacks which underlined once more the power of the Senusi, despite widespread and indiscriminate Italian bombing. In the words of the March *Notiziari*:

The air force has not failed, when weather conditions have permitted, to carry out its reconnaissance flights throughout the region, bombing any rebel encampments and groups that it sighted. These have been kept in continual turmoil as a result of the bombardments; and although recent reports indicate that such attacks have not been very effective in view of the fact that the soldiers have easily managed to withdraw, hiding in the caves of the high *wadis*, bomb fragments have caused heavy losses among livestock.

The rebel *duar* continue to roam about in the Goscia, with occasional sightings in the Sirual; they may again have their families and flocks with them. Hassan er-Redà is still with Omar al-Mukhtar. Each *dor* constitutes a separate encampment, but in sight of one another.

The *duar* are made up as follows: (1) Brahasa: about 400 men, 60 of whom are on horseback. They are divided into four *tabur*. . . . (2) Hasa-Abeidat: about 300 men with 50 riders. (3) Abid: about 100 warriors, almost all

[28] The air force was especially used against movements of men and flocks south of the line of garrisons, as is reported, for example, by the 'Notiziario' of 28 January 1928, when planes 'carried out a bombardment, with 2-kilogram bombs, of several small groups of Bedouin tents, an encampment surprised on the move, and a herd of camels that appeared to have been abandoned'.

[29] 'Notiziario' of 4 February 1928.

[30] 'Notiziario' of 3 March 1928.

mounted. . . . They are well armed, mainly with model 91 and Mannlicher (rifles); there are plenty of the former, few of the latter[31].

Every day small groups of *mohafdia* are detached from the single *duar*, with the responsibility of keeping a watch on our garrisons. In addition to the afore-mentioned groups of raiders south of Benghazi (two groups of 20 or 30 men), others have been sighted around Kaulan, Fiadia, Wadi el-Kuf, Sidi Gibrin, and approximately 150, in three groups, in Marmarica. . . . They are chiefly engaged in collecting payment of tithes in livestock, and this activity is often covered by simulated raids[32].

The increasing guerilla activity[33] forced Mezzetti to recall his troops from Sirtica for a large-scale mopping-up action, and this led, on 31 March, to the destruction of a large caravan in the Sciaafa, at Baltet es-Zalgh, with 200 dead, 1500 camels killed and 60 rifles taken[34]. The resumption of offensive activity by the Italian forces slowed down but did not interrupt rebel action; so Mezzetti stationed in the Gebel 'mobile groups designed to keep continuously on the move, independently of the territorial organization, in sufficient numbers to confront and attack, on their own, almost any rebel formation'[35]. But after a partial success on 30 June at the head of the Wadi Gherma[36], the mobile groups found themselves facing only emptiness: the *duar*, in fact, had scattered in small groups, protected by the population, and these kept up their guerilla activity behind Italian lines. The very close link between rebels and *sottomessi* was mentioned by the *Notiziari*:

Many of the Hasa-Abeidat rebels (reinforced by a hundred or so armed Brahasa) have infiltrated the ranks of the Abeidat *sottomessi*. So-called dissidents, moreover, have sent all their livestock into Abeidat territory, where it has mingled with the animals of the *sottomessi*; they have also done the same with their families and much of their chattels[37].

---

[31] 'Notiziario' of 10 March 1928. As in all quotations, the text of the original has been reproduced without correcting errors of grammar and syntax.

[32] 'Notiziario' of 24 March 1928. According to this source, the Brahasa *dor* was commanded by Osman Sciami, the Hasa-Abeidat *dor* by Fadil Bu Omar, and the Abid *dor* by Jusef Bu Rahil el-Musmari; Omar al-Mukhtar was with the Abid, and Hassan er-Redà with the Abeidat. The same 'Notiziario' noted that a large caravan with an armed escort of more than 100 men, en route from Egypt to the Gebel, had routed the Italian border garrison forces.

[33] The 'Notiziario' of 31 March 1928 mentioned eight raids in one week, the crossing into Egypt of 300 tents, 2500 camels and horses, and over 15,000 sheep; also Omar al-Mukhtar's forces now had 1500 rifles.

[34] 'Notiziario' of 7 April 1928; MEZZETTI, *op. cit.*, pp. 251–3.

[35] 'Notiziario' of 18 August 1928.

[36] MEZZETTI, *op. cit.*, pp. 254–5.

[37] 'Notiziario' of 30 June 1928; in it is a report of an ambush of a unit of 80 carabinieri and *zaptiè*, routed with heavy losses near Barce. A similar action took place a week earlier near Derna. In a footnote to the 'Notiziario' of 23 June 1928, General Graziani (who was reviewing the

The rebels have found the usual assistance from the people of the Abeidat territory; according to reports coming from the force (i.e. the *carabinieri*) at Derna, encampments in certain zones have accommodated two to three rebels per tent. Some of these have got rid of their weapons so as not to be recognized in the event of Italian searches and forays[38].

The rebels' new tactics have encouraged the Italian authorities to issue somewhat exaggerated victory bulletins.

The overall situation in the Gebel is fairly quiet. The continuous pressure of our regular and irregular forces continues to keep the rebels in a state of agitation, divided and dispersed, without any chance of offering us serious hostility, and experiencing great difficulty in replenishing their provisions and arms[39].

Actually, the *duar* were still very effective and could always rely on the support of the people, as Mezzetti himself was forced to admit in his report of 1 December 1928, which nevertheless gave an exaggeratedly optimistic account of his almost two years of command:

Since 1 April 1927 not one action of the rebel forces has met with success, apart from the insignificant capture of two small riderless military caravans. This applies to the area behind the Gerdes Abid-Maraua-Gerrari-Kaulan line as well as to the rest of the colony.

This fact should demonstrate, in the humble opinion of this command, that control of the territory behind the afore-mentioned line is militarily complete.

There still remains, it is true, the raiding phenomenon, but this is a rather complex matter, since it includes the payment of tithes to the Senusi, simulated raids that conceal actual exchanges of livestock and provisions, the overland consignment and sale by the rebels of livestock to Egypt according to age-old custom, cattle-stealing among the *sottomessi*, etc.

This phenomenon is likely to diminish or cease only when progress is made in the political and military organization of the territory. *And this is the nub of the question.*

Absolute control of the territory can be achieved only by the destruction of the rebel forces as a politico-military organization. This destruction must be the crowning result of efficient military and political action. On the basis of long colonial military experience, it can be said that the essential condition for destroying the politico-military organization of the rebels is the politico-military organization of the territory, which, as it proceeds towards the

---

situation prior to his arrival in Cyrenaica, as indicated by several notes in his own hand) remarked: 'by and large, matters stand as they did last year. We still cannot accept that the rottenness in Cyrenaica is due to the armed *sottomessi*.'

[38] 'Notiziario' of 14 July 1928.

[39] 'Notiziario' of 13 October 1928.

borders of the colony, drives the hotbeds of rebellion ever farther back, while well prepared and repeated strikes against the rebels by our troops will extinguish the hotbeds themselves[40].

In conclusion, Mezzetti was compelled to admit that the Senusi organization was still functioning efficiently, in spite of the strongest Italian presence in the Gebel and in the semi-desert hinterland; the only practical plan suggested by the general was to increase Italian pressure for an indeterminate period until the enemy was exhausted, but without any greater guarantee of success than the previous plans.

III. The truce of 1929.

1. The June agreements

In December 1928 Mussolini assumed responsibility for the Colonial Ministry, though leaving affairs to be handled effectively by sub-secretary De Bono, one of the leading lights of the Fascist government, who had ruled Tripolitania as governor from July 1925 to 1928[41]. The appointment of joint governor of Tripolitania and Cyrenaica (which, nevertheless, retained two distinct administrations) went to Marshal Badoglio, most distinguished of army commanders, who kept his high rank of chief of the general staff. Badoglio chose as vice-governor of Cyrenaica (with wide autonomy, since Badoglio resided in Tripoli) General Domenico Siciliani, his most loyal colleague, who was, however, new to the colonial scene and lacked personal prestige. Command of the troops was assumed by General Ronchetti, who had already seen service in the two Libyan colonies.

Badoglio had requested and obtained five years as governor to bring about the pacification and development of the two colonies. He began by issuing a widely circulated proclamation, in which he promised pardon for any rebels laying down their weapons and making full submission, but also threatened bitter repression for those who refused to surrender. 'If obliged,' he declared, 'I will wage war with powerful systems and means, which they will long remember. No rebel will be left in peace, neither he nor his family nor his herds nor his heirs. I will destroy everything, men and things'[42]. At the same

[40] Mezzetti report of 1.12.1928, cit. A few lines previously Mezzetti wrote that 'defeats inflicted on rebel formations may wear down their forces but cannot lead to final success'.

[41] In September 1929 Mussolini handed over the ministry to De Bono, with Lessona as his under-secretary. This was a formal change, since both before and afterwards Mussolini continued to show some interest in Cyrenaica and to intervene in all major decisions, leaving De Bono, however, with the direction of the ministry.

[42] The proclamation appears in GIGLIO, La confraternita senussita, cit., p. 133. For this reconstruction cf. ROCHAT, cit., pp. 9 et seq.

time Badoglio circulated two general directives to the political and military authorities of the two colonies, which voiced a critical opinion of the situation as he found it: the marshal called for more discipline, more order, greater correctness towards superiors and colleagues, more respect for the population and genuine interest in their conditions. Here is, in some detail, the final part of his circular of political directives dated 9 February, which summarizes the programme of Badoglio's government and outlines his attitude towards the Libyan people with a clarity that requires no comment:

We are here as the ruling nation which has driven out that incompetent ruling power, the Turk, and in its place are carrying out a noble civilizing mission. The Arab, or to be more precise, the entire native population must acquire this deep conviction, that we are here and that we shall stay here for ever, that we are here not to exploit but to improve the state of affairs of these lands in all fields of human endeavour, and that we shall accomplish this task whatever the cost.

This being axiomatic, we must, nevertheless, draw from it the following deductions. We have not merely occupied a land for the purpose of exploitation. We have also brought under our government a population that we must care for and steer towards a more civilized way of life. It is obvious that we shall never achieve our goal if this population does not feel the moral and material benefit of siding with us, submitting to our customs, to our laws. If this does not happen, we shall be in a state of perpetual strife which would make our already burdensome effort that much heavier. If this does not happen, we shall always be living over a powder barrel ready to explode. Finally, if this does not happen, we may, in the fury of the struggle, even destroy the entire population, and we shall have peace, but a peace of the graveyard. And graveyards are places of sad memories, not of positive actions.

Therefore we must:

—always stand on a higher step, but stand there austerely;

—always make our intellectual superiority felt, but with actions, not with words, and least of all with words that give offense;

—never forget that beneath the dirty barracan of the fellah, as beneath the elegant barracan of the well-to-do, there is a heart capable of hatred and of love, and never sow hatred, which always reaps bitter fruits;

—care for the wellbeing of the native population in all manners consistent with the law;

—not offend religious and family feelings.

To sum up, I intend:

—to have officials who carry out, with full awareness and with a complete sense of their own responsibility, all, *I repeat all*, the functions of law and regulations that have been assigned to them;

—in all relations with the native population to pursue a policy of national pride, tempered, however, by justice, of continual concern, of nobility in bearing and conduct.

Adventurers discovered new lands but were not colonizers; they lacked the essential qualities. Colonizing does not mean conquering, it means, especially, organizing, that is ruling methodically, with justice, with intellectual and moral superiority. That is our task. In the name of the King and the Duce, we will carry it out[43].

The proclamation of pardon and threat issued to the rebels met with no success in Tripolitania, where the Italian conquest was by now almost finished (at the end of 1929 General Graziani's columns reached Fezzan, completing the territorial occupation and dispersing the last pockets of resistance), nor initially in Cyrenaica, where guerilla warfare flared up anew in February and March with a series of impressive raids, sudden attacks and ambushes[44]. Even so, Badoglio did not renounce his programme of pacification and, as a sign of his goodwill, brought Mohammed er-Redà back home from exile on Ustica, in March. In April and May secret negotiations, about which we do not have much information, were conducted; these led to a slowing down of hostilities and then, in June, to a proper armistice, ratified by meetings between the higher-ranking commanders on both sides.

It is not easy to discover much about the peace efforts conducted by Badoglio and Siciliani in the summer of 1929 because of the lack of documentation and because all the versions and reconstructions from the Italian viewpoint, starting with Graziani's in 1932 and concluding with De

[43] Circular from Badoglio dated 9 February 1929 containing policy instructions, with a copy up to company command level, in AUSE-FL, 174/10, partly published in VITALE, *Avvenimenti militari, cit.*, pp. 199–201. In a letter to De Bono of 1.7.1930, Badoglio voiced weightier criticisms: 'During the period of operations, many have profited or at least tried to profit from them. They are the various suppliers and transport contractors. Scandalous profits have recently been made by those who have charge of transport. In the period of reorganization all this money-grabbing will come to an end. However, as we all know, there are certain types of people for whom the state of rebellion creates an environment conducive to more or less lawful profits. . . . Moreover, we need to face the truth, very bitter though this may be. The troops themselves have not proved immune to this speculation. A number of cases have come to light, and it is impossible to affirm that such incidents are admittedly serious but sporadic. Until now there has been a widespread opinion that a state of rebellion affords opportunities for career betterment. This has led to the tendency not to pursue actions to their conclusion, to exaggerate every encounter, however insignificant, to put in floods of commendations (for medals and promotions) and also to use the well-worn phrase—'another time it will be all right'—whenever the enemy managed, without too much effort, to break off an engagement.' (ACS-FG, 1/2/2).

[44] During this period Omar al-Mukhtar had reorganized his forces into two solid *duar*, the more westerly of which, comprising 350 Auaghir, Abid and Brahasa, gave battle on 13 March in the neighbourhood of Gerdes Abid to two Italian battalions and two squadrons, losing 20 men, 20 camels and 16 rifles, but killing 23 Italians and *ascari* (*Dieci anni, cit.*).

Leone's in 1960, are so markedly one-sided[45]. According to them, Omar al-Mukhtar, compelled to open peace negotiations because of the weariness of the local people and the internal disputes among the Senusi leadership, took advantage of the inexperience and ambition of Badoglio and Siciliani to bring about an act of submission that he had no intention of respecting, but which was essential to him for the reorganization of his exhausted forces, so enabling him to regain control of the situation and relaunch his guerilla warfare. We have no way of estimating the seriousness of the internal Senusi crisis and thus of assessing Omar al-Mukhtar's true motives, because Italian accounts of the rebellion are comparatively unreliable (though the tragic effects of the war on the ordinary people were real and evident); in any event, it was Graziani himself who, in April–May reported that the negotiations had not, in fact, been conducted on the basis of the unconditional surrender terms laid down in the Badoglio proclamation[46]. In exchange for the end of guerilla warfare and acceptance of Italian sovereignty and presence, Siciliani offered recognition of all the traditional Senusi organs and functions, virtually envisaging an ambiguous sharing of power, in which a partial disarming of the population (the handing over of half its rifles against a payment of 1000 lire for each one) was to be counterbalanced by retaining strong detachments nominally controlled by the Italian government but in practice by Senusiya[47].

At the beginning of June an agreement was reached, of which we possess only contradictory and summary versions, but which, as far as can be seen, followed the lines of the compromise noted above, leaving the concrete definition of the status of Cyrenaica for subsequent negotiations. The end of hostilities was marked by meetings that Omar al-Mukhtar and the other guerilla leaders had on 13 June with Siciliani, on 18 June with Badoglio, and on 28 June again with Siciliani in various places in the Gebel. According to Italian sources, on these occasions Omar al-Mukhtar and his companions fulfilled the formal and unconditional submission demanded by the Badoglio proclamation, even though Graziani, more honest than later historians, wrote explicitly that the submission was only the first stage of a comprehensive agreement which was to provide for the restoration of Senusi authority and the preservation of its armed forces[48]. According to Omar al-Mukhtar, all that

---

[45] GRAZIANI, *op. cit.*, pp. 21–46, and DE LEONE, *op. cit.*, pp. 549–55. Between these two versions and the many others expressed in colonial circles, like Canevari's, there are minor differences (for instance, Graziani could not openly attack Badoglio, his direct superior, who was, nevertheless, the principal target for all the other authors); what they have in common is their anti-Arab attitude, their whole-hearted defence of a policy of force, and their offhand manner of manipulating the documentation.

[46] GIGLIO, *La confraternita senussita, cit.*, pp. 134–7.

[47] GRAZIANI, *op. cit.*, pp. 24–8.

[48] GRAZIANI, *op. cit.*, pp. 29–30. This did not prevent Graziani attributing the failure of the peace effort entirely to the double-dealing and wickedness of Omar al-Mukhtar and Senusiya.

was agreed at these meetings was a truce for two months, necessary for continuing the negotiations already begun[49]; and circumstances would appear to prove him right, because he went to meet both Siciliani and Badoglio with a strong retinue of warriors, without performing any of the traditional acts of submission[50]. What is certain is that the validity of the June agreements was of lesser importance than the actuality of the situation, since the Senusi rebellion had not been defeated in the field but was clearly capable of negotiating a compromise peace from a position of strength[51].

Given this situation, it is hard not to be surprised at the decisive way in which Badoglio informed De Bono and Mussolini that the submission of Omar al-Mukhtar and his colleagues was to be regarded as unconditional and definitive. Reporting to Mussolini on the meeting of 13 June, he put the following words into Omar al-Mukhtar's mouth:

It is not true to say that I was a rebel because never before today did I submit to the government, and thus I have always fought it. . . . Today I submit; for me General Badoglio is the first Italian governor who has ruled Cyrenaica. From today there is in Cyrenaica a government, an Italian one. From today there are government soldiers in Cyrenaica. Cyrenaica enters, from today, into a new era, that of peace. I am at the disposal of the government[52].

'I leave tomorrow for Benghazi,' continued Badoglio, 'to receive the solemn act of submission. With rejoicing heart I send this telegram to your excellency (Mussolini) since I am confident that a new life is beginning for Cyrenaica'[53]. At the same time the marshal telegraphed De Bono:

I have strongly refused all proposals made to me, stating that the sole basis of peace must be my proclamation, which is explicit and can leave no cause for doubtful interpretations. The present submission is based solely on two conditions: (1) disarmament; (2) pardon. I fully share your excellency's conclusion that Senusiya is done for and has lost all credit[54].

---

[49] See the declaration of Omar al-Mukhtar dated 20 October 1929, in GRAZIANI, *op. cit.*, pp. 44–6.

[50] This point is forcefully underlined, in discussion with Badoglio, by CANEVARI, *op. cit.*, pp. 325 *et seq.*

[51] In fact, Omar al-Mukhtar pointed out that his meetings with Badoglio and Siciliani were held between those of equal rank, representing the governments who alone could be expected to decide on peace, and he demanded as a condition for progress in the negotiations that the Italians should call upon Idris es-Senussi, thus recognizing his authority as head of state.

[52] Quoted in DE LEONE, *op. cit.*, p. 551. De Leone himself, who justified all aspects of Fascist policy, admitted that Omar al-Mukhtar had never submitted (p. 559).

[53] Quoted in DE LEONE, *op. cit.*, p. 551.

[54] Badoglio to De Bono, 16 or 17 June 1929, in ACS-SPD/cr, b. 224/R, fasc. colonial ministry, sf. De Bono (already published in ROCHAT, *cit.*, p. 10).

In the days that followed, Badoglio several times repeated his conviction that the Senusi unconditional surrender had been due to the depth of its internal crisis, persuading the leaders of the rebellion to bring it to an end:

There has never been a distinction here between non-combatants and rebels. Those killed in battle have almost always carried non-combatant identity. The rebellion has been fed by the *sottomessi*, to the extent that Omar al-Mukhtar, in spite of the losses sustained in battle, was always able to replenish his forces from the ranks of *sottomessi*. Disastrous living conditions for everyone and the natural wish for a quiet life after so many years of bitter warfare, during which time the *sottomessi* were treated in the same manner as the rebels, resulted in my proclamation being welcomed as the only possible solution. The rest is known. Now it is up to us to ensure that our conduct remains unchanged, looking for ways to improve the lot of these unfortunate people. The government can rest assured that this will be done[55].

All the Senusi leaders are being, and always will be, closely watched, but I have to say again that Senusi political influence in Cyrenaica is completely destroyed. This is especially true since the members of the Senusi family, with the exception of Ahmed esc-Scerif, are a bunch of degenerates who are interested only in living as comfortably as possible. There are no foreseeable Senusi elements here that can possibly cause any further disturbances[56].

It is useless or at any rate unrealistic to get in a lather any more over the Senusi bugbear. As a political force, Senusiya, run by the present Senusi people, who are either stupid or immoral or a combination of both, is done for[57].

Badoglio's boastful optimism reflected, first of all, the verifiable incapacity of the army commands and of Italian colonial circles to appreciate how deeply rooted the rebellion was, and their failure to understand the behaviour of the Senusi leaders; but the attitudes of the marshal and of the faithful Siciliani had other origins as well. Badoglio's pacification policy had, in fact, encountered strong hostility in colonial quarters, where it was firmly believed, for a number of reasons (national pride, career and commercial interests, racism and so forth) that a policy of force was the only answer; and De Bono, jealous of the autonomy enjoyed by a man of high rank and prestige such as Badoglio, lost no opportunity to denounce, when reporting to Mussolini, the unfortunate effects of a policy based on weakness and compromise, which was inconsistent with the image of imperial strength and grandeur sought by the regime. Badoglio himself had not pursued the path of peace from any deep conviction, but in the hope of chalking up a personal triumph by obtaining

---

[55] Badoglio to De Bono, 21 June 1929, in ASMAI, 150/21/90.
[56] Badoglio to De Bono, 22 June 1929, in ASMAI, 150/21/90.
[57] Badoglio to Mussolini, 24 June 1929, quoted in DE LEONE, *op. cit.*, p. 552.

an end to the state of war within a few months; nor, what is more, did he really envisage a sharing of power with the Senusi, but merely a more pliable and effective form of Italian penetration than might be achieved by the traditional recourse to armed force. His position was none too easy, since he found himself fighting on two fronts, against the Senusi and against the colonists, both eager to take advantage of any false step on his part; this would apparently explain his decision to play a dangerous double game, which led him on the one hand to guarantee the colonists and his superiors in Rome that Omar al-Mukhtar's surrender was unconditional and final, enabling him to carry through his policy without any outside interference, and on the other hand to negotiate with the Senusi a compromise peace based upon power-sharing in Cyrenaica, in the conviction (derived from his very inability to comprehend the mass roots of the rebellion) that a few months' armistice and a brief interval of corruption and discord would be sufficient to shatter the Senusi front and lead to real pacification on the basis of unopposed Italian rule. Badoglio was thus prepared to grant a good deal in the short term to Omar al-Mukhtar, but not concede to the written, formal agreements which the Senusi asked for (and which Siciliani promised), because he was convinced that the rebellion's internal arguments (encouraged by the Italians with rewards and promises) and the weary state of the Gebel populations would, within a short time, make the resumption of guerilla activities impossible, opening the way, gradually and inevitably, towards full Italian rule.

2. The truce

'The satisfactory general and political situation in Cyrenaica, in my opinion, is on the way to becoming excellent both in substance and appearance,' wrote Siciliani on 29 June, showing complete faith in the future:

It has been the people who have obliged Omar al-Mukhtar firstly to abandon aggressive behaviour and then to submit. It will again be the people who will prevent the rebel armed forces from breaking the pledges they have given or allowing the rebellion to degenerate into brigandry. . . .

The *duar* have taken on the guise of peaceful encampments and their numbers have greatly diminished because many of the people composing them have quietly dispersed in various directions to test the ground and find out what the real intentions of the government are. Many of them are without arms, others have deposited their weapons at control posts, after receiving the promise that they will get them back on demand once they have withdrawn from built-up areas and garrisons[58].

---

[58] Siciliani to Badoglio, 29 June 1929, in ASMAI, 150/21/90. Omar al-Mukhtar fully collaborated, wrote Siciliani, on condition that dealings were with him alone; instead Italian policy aimed to set off the *sottomessi* against the leaders of the rebellion.

Actually the situation was more complex. The *duar* had not been broken up nor had the population been disarmed, so that the quiet conditions in the Gebel really demonstrated the authority of Omar al-Mukhtar rather than the strength of the Italian armed forces; furthermore, the Senusi organization was once again exercising its powers in broad daylight, from the administration of justice to the collection of taxes[59]. In mid-August Siciliani had to admit that the course of pacification was proving 'laborious', principally because Omar al-Mukhtar, although scrupulously observing the truce, refused to dissolve the *duar*, and was publicly receiving the traditional taxes in order to maintain them[60]. Nevertheless, Badoglio and Siciliani continued to avoid using any force which might hasten matters, preferring to concentrate on wearing down the Senusi organization, torn as it was by serious internal disputes. According to Italian sources, which, as we have already pointed out, are not to be taken as very reliable, Mohammed er-Redà and his son Hassan er-Redà headed the faction inclined to accept a compromise peace, while Omar al-Mukhtar was the most authoritative exponent of the school of thought which preferred the renewal of hostilities to any peace that might restrict the independence of the Gebel tribes and of Senusi authority. The tensions between these two factions must have been strong if it is true that the Brahasa-Dorsa *dor*, under the influence of Hassan er-Redà and the *sottomessi*, withdrew from the command of Omar al-Mukhtar and, whilst retaining its organization, accepted Italian funds for its maintenance[61]. It does not seem, however, that the gravity of these disagreements was exaggerated, so much so that in mid-September Badoglio was encouraging Siciliani to step up pressure on the Gebel:

On the orders of his excellency Minister De Bono, I confirm the following directive actions. Firstly, try to get as many dissidents as possible under our control without approaching their leaders. Persuade the *sottomessi*, particularly the Brahasa Dorsa, to act against the dissidents not only by word but also by deed, wherever they can count on the support of our units. Try, as soon as possible, to initiate public works, in accordance with today's telegram, so as

---

[59] De Bono claimed that it was because of his direct intervention that the Senusi leaders were prohibited from again setting up gallows—their traditional symbol of sovereign authority (De Bono to Badoglio, 14 July 1929, in ASMAI, 150/21/90).

[60] Siciliani to Badoglio, 16 August 1929, in ASMAI, 150/21/90. The Italian authorities offered the armed soldiers of the *duar* the same treatment conceded to the men of the *daurie*, those irregular bands attached to the local commissioners with police duties, but Omar al-Mukhtar preferred to resort to traditional taxation, despite the poverty of the people, in order to maintain full control of his forces and to affirm Senusi sovereignty.

[61] GRAZIANI, *op. cit.*, pp. 31–5, and Badoglio to De Bono, 25 August 1929, in ASMAI, 150/21/90.

to employ the maximum local manpower. This action must be undertaken in such a way that the situation is not suddenly and inopportunely upset[62].

From the few available accounts of the events of the summer, we get the impression that the disruptive action taken by the Italians achieved limited results, but that the Senusi leadership considered the protection afforded by the truce to be dangerously unbalanced. Badoglio, in fact, showed himself generous with under-the-counter concessions but refused to give any formal pledges guaranteeing to the Senusi the role they hoped for; in particular, he refused to negotiate with Idris es-Senusi for fear of recognizing his political authority. Italian superiority in all departments was so great that for the Senusi to have accepted a real peace without precise guarantees would have meant them running the risk of progressively losing ground. Therefore, on 20 October, faced by new Italian attempts to protract the armistice without offering adequate political negotiations, Omar al-Mukhtar announced his decision not to accept further adjournments and to resume hostilities from 24 October. After briefly summarizing the intervening negotiations, and emphasizing that it was the Italians who had found the pretext of curtailing them by refusing to recognize Idris's authority, Omar al-Mukhtar continued by saying:

The armistice is now on the point of expiring and I have received no answer from the Italian government regarding its proposal to get in touch with our emir Saied Mohammed Idris es-Senusi. I intend, therefore, to resume the war and to take no notice of any conversation and of any intermediary, not even if they were those of the Senusi family, unless the choice is made as a result of the nation's trust. But I do not understand why the Italian government shrinks from making contact with the above-mentioned leader, knowing very well that it alone has the power to make and destroy. If it were truly committed to pursuing peace, it would not hesitate for an instant to get in touch with him.

Let every fighter know, therefore, that the sole aim of the Italian government is to stir up discords and plots among us in order to destroy our bonds and break up our union, and to be able to prise away and snatch from us all our legitimate rights, as has already happened many times. But, thanks to God, they have not managed to do any of this.

Let the whole world bear witness that our intentions towards the Italian government are noble, that we have no other aim than to claim our freedom

---

[62] Badoglio to Siciliani, 13 September 1929, in ASMAI, 150/21/90. Siciliani, on the other hand, displayed the utmost confidence; the situation was quiet, submissions were continuing, refugees were returning, and in the Gebel 'ex-rebels, in large numbers and disarmed, visited our positions, behaving in a deferent and correct manner' (Siciliani to the ministry, 23 September 1929, in ASMAI, 150/21/90).

and that the objective of the Italians is to repress any national movement which aims at the reawakening and progress of the Tripolitan people. . . .

We are now defending our very existence and are sacrificing our blood in order to redeem our country and to achieve the ends that we have mentioned. Nevertheless, we undertake that such a situation will only last until the individuals who are set upon using violence against us change their ways, start out on the right path and treat us with fairness rather than with flattery and deceit[63].

3. The resumption of hostilities

The denunciation of the armistice was not immediately followed by an outbreak of hostilities, but it alarmed the Italian military command (even if Italian colonial historians prefer to ignore the proclamation so as to be able to accuse Omar al-Mukhtar of treason). When, on 8 November, a *zaptia* patrol fell into an ambush at Gasr Benigdem, leaving four men dead, Siciliani's reaction was prompt: resume combing operations, arrest 'ex-rebels' and shoot anyone offering resistance. 'The utmost aggressiveness and no quarter,' ordered the vice-governor, who regretted not being able to swoop down at once on Omar al-Mukhtar, at that moment in another part of the Gebel. 'Although different sources absolve Omar al-Mukhtar of direct responsibility for the Gasr Benigdem episode, events of the last 24 hours confirm that he has resumed hostilities,' telegraphed Siciliani; 'it is now useless to fool ourselves: as long as Omar al-Mukhtar is here, we cannot bring about peace in Cyrenaica'[64].

De Bono took advantage of the occasion to obtain from Mussolini a repudiation of Badoglio's policy, which he telegraphed on 10 November:

Unfortunately, what I foresaw and pointed out in my various communications has now come to pass. The head of government, being acquainted with the situation, approves my proposals, as follows: (1) break off any form of negotiation with, and toleration for, the rebels, attacking them and giving no quarter; (2) all Senusi persons in our hands to be strictly and manifestly supervised, without any considerate treatment; (3) no more talk of sub-

---

[63] For the date as well as for the text of Omar al-Mukhtar's proclamation we are forced to depend on GRAZIANI, *op. cit.*, pp. 44–6, from which it is unclear when precisely the proclamation reached the Italian authorities and when it was circulated among the people.

[64] Siciliani to Badoglio, 8 and 9 November 1929, in ASMAI, 150/21/90. It seems unlikely that Omar al-Mukhtar had any direct responsibility for the Gasr Benigdem ambush (the legendary chief could have used a number of other methods if he had wished to resume hostilities with a surprise action), but the episode is nevertheless part and parcel of Omar al-Mukhtar's and Senusiya's decision to take the offensive again in the Gebel, as attested by his denunciation of the armistice.

missions if they have not actually happened (sic); (4) captured leaders to be hanged. . . .

It is necessary that this serious political failure should have the least possible repercussions. Every care must be taken not to publicize it. . . .

Vice-governor Siciliani has by now demonstrated all too clearly that he is not equal to his position. He must be replaced as soon as possible, without giving the impression that we have suffered a setback[65].

Aware of the insecurity of his position and strongly urged by Badoglio (who, however, continued to back him before De Bono), Siciliani threw himself into frantic activity, organizing patrols and large-scale encircling manoeuvres, relaunching terror raids from the air, and issuing proclamations intended primarily for the ministerial and colonial circles that were accusing him of weakness. Here is the resounding order of the day dated 12 November:

Omar al-Mukhtar's treason has compelled us to resume hostilities against the rebels. War without let-up and without quarter against anyone who uses arms against the government and who carries them without its permission.

The honour of the first engagement has gone to the air force. The manner in which it has acted will always be a matter of congratulation and pride for the force itself, and a source of great admiration for us. The airmen have returned to base covered with glory, and if a machine that has been hit has been forced to land on the battlefield and its brave crew captured by the enemy at gun-point, this cannot be counted as a loss but must rank as a display of courage in the long record of heroic deeds and glorious sacrifices by the Italian air force. My heart, both as vice-governor and soldier, together with the hearts of all Italians and soldiers serving in the colony, beats more rapidly in unison to the rhythm of the engines and with the no less iron hearts of our brave airmen[66].

On 16–17 November the *dor* of Omar al-Mukhtar, which clearly did not yet expect a full-scale attack, was surprised at Gasr Mragh by a coordinated manoeuvre of the Italian troops and forced to scatter, with losses[67]. The success strengthened Siciliani's conviction that Omar al-Mukhtar could by now rely only on reduced forces because of his diminishing influence with the

---

[65] De Bono to Badoglio, 10 November 1929, in ASMAI, 150/21/90; the telegram had already been partially published in DE LEONE, *op. cit.*, p. 554. De Bono judged the situation so grave that he suggested to Badoglio that the start of operations for occupying Fezzan be delayed. Badoglio replied that he had enough strength to cope with the situation in Cyrenaica (14,000 well organized men) and at the same time to complete the reconquest of Tripolitania (Badoglio to De Bono, 12 November 1929, in ASMAI, 150/21/90).

[66] Order of the day from vice-governor Siciliani, 12 November 1929, in ASMAI, 150/21/90; on the air force cf. LIOY, *op. cit.*, pp. 159–60. Between 12 and 25 November the Cyrenaican air force carried out ten bombardments and machine-gunnings, and 360 hours of operational flights, attacking rebel formations and caravans, and suspect encampments.

[67] Siciliani to De Bono and Badoglio, 18 November 1929, in ASMAI, 150/21/90.

non-combatant population[68]; and, in fact, the Brahasa-Dorsa *dor* did not immediately take the field, but retreated into a kind of armed neutrality, which Siciliani encouraged by refusing De Bono's orders to disarm the *dor* by force. Yet this time, too, the Italian authorities underestimated the depth of the rebellion's roots, because Omar al-Mukhtar quickly regained control of the Gebel, with the support of the great majority of the population, and roused the Brahasa-Dorsa *dor* against Hassan er-Redà, who continued in his refusal to return to battle. In early January the *dor* rebelled against Hassan er-Redà, escaped the surveillance of the Italian troops and took up its position again alongside Omar al-Mukhtar, sealing the definitive failure of the policy of pacification and disintegration. De Bono took the opportunity of issuing a stern rebuke, on 10 January, to Siciliani (and implicitly to Badoglio, who was still backing him):

So what I foresaw has once again happened. Months ago I warned you not to trust anyone. I have insisted at least five times that steps should be taken to disarm the *dor*, but your excellency has always nourished illusions. Your excellency will agree that yet again we have not cut a very fine figure. I tried to make it clear in every possible way that any concession to the rebels would be taken as weakness. This latest incident smacks of rebellion. Your excellency must make sure that Hassan does not act in the same way. Your excellency will therefore hold him prisoner. Take measures to prevent the rebellion spreading and ensure that those who have rebelled do not join up with Omar al-Mukhtar[69].

At the same time De Bono telegraphed Badoglio, demanding Siciliani's head and an intensification of repressive measures:

We have had the encore as I predicted. That is why I have telegraphed Benghazi. Siciliani, I repeat, does not seem to be up to his job. Your excellency must see what measures we need to take so as not to waste our efforts. *My opinion is that we shall have to resort to concentration camps*, and that we should do this as soon as Tripolitania is sorted out. Thus it is necessary to give the impression (in) Cyrenaica that the system is going to be changed once and for all[70].

In a desperate attempt to retrieve his declining position, Siciliani, on the same day, issued a proclamation announcing a stepping-up of repressive measures:

---

[68] Siciliani calculated that Omar al-Mukhtar had lost two-thirds of his soldiers during the armistice and could rely only on a maximum of 500 men on foot and 300 on horseback, with a caravan of a thousand camels.

[69] De Bono to Siciliani, 10 January 1930, in ASMAI, 150/21/90, already published in DE LEONE, *op. cit.*, p. 554.

[70] De Bono to Badoglio, 10 January 1930, in ASMAI, 150/21/90. Here the italics are ours.

To the people of Cyrenaica.

Between the months of April and November you have tasted all the joys of peace. The country has benefited from it. The government has helped the people, has pardoned crimes, has emptied the prisons. I have waited patiently for the desire for peace to enter the hearts of the rebels and to get them to lay down their arms.

It has all been in vain! Omar al-Mukhtar has turned traitor and, in the name of Idris and of Senusiya, has resumed hostilities, causing blood to be spilled anew. His propaganda has even swayed those who, mistrusting him, had declared themselves loyal. In fact, some of the soldiers of Hassan er-Redà's *dor*, forgetful of the responsibilities and benefits received from the government, have carried out raids which have harmed the *sottomessi*, and when the government has tried to punish them have gone over to Omar al-Mukhtar. Others have rebelled against the government's first lawful order and have fired against government forces. They have been destroyed!

Hassan er-Redà, who recognized these grave faults, was not prepared to remain with those who had rebelled against the government, and has retired to live happily in Benghazi with his family.

New blood has been spilt and new riches have been lost. The prisons are again being filled! The horror of all this damage is due to Omar al-Mukhtar, to those who force him to remain a rebel and to those who are with him.

Listen to what I say. Remember the words of his excellency the governor Marshal Badoglio. Whoever stays loyal and does not make common cause with the rebels will continue to enjoy peace, tranquillity and prosperity. Whoever is still a rebel and who comes forward with his rifle and ammunition will be pardoned and be as safe as those who have already taken this sensible step. War without respite and without quarter for anyone who stubbornly remains a rebel and for those who assist the rebels, so prolonging the actions that will end up by completely destroying the country's welfare[71].

It is symptomatic that Badoglio, too, continuing to lend support to Siciliani, proposed new terrorist measures of extreme gravity, the only point on which all Italian commanders agreed:

I give my complete approval to action. Continue mopping up and something will surely come of it. Remember that Omar al-Mukhtar requires two things: firstly, an excellent information service; secondly, *a nice surprise with aircraft and mustard-gas bombs. I hope that such bombs will be sent to him as soon as possible*[72].

[71] Proclamation by vice-governor Siciliani, 10 January 1930, in ASMAI, 150/21/90.
[72] Badoglio to Siciliani, 10 January 1930, in ASMAI, 150/21/90. Here, too, the italics are ours. We do not believe that the Italians used asphyxiating gas in repressing the Libyan resistance; see, however, the documentation by Eric SALERNO, *Genocidio in Libia. Le atrocità nascoste dell'avventura coloniale 1911–31*, Milan, Sugarco, 1979, pp. 45–63, which claims that gas was used on various occasions.

The marshal then came to the defence of Siciliani's policies with a telegram that requested De Bono to delay any decision[73] and with a full report which summed up the results achieved in Cyrenaica in twelve months. In January 1929, wrote Badoglio, 'there was not the slightest security in any part of the colony. Anyone venturing a short distance from our garrison was sure to be the object of some attack.' The Italian military apparatus was in a critical state: 'an inflated occupation force, with far too many detachments scattered all over the place, with units that had little organic cohesion, incapable of virtually any offensive action because they were deprived of adequate logistical services, and, moreover, very low in morale as a result of the continual state of siege in which they found themselves'. The people were caught between two fires, apparently submissive to the government, but actually compelled to support the rebels; and even the Italian colony was going through a serious crisis: 'distrust and consequent apathy on the part of many officials, civil and military, slander and gossip that spread abroad to Italy, and corruption in the administration which resulted in accusing notes being sent to the public prosecutor'. In this difficult situation, continued the report, Badoglio and Siciliani had been forced to work on a long-term basis, accepting the offered truce primarily as an expedient to buy precious months. Their programme envisaged a complete reorganization of the troops, which would make them truly mobile (it was the very lack of trained mobile units in the summer of 1929 that had prevented Siciliani from disarming the *duar*), the building of a road network in the Gebel which would provide work for the people and freedom of movement for the troops, and the setting up of a fortified line which would genuinely protect the *sottomessi* from attacks by the rebels. This programme, insisted Badoglio, had in its essential points been brilliantly realized by Siciliani, and even Omar al-Mukhtar's betrayal, which had so alarmed De Bono, had been faced calmly. Certainly, the achievement of complete pacification had had to be delayed, but the resumption of guerilla activities occurred in far less favourable circumstances for the enemy, giving rise to hopes that it might be crushed within a short period. The balance sheet over a year of government was thus, in Badoglio's view, largely positive; and he concluded his report by stating firmly that 'vice-governor Siciliani, I repeat, has my unconditional confidence'[74].

Badoglio's intervention was, however, overtaken by events, for De Bono had lost no time in persuading Mussolini to replace Siciliani with General

---

[73] Badoglio to De Bono, 10 January 1930 (in reply to a telegram from De Bono of the same day), in ASMAI, 150/21/90. 'No special measure need be adopted,' promised Badoglio, 'Situation is completely clarified and our forces fully able to cope.'

[74] Badoglio to De Bono, 10 January 1930, in ASMAI, 150/21/90. Badoglio asked for any decision to be delayed until February, when he would have had time to return to Rome to discuss the situation in Cyrenaica with Mussolini and De Bono.

Graziani from 10 January. Graziani was the man in charge of the reconquest of Tripolitania, and was then engaged in completing the occupation of Fezzan. Badoglio had to give in[75]; but he kept the faithful Siciliani with him as commander of the troops in Tripolitania, the post left vacant by Graziani and a prestigious one, even if of lesser importance now that this colony had been pacified.

IV. The operations in the Gebel in 1930–1

1. *Graziani and the policy of punishment*

The crushing of Cyrenaican resistance in 1930–1 is associated with the name of Graziani, who not only carried it out but who, in many respects, planned it as well. In fact, the propaganda of the Fascist regime and, in due course, colonial historiography placed so much emphasis on him and on the action he took that the credit and responsibility of his superiors and subordinates are largely overlooked. Little mention is made of the extraordinary combination of circumstances that made his victory possible, there is silence concerning his errors, and the high cost of his punishment programme in terms of human lives is conveniently forgotten or ignored.

The official propaganda and the pages of colonial history offer diverse reasons for his success. Thus Graziani was the most famous of all Italian 'colonial' generals, active in all the Fascist campaigns in Africa, undoubtedly able and fortunate, with a powerful physical presence, an inclination for poses and spectacular gestures, and an ability to mouth rhetorical slogans which made him a genuine 'Fascist hero'. He was, furthermore, far closer to the regime than most of the other high-ranking commanders, since neither by virtue of his origins nor his career was he part of the monarchic army establishment (he came from the ranks of the reserve officers and had not attended either an army school or academy, but won his promotion in the field); consequently he parted company with the traditional hierarchies and sought support from the Fascists and their friends (De Bono during the period under discussion, and later Mussolini himself), protesting his loyalty repeatedly and giving proof of his ability and efficiency. One proof of his awareness

---

[75] Badoglio to De Bono, 11 January 1930, in ASMAI, 150/21/90. Badoglio said he would obey the peremptory order to dismiss Siciliani, approved his replacement by Graziani (on condition the latter would complete the operations in Fezzan before going on to Cyrenaica) and requested General Pintor as replacement for Graziani (to which Mussolini and De Bono would not agree).

of the importance of propaganda is the weight of autobiographical material he turned out so rapidly: *Cirenaica pacificata*, the book which reconstructs the two decisive years of the breaking of Senusi resistance, was published within a year of the events described, and it constitutes, even today, an extremely important and valuable document (Graziani did not have much respect for the truth, when he could be harmed by it, but was so confident of himself and of the regime's protection that he felt no need to conceal the harshness of the repressive measures carried out), but remains, above all, a monument of self-publicity, which colonial historians have always accepted uncritically.

The Graziani who emerges from our archival investigation is rather different from the man as traditionally depicted. His most obvious character-istic is an impatient need for self-assertion, to the extent that he was led to regard both friends and enemies as stepping stones towards his further success and therefore to take upon himself responsibility for the most severe and heinous measures if they seemed useful to him; furthermore, he would plot, without scruple, against superiors and subordinates in order to retain all credit for himself, showing ever more explicitly a persecution mania which was only partially justified in the climate of social climbing and corruption which distinguished Fascist colonialism. His proven ability as an organizer and leader of modern forms of desert warfare (an area where Graziani was undeniably the greatest expert in colonial Africa between the two World Wars), was only partially tested during his period of government in Cyrenaica, notably when he conquered Cufra, because the Gebel presented a diversity of geographical and social conditions. As we shall see in detail, in repressing the Senusi resistance, Graziani showed himself to be a capable organizer and a ruthless executor rather than a genius in political and military affairs, even if he subsequently chose to claim the entire merit of the victory for himself. Even his vaunted understanding of the mentality and environment of the Arabs needs to be reassessed, for it was not the fruit of genuine interest in Arab society and culture, but of long experience in colonial government, and therefore focused attention merely on the most obvious and traditional elements of paternalism and racism.

The choice of Graziani as vice-governor of Cyrenaica after the downfall of Siciliani was logical, given his prestige as a commander and his reputation for toughness just at the moment when all the people responsible agreed on the need for a return to a policy of indiscriminate repression, but it also represented revenge for De Bono and the colonial administrators, who were aiming to rid Badoglio of his authority. When in March 1930 he was in Italy to receive ministerial instructions prior to taking over the vice-governorship (he had completed the conquest of Fezzan in January-February), Graziani obtained from De Bono and colonial officials explicit promises of support if Badoglio, his direct superior, attempted to restrict his freedom of action by continuing his pacification policy[76]. The directives imparted to him by Mussolini were unequivocal, though certainly not new:

(1) Clear and effective distinction between those who had, and those who had not, offered submission, in their homes, their places of work and their dealings.

(2) Give safety and protection to the *sottomessi*, but keep a watch on their every activity.

(3) Remove the *sottomessi* entirely from all Senusi influence, prohibiting absolutely collections by any Senusi representatives or anyone demanding any kind of tithe or *zachat*.

(4) Constant and complete control of goods, and strict closure of the Egyptian frontier so as to avoid any chance of the enemy receiving fresh supplies.

(5) Systematic but firm purging of the native quarters, beginning with the bigger towns and especially Benghazi.

(6) Use of irregular elements to fight enemy brigandry and to initiate vigorous reprisal actions, the final objective of these being to clear the territory completely of every enemy formation[77].

In Benghazi, where he landed on 27 March[78], Graziani found the guerilla war raging fiercely; in the five months since the renewal of fighting, the rebels had lost 380 men and 150 rifles (in January Omar al-Mukhtar himself had been wounded at Wadi Mahaggia), but had themselves killed six officers, six Italian non-commissioned officers and 102 *ascari*; furthermore, 'Omar al-Mukhtar still held the initiative in the operations because his freedom of movement in the Gebel had not in any way been restricted'[79]. Graziani's first preoccupation was to analyze the situation, about which he already had definite ideas, so that he was able immediately to produce reasoned arguments underlining the links between the people and the Senusi forces:

(A) Senusi activities have an impact everywhere. *They all* hope that if they do not manage to establish peace by force the government will be induced to yield, making a variety of concessions. *All of them*, be they important or ordinary people, *sottomessi* or not, are doing everything possible to keep the rebellion alive, thus disturbing public tranquillity. This is an absolute reality, and to deny it is a refusal to see matters clearly. All that is necessary, however,

[76] See in the Graziani archive the letters previously addressed to him in February by De Bono and head of the cabinet De Rubeis, with an explicit offer of an agreement (ACS-FG, 1/2/2).

[77] De Bono to Badoglio and Graziani, 24 March 1930, in ACS-FG, 1/2/2, and in ASMAI, 150/22/98; published with slight changes in GRAZIANI, *op. cit.*, p. 49.

[78] Graziani called himself a Fascist from the time of his first greeting to his compatriots of Benghazi: 'My action,' he said, 'will be loyally marked with the principles of the Fascist state, because I, who am divisional general on active service with the army, hereby declare my principles to be wholly Fascist.' (GRAZIANI, *op. cit.*, p. 51.)

[79] *Dieci anni di storia cirenaica*, cit.

is to recognize it and try to cut off at the roots the sectarian influence which originates it and which guides the thread of the tangled skein through narrow, often unattainable, channels.

(B) Omar al-Mukhtar does not now possess more than 600 rifles, with which he levies the non-combatants, tries to attack our organizations, and carries out costly reconnaissance forays even in built-up areas, as happened recently at Tocra, Cyrene and Derna, where a handful of men were able to infiltrate the towns, without anyone striking a blow in return, and withdraw unpunished after committing acts of brigandry.

(C) The *sottomessi* are linked to the old *akuan* (Senusi chief) and to his proselytes by sectarian bonds and by blood, because his *dor* is made up of men belonging to every tribe who pay, willingly or unwillingly, tribute. However, this limits their action to passive defence and to counter-offensives which, nine times out of ten, are simulated or sterile. They never really take the offensive initiative. If this were to happen, the rebellion would end within a fortnight.

This is how things are, and unless there is a radical cure of the entire organism they will continue like this for dozens of years to come, because I rule out military action, intensive though it may be, as a means of destroying the *duar*, which are always ready to regroup by a phenomenon of endosmosis, turning up leaders in the encampments of the *sottomessi*.

I see the situation in Cyrenaica as comparable to a poisoned organism which produces, in one part of the body, a festering bubo. The bubo in this instance is the *dor* of Omar al-Mukhtar, which is the result of a wholly infected situation. To heal this sick body it is necessary to destroy the origin of the malady rather than its effects[80].

This analysis (like all other similar ones previously mentioned) was typical of colonial thinking, i.e. sufficiently realistic to grasp the central issue of the problem, the basis of Senusi mass-resistance, but totally uninterested in the real reasons for the rebellion and in the nature of the Gebel society. For Graziani, as for his predecessors, the only thing that mattered was how to gain absolute control of the situation by breaking down the traditional political and social structure; and in 1930 the path to follow appeared to be an intensification of the punitive measures already attempted. In the course of the spring and summer, Graziani proceeded to close the Senusi *zavie*, to deport the *zavia*

---

[80] Graziani to Badoglio and De Bono, 5 April 1930, in ACS-FG, 1/2/2, and in ASMAI, 150/22/98 (previously published in ROCHAT, *cit.*, p. 13). A fuller and clearer analysis, though not a more profound one, appears in Graziani's afore-mentioned book, and this is the concise conclusion: 'We had against us all the people of Cyrenaica who were part and parcel of the rebellion; on the one hand, in a potential state, the so-called *sottomessi*, and on the other, openly in the field, the soldiers. The whole of Cyrenaica, in a word, was rebellious.' (GRAZIANI, *op. cit.*, p. 57.)

leaders and to confiscate Senusi property, movable and immovable (a measure thus far avoided because Fascist Italy did not want to alienate Moslem countries); he conducted a drastic purge of salaried Arab government officials, many of whom were tried for treason, and combated every form of neutrality and absenteeism in the fight against the rebellion; he ordered the *sottomessi* to be completely disarmed and he punished connivance with the *duar* by staging spectacular trials which carried the death penalty for possessing a weapon or for paying a title to the Senusi organization[81]; he dissolved the Libyan battalions and reduced the Savari squadrons and police forces (*daurie* and irregular bands), which had often given direct or indirect assistance to the rebellion; he prohibited all forms of commerce with Egypt to facilitate the control of contraband, which played an important role in the economy of the Gebel and in feeding the guerillas; and he embarked on the construction of a road network in the Gebel, an objective that none of his predecessors had ever managed to realize[82].

These measures were announced with a great flourish of bombastic declarations concerning the firmness and far-sightedness of Graziani's policies, in the traditional style of Fascist propaganda, which irritated Badoglio[83] but was highly appreciated in Rome. For example, De Rubeis, De Bono's principal private secretary, telegraphed Graziani in these terms: 'Measures introduced have won full ministerial approval and aroused great enthusiasm

[81] Graziani set up the 'flying tribunal', which moved by air to various places in Cyrenaica for trials of red-handed crimes, held in front of the people and concluding with the immediate execution of those condemned to death. During his first year of government Graziani was responsible for ordering 520 judicial procedures, in which 119 prisoners were condemned and executed, and 117 sentenced to detention (GRAZIANI, *op. cit.*, p. 144). The president of the special tribunal was General Olivieri, a military lawyer, who in 1937 was to defend the massacres carried out by Graziani in Addis Ababa (cf. Giorgio ROCHAT, *L'attentato a Graziani e la repressione italiana in Etiopia 1936–7*, in 'Italia contemporanea', 1975, no. 118). According to a widely diffused rumour, Graziani introduced into Cyrenaica the practice of judging rebels and suspected persons by making them jump out of an aircraft; we have found no confirmation of this in any documents, nor were any planes then in Cyrenaica used for this macabre game.

[82] We return for more details to the afore-mentioned book by Graziani, often imprecise and always tendentious, but nevertheless full of first-hand information. On Italian repression in Cyrenaica see also SALERNO, *op. cit.*, informative, but disordered and not always clear or correct.

[83] Badoglio, who knew quite well how these statements were designed to increase Graziani's credit, never ceased advising him to adopt a more sober style. Here are some passages from his telegrams: 'Remember that the best propaganda consists of facts' (10 April); 'Disarming is the only positive thing, all the rest is blather' (12 April). And when Graziani cabled: 'Continuing the systematic work of unhinging and dismantling all the previously established positions and all the prejudices which have in the past lessened our prestige and maimed our affirmation of absolute dominion, I have on today's date arrested all the Senusi *zawia*-leaders. . . .' (29 May), Badoglio drily replied: 'Point of this telegram has already been made many times by your excellency. I consider it by now superfluous to repeat it for every action taken. Will your excellency therefore limit yourself to saying what measures you are taking' (30 May). All the telegrams quoted are in ACS-FG, 1/2/2.

among ministry officials. Style of telegrams very much liked. Bravo Graziani'[84]. And De Bono handed one of these telegrams to Mussolini with these words: 'From this you can see the new style of government, the intuitive grasp of the situation and the confidence of success. Let us hope only that Badoglio allows him to do it'[85]. A correspondence on this pattern then ensued between Graziani and the minister, behind Badoglio's back; the latter wrote in vain on 14 May to his restless subordinate:

Unhappily, the attempt to cause trouble between us originated in the ministry. For my part, you are still the Graziani whom I knew in 1922 and with whom I have always worked in perfect harmony. . . . In the course of my long military career I have never had an argument with any subordinate. And certainly I shan't have one with you, whom I know to be an impetuous man but basically loyal and generous[86].

Graziani's keenness for action, however, still had to be put to the test and justified by victory in the field, for although his punitive policy might weaken the rebellion, positive action was needed to destroy the *duar*. Graziani, well aware of this, therefore set about reorganizing the troops under his command; during the summer the 13,000 men at his disposal (1000 officers and non-commissioned officers, 3000 Italian soldiers and 9000 *ascari*, mainly Eritreans) were formed into eight Eritrean battalions, three squadrons of armoured cars, one special frontier company of motor lorries, two Saharan groups, four Savari squadrons and two mobile batteries; in addition, he had a militia legion and a battalion for garrison duties, a motorized unit with 500 vehicles, and 30–35 reconnaissance and light bomber aircraft[87].

These forces appeared sufficient to destroy the *duar*, despite the unhappy experiences of former years; and, indeed, Graziani took great pains to prepare a coordinated operation with ten columns of varied composition and provenance, heavily supported, the aim being to encircle and destroy Omar al-Mukhtar's forces in the Fayed zone. So confident was he of success that he asked Badoglio to be present to celebrate the victory[88]. The operation began

---

[84] De Rubeis to Graziani, 2 April 1930, in ACS-FG, 1/2/2.

[85] De Bono to Mussolini, 1 April 1930, in ACS-SPD/cr, b. 389/R, fasc. Badoglio.

[86] Badoglio to Graziani, 14 May 1930, in ACS-FG, 1/2/2. The arrogance and superficiality of the ministry was such that on 13 June De Rubeis wrote to Graziani that, on the occasion of the imminent visit of Badoglio to Cyrenaica, 'the instruction given you is to avoid old-style top-level reunions and communications', so that the impression of energy given by Graziani should not be dissipated by Badoglio's weakness of character! (ACS-FG, 1/2/2). Cf. also ROCHAT, *cit.*, pp. 14–15.

[87] GRAZIANI, *op. cit.*, pp. 80–4; LIOY, *op. cit.*, pp. 165 *et seq.*

[88] On the action in the Fayed zone cf. GRAZIANI, *op. cit.*, pp. 151–3, and *Dieci anni di storia cirenaica*, *cit.*; for the request of Badoglio's presence see the exchange of telegrams between Graziani and Badoglio, 3 and 4 June 1930, in ACS-FG, 1/2/2; there too is the request by Badoglio to Graziani, dated 8 June, to be minutely informed as to the preparation of the operation in hand, 'so that responsibility for all that happens in the two colonies is entirely mine'.

on 16 June, but once again the *duar* were quickly informed by the people and by *ascari* deserters; breaking up into small groups, they managed to find their way through the Italian columns, with relatively light losses (50 dead and 32 rifles captured during the entire operation). Graziani could only boast that he had overrun some territory; and Badoglio was not slow to underline his setback:

I await more precise information that your excellency will send me. I note, however, that the principal objective, with concentric movements from the north and the south, was to teach the rebels a bitter lesson, as we did together in the Sciueref, and certainly not just to occupy a particular locality, something that your excellency can do whenever he wishes[89].

Graziani was forced to defend himself by protesting that he had always said it was 'impossible to destroy a rebel armed organization merely by resorting to military action'[90].

2. *The deportation of the people*

At this point Badoglio took the initiative once more, very firmly and clearly proposing that repressive measures assume a new dimension by deportation of the people of the Gebel, the only action that could literally create an empty space around Omar al-Mukhtar's *duar*. Here, in full, is the letter which he signed at the beginning of the final phase of resistance in the Gebel:

I have wanted your excellency (Graziani) to carry out the first cycle of operations without my direct intervention both in order not to impede the work but also to fall in with your excellency's request, as telegraphed to me, to postpone my arrival there until the operation is concluded. But it is now my strict duty to intervene, because responsibility for the action devolves directly on me, prior to reaching the ministry.

In Cyrenaica all operations of columns moving concentrically from distant departure points, i.e. all so-called long-range manoeuvres, have always failed and will always continue to be destined to failure as long as present conditions last. This is because the people and also the deserters (as has happened in this instance, and certainly not for the first time) collaborate so closely with the already highly vigilant protection and information service of the rebels that every move of ours is signalled to them at the appropriate time.

This valuable information service is matched by the ability of Omar al-Mukhtar, who is not consumed by megalomania as were the Sef-en-Nasser brothers at Bir el Afie and at the Sciuref, but, guided by a cold, calm

---

[89] Badoglio to Graziani, 19 June 1930, in ACS-FG, 1/2/2.
[90] Graziani to Badoglio, 20 June 1930, in ACS-FG, 1/2/2.

assessment of his forces and the consequent possibilities, refuses to fight and disperses his men. Such dispersal can always be carried out at short notice because information about our movements gets to him in time and because he can send his men to behave like *sottomessi* in single kabyles until the right moment comes for reuniting.

If your excellency will examine the course of all the operations, you will see that we have often captured flocks but have never inflicted serious damage on the enemy because of the persistence of the above-mentioned conditions. I have repeatedly cabled your excellency that the objective of this cycle of operations could not possibly be the one stated by your excellency, namely to invade the territory occupied by the enemy and to rout him. Your excellency is too experienced in such matters to maintain this argument. The true purpose was, or should have been, to eliminate the cause or at least to inflict a serious setback on the enemy. The result has not been achieved, not by reason of any fault in the orders or deficiency in execution, but purely and simply because of what I have said. Omar al-Mukhtar will go on dispersing his forces as long as he senses that there is movement around him. Then he will reunite them ready to carry out a quick attack to give the impression that we have achieved nothing.

What path should we follow? Your excellency has already provided the answer quite by chance when you informed me that you had decided that a tribe suspected of connivance was to be moved towards Tolmeta.

We must, above all, create a large and well defined territorial gap between the rebels and the subject population. I do not conceal from myself the significance and gravity of this action, which may well spell the ruin of the so-called subject population. But from now on the path has been traced out for us and we have to follow it to the end *even if the entire population of Cyrenaica has to perish.*

It is therefore urgent that the entire subject population should be herded into a restricted space, in such a way that we can keep suitable watch over the people and maintain an absolute gap between them and the rebels. Having done that, we can then go on to direct action against the rebels. . . .

Your excellency has for more than a year operated under my direct orders and in daily and amicable contact. Know that I am not refusing discussions and that I am always ready to go back on my decisions if you come up with an idea which I consider to be better than mine. I have expressed my thoughts to you as clearly as I could. If your excellency has objections to them, tell me what they are. If not, *put into effect immediately what I have said*[91].

Actually, the first movements of people were already under way in May, but these were simply regroupings of different tribes in one single zone of

---

[91] Badoglio to Graziani, 20 June 1930, in ACS-FG, 1/2/2 (partially published in ROCHAT, cit., pp. 16–17). The italics are ours.

their territory lying close to the Italian bases and easy to control; for example, 900 Abid tents were assembled on the Barce plain, 1400 Dorsa tents around Tolmeta, and 3600 Abeidat tents in the Derna zone[92]. Now, however, the forced transfer programme was immediately expanded, and on 25 June Graziani implemented the Badoglio directive by ordering 'the total clearance of the Gebel by moving the entire population, under its first phase, from Tolmeta to the sea'[93]. On 1 July Badoglio, after a series of talks with Graziani plus inspections, summed up the new strategy in a detailed memorandum for De Bono, several passages of which follow, beginning with this one, alluding to Omar al-Mukhtar:

The rebellion hinges on a single man who enjoys absolute authority and prestige. Omar al-Mukhtar does not share his power with anyone. He only has devoted and disciplined lieutenants. Thus it is not possible to employ the usual system of hemming him in among the jealousies, the rivalries and the hatreds which always exist when there are a number of leaders. At every moment and in every circumstance his firm will is law. He is extremely able both as commander and as organizer. A perfect information service enables him to refuse battle when the situation does not definitely favour him. A tight-knit counter-espionage service ensures that the only information that circulates is that which he has sanctioned. He is thus doubly safeguarded. Perfect knowledge of the terrain, especially that vast tableland zone of woods and ravines, facilitates his every move. His followers are people who for years have had no other trade than rebellion. By now they are accustomed to a life of adventure, of vagabondage and of struggle, ennobled by the halo of heroism. They are somewhat like the one-time bravos and brigands of our southern provinces. Woe to anyone who hesitates; at the faintest suspicion, wipe them out!

It is evident, nevertheless, that a group such as this, comprising a supreme chief and followers prepared for any hardship and any risk, cannot last long against forces ten times as big unless it can rely upon a strong and complex organization to ensure its existence. And here analysis becomes minute and extremely difficult. . . . To avoid confusion we have to focus on what is positive, on what must indisputably happen: the population has to share in the rebellion in every way, furnishing it with the means to live and to fight. . . .

In such a situation the action of the high command encounters numerous serious difficulties. One principle has to be stated at once: after Omar

---

[92] GRAZIANI, *op cit.*, p. 99.

[93] GRAZIANI, *op cit.*, pp. 101–2. The camps were to be concentrated during the month of July in the zones of Ain Gazala-Acroma-Tobruk, Derna, Cyrene, Tolmeta, el-Abiar, Agedadia and el-Agheila.

al-Mukhtar's betrayal of last year, no negotiation of any kind is possible. No more emollients, but surgical operation. We must therefore resolutely refuse any intervention by members of the Senusi family, and by other high-ranking representatives of this or that tribe. Let us start again from the beginning: but now is the time to make every effort for a complete settlement.

Having agreed that only the use of force will enable us to untie this Gordian knot, let us see how to employ this force. Concentrating exclusively on the *dor*, as has been done in the past, cannot yield any different results from those we have already achieved. The *dor* will break up, avoiding any activity for a certain time, and will then regroup as soon as pressure is lifted. The only course to pursue is, first of all, to isolate the *dor* from the rest of the people and cut the organizational link between them and the *dor*. It cannot be denied that this procedure is grave, complex and certainly not immediately effective. But it is the only one that I judge possible. It is already being set in motion. All the tribes will be removed from the tableland and concentrated in the foothills, between the slopes and the sea.

How will the rebels react? If they want to survive they will have to follow the movement of the population at some remove, otherwise communications and exchanges will become too difficult and hazardous. We will therefore have two advantages: removal of the rebels from the most dangerous tableland zones, and curtailment of the space requiring surveillance, thus giving greater efficacy to our action. At the same time, we must try to profit from every occasion to deal blows to the rebel forces.

In order to carry out this task two things are essential: (1) a nucleus of troops which, by dogging the heels of the rebels, can give us, even if only to a limited degree, a few grains of information, which at the moment we lack. This will be the job of the Akif band; (2) mobile nuclei of troops, notable for their great offensive spirit and guaranteed loyalty, and thus composed of Eritreans, which will survey a special zone and scour it incessantly. So we shall not have, because that is not possible, conclusive feats of arms, but we will have a wearing-down action, giving us cause to hope for a solution of exhaustion. Time, no impatience, solid nerves, and no deflection ever from the line taken, even if there seems to be a favourable occasion, because we ought by now to be thoroughly persuaded that these are shining yet false hopes[94].

A week later it was again Badoglio informing De Bono about what was going on, on the eve of the latter's visit to Cyrenaica:

The operation for concentrating the *sottomessi* continues in orderly fashion.

---

[94] Badoglio to De Bono, 1 July 1930, in ACS-FG, 1/2/2 (partially published in ROCHAT, *cit.*, pp. 17–18). Badoglio's programme for the population was summarized in the closing section of his memorandum as follows: 'To adopt for those people concentrated in the indicated zones all such measures as are designed to alleviate the worst hardships, but not to slacken the pressure on them whatever consequences this may incur.'

The Auaghir are all assembled between Giardina Soluk and Ghemines. I spoke to them quite severely yesterday morning. Tomorrow the Brahasa, Dorsa and Abid concentration will be complete between Tolmeta and Tocra. On Tuesday a start will be made on moving the Abeidat, about 7000 tents to be removed to the area between Tocra and Benghazi. This huge move will be completed around the 20th. As soon as the concentration camps are formed, we shall go on to rearrange the *ailet* and to carry out a strict census of people and livestock. For the first time we will thus have a true census. Gathering of barley on the tableland will be completed with concentric operations whereby no native will any longer remain in the area, and anyone who is encountered will be executed as a rebel. The entire population is truly filled with a sense of dismay and disorientation, because they now realize that rebels isolated in this manner cannot last long[95].

During the second week of July Badoglio and De Bono, visiting Cyrenaica[96], re-examined the new line of politico-strategic policy, which could not fail to have international repercussions as a result of predictable protests from nationalist Arab quarters. It was Badoglio, again, who, according to all the documentation, appears to have assumed the initiative and responsibility for the deportation policy, to sum up the conclusions in operative instructions for Graziani:

His excellency the Colonial Minister has been pleased to show his approval of the way in which the politico-military problem of the colony has been tackled. All that remains, therefore, is to persevere unswervingly with this line of conduct. To be more precise, from the political point of view, it is necessary:

(1) that the concentration movement of the *sottomessi* be completed and the security service relating to it properly arranged;

(2) that our civilian officials be set to work drawing up an exact census of people and livestock;

[95] Badoglio de De Bono, 7 July 1930, in ASMAI, 150/21/90. On the same day Badoglio wrote in a circular to the Cyrenaican commands: 'The operations to concentrate the so-called *sottomessi*, notwithstanding their scale, are being carried out in the most orderly manner. . . . The people have accepted the serious measure without any reaction, thus with supine obedience, in exactly the same way as they had accepted the removal of their weapons. They have understood perfectly that power is in the hands of the government and furthermore that the government has decided on any form of extreme measure to see that the orders it gives are completely carried out.' (ACS-FG, 1/2/2.).

[96] Graziani dates De Bono's visit in June and plays down Badoglio's stay (GRAZIANI, *op. cit.*, pp. 99–100). Comparison of documents, however, shows that De Bono was in Cyrenaica in the second week of July, while Badoglio remained there for almost a month, evidently for an overall examination of Graziani's work and to introduce the next stage of the repression, i.e. the deportation of the population. Nevertheless Badoglio did not subsequently claim he had played the decisive part in breaking the Cyrenaican resistance, which would have redounded little to his glory, allowing Graziani to take all the credit for himself.

(3) that continuous pressure be put on the *sottomessi* to bring in their relatives, persuading them to abandon the *dor* and come back into the camps.

We shall therefore have to pause a while awaiting the repercussions that all these actions will be bound to provoke. *We must not be in a hurry and we must make absolutely certain not to take any false steps.*

If the rebels' acts of surrender do not increase, it will be necessary to go on to another series of more severe measures, namely:

(1) assemble all relatives of the rebels in a crowded, high-surveillance concentration camp, where their living conditions are quite uncomfortable;

(2) arrest, in the kabyles and in Benghazi, important men who have traditionally opposed us, sending them to internment in Italy, the locations to be indicated by the Ministry.

It is useless to prepare a longer-term programme than this. Time and events will suggest to us what measures to take, always bearing in mind the thought that our pressure has to be stepped up equally on both rebels and *sottomessi*[97].

The movement of the semi-nomads of the Gebel (for information on numbers, we shall revert in the next chapter) was completed in July and August without incident, under the protection of all mobile Italian troops. The *duar* did not dare give open battle, but the Senusi organization managed to maintain contact with the new camps, so much so that in mid-August Badoglio let out a cry of alarm:

From the last report of your excellency (Graziani) it would appear that notwithstanding the concentration of the *sottomessi* in camps along the coast, the people are still giving various types of assistance to the rebels. Your excellency refers to the possibility that they are still paying tithes, and to the fact that flocks have been taken outside the assigned limits, the explanation being that they have partly been stolen, whereas everything points to the fact that this is one of the customary ways of getting livestock to the rebels. What this means is that the protective, or, to put it more precisely, isolating net that we have cast around these people is not yet sufficiently tight or efficient to guarantee us that all contact with the outside is cut off[98].

Graziani replied, asking for time to complete his new arrangements:

On the understanding that I shall give you a fuller report, I am taking the opportunity meanwhile to underline the essential points of the situation. Movement of the *sottomessi* in the coastal zones is not yet concluded, since that of the Hania encampments is still in progress and will be completed by the

[97] Badoglio to Graziani, 16 July 1930, in ACS-FG, 1/2/2 (partially published in ROCHAT, *cit.*, p. 19). Leaving Cyrenaica, De Bono expressed his complete approval to Badoglio, underlining the unity of purpose and action that he had created among those responsible for handling Italian policy in the colony (De Bono to Badoglio, 17 July 1930, in ACS-FG, 1/2/2).

[98] Badoglio to Graziani, 13 August 1930, in ACS-FG, 1/2/2. Badoglio proposed devoting a bigger proportion of mobile troops to guarding the camps.

end of the month. Transfer of such enormous numbers of animals, tents and people has entailed a tireless service of protection by the troops, who have almost all been engaged in the task and who, at the same time, have had to fight off rebel attacks, with useful results, preventing, additionally, any further raids on the columns of prisoners, which in the case of Abeidat, were up to 16 kilometres. Road-building work is also proceeding, protection being provided by removing one company from each battalion, so that these are, in effect, three companies short.

After final operations in June the rebel *duar* were broken up from Marmarica to Sirtica, thus necessitating a constant control over the entire area. A definitive arrangement of the troops to form a complete blockade of the *sottomessi* encampments, which is gradually taking shape, can therefore be made when the transfers are concluded. . . .

I am convinced that this business of connivance has lost much of its *raison d'être*, but that it has not disappeared, so that we shall need to ensure that there is no let-up in the rhythm of current punitive measures in order to curtail it, seeing that it tends to be increasingly linked with factors of greater spiritual solidarity. To conclude, I do not consider that the process of first clarifying the situation is yet complete, and that this must certainly be followed by a long period of normalization[99].

To sever links between the deported people and the guerilla fighters of the Gebel, it was decided at the end of August to shift the camps again, and during the autumn and winter these were concentrated in the coastal strip between Benghazi and el-Agheila. At the same time, conditions in the camps took a turn for the worse: 'all the camps were encircled by a double barbed wire, food was rationed, the pastureland area was reduced and patrolled, and nobody was allowed out except by special permit'[100]. As Graziani pointed out, when he ordered all livestock found outside authorized limits to be confiscated, '*the government is calmly determined to reduce the people to most miserable starvation* if they do not fully obey orders. The same severity will be meted out to all those outside who act on their behalf'[101]. Following

[99] Graziani to Badoglio, 21 August 1930, in ACS-FG, 1/2/2. Note the unaccustomed recognition of the basis of 'greater spiritual solidarity' for the rebellion.

[100] GRAZIANI, *op. cit.*, p. 104; but for the whole question see pp. 103–9, bearing in mind that the dates furnished are generally imprecise and tend to anticipate decisions and events.

[101] GRAZIANI, *op. cit.*, p. 15; the italics are ours. In order to gain the obedience of the *sottomessi*, the principle of collective responsibility was introduced, which called upon an entire camp to answer for the action of single individuals. Here is an example of this taken from Graziani's circular of 7 October 1930: 'Let a proclamation be made so that all the people know that as a result of the desertion to the *dor* of five men from the Abadla el Bid kabyle, I have punished the whole community consisting of 80 tents by confiscating all their livestock and transferring the entire community to Agheila. The same measure will be taken in future in the

Badoglio's instructions, a punishment camp was then set up at el-Agheila for the families of rebels and for trouble-makers, accommodating 7000 people. Meanwhile Graziani arranged for the deportation to the island of Ustica of about forty Senusi spokesmen and leaders[102], and then returned in November to propose banishing to Italy another 120 chiefs who had just been arrested: 'The people (he wrote) can thus genuinely be governed without chiefs and under the direct influence of commissioners, alongside whom will be placed the *mudir*; I will try to find the latter among the old sergeants of the Libyan battalions and police'[103].

3. The turning-point in the Gebel operations

After the failure of the major encircling operation in the Fayed zone which had been attempted in June, Italian strategy in the Gebel underwent a thorough transformation. In fact, all hopes of destroying the *duar* through a series of successful pitched battles were abandoned, to be replaced by a long-term strategy of attrition, the first essential premise of which was the mass-deportation. According to one of Mao Tse-Tung's famous definitions, a guerilla fighter has to move in his element like a fish in water; and, in fact, the real strength of the Senusi guerilla war derived from the solidarity of the people, plus the characteristics of the rough, mountainous terrain. Developing Mao Tse-Tung's image, the safest way to eliminate the fish-guerilla is to remove him from the water, namely to destroy the environment in which he lives, the human, economic and political costs being easily imaginable and generally prohibitive. Fascist Italy, however, was ready to meet these costs, all the more as national public opinion was kept wholly in the dark concerning the horrors of the repression, and because European public opinion was hardly interested in the fate of a small North African people (massacres of far greater dimensions had been perpetrated by French, English, Belgians and Spaniards). Mussolini and De Bono were thus able to authorize Badoglio and Graziani, without worrying too much about the consequences,

---

case of any kabyle which is found guilty of the same misdeed, because it is unbelievable that the intention of the defectors should not be known to the leaders and the other people.' (GRAZIANI, *op. cit.*, p. 105).

[102] We do not have complete data on the deportation of Italy of rebel leaders. Evidently on 28 September 31 *zavia* chiefs and Hassan er-Redà were put on board ship for Ustica (GRAZIANI, *op. cit.*, p. 127) and on 11 October eight other important rebels followed them (Graziani's correspondence with the ministry, in ASMAI, 150/22/98). In the following February a Senusi leader captured at Cufra was sent to Ustica. From the latter place several internees were transferred to Ventotene and Tremiti.

[103] Graziani to Badoglio and De Bono, 4 November 1930, in ASMAI, 150/22/98. Confinement of these leaders in Italy was no financial problem, noted Graziani, because at the same time as their arrest the payments assigned to them had been stopped. Nevertheless, Mussolini refused to receive these 120 leaders in Italy, and they were therefore interned in Benina.

to deport the people of the Gebel, in such a manner as to deprive the Senusi guerillas of their mass base, their source of supplies and their very environment; if, in fact, the technology of the time had not ruled out the destruction of the Gebel's mountains and vegetation, the transfer of its 80,000 inhabitants and the disappearance of their hundreds of thousands of heads of livestock would have transformed the green tableland into a desert empty of life and resources. From July 1930 Badoglio and Graziani were therefore able to count confidently on the collapse of the guerilla movement within a reasonable period, provided two conditions were met: the blocking of any source of new supplies and constant military pressure on the Gebel which, if it did not register major successes, would at least deny breathing space to the *duar* and give them the chance to find tactical alternatives.

For this new strategy it was not so much a matter of modifying the Italian military organization in the Gebel, hinging as before on mobile groups composed of one Eritrean battalion and one Savari squadron, as a change of attitude on the part of the Italian commanders, accustomed to break a tranquil routine only for rare, brief cycles of operation, described every time as decisive. Badoglio and Graziani, both highly critical of Cyrenaican military circles, exploited all their prestige to convince Italian officials of the necessity and value of a new approach to waging guerilla warfare, onerous in the sense that it was based on continual movement over rough ground, and visibly poor in results because it aimed to keep the *duar* in a perpetual state of alarm and engage them in minor skirmishes rather than in large-scale pitched battle. Badoglio, in a circular to the Cyrenaican commands, on 7 July, announced:

Gentlemen, I want you all to heed my urgent words of warning. It is absolutely vital to abandon the Arab system of shooting from a distance and regarding it as a success if the enemy is forced to withdraw. This system, capable only of prolonging hostilities indefinitely, is also contrary to the fighting spirit and aggressive instincts of our brave Eritrean *ascari*. We must therefore restrict our fire to the indispensable minimum, and seek a radical solution by attacking with sidearms and pursuing the enemy to the limit, fiercely and inexorably. This must be a real hunt for rebels, in which any act of unrestrained daring will be appropriate. . . .

The pressure cannot be allowed to let up in the slightest, and the action must always be maintained uncompromisingly and unceasingly. We cannot impose limits to our line of conduct. Thus we must remember that in order to resolve matters absolutely and finally, it will have to continue not for weeks and months, but for years[104].

[104] Badoglio circular dated 7 July 1930, *cit.*

In a circular a month later it was Graziani who demanded aggressiveness and action:

With the complete removal of the Gebel encampments, which will be finished in a few days, the field will be free for the troops. They must operate in mobile groups in the various sectors. Every sector commander . . ., employing one Eritrean battalion and one squadron, will thus always have the upper hand on any occasion, given the present situation. We have to keep on the move. Always. Even in empty space. Take no notice of information which, 99 times out of 100, is tendentious, and do not follow it up, which would be playing the enemy's game. Instead, you must search the terrain, every corner of it and in every direction. Look for the rebels. Whittle them out of their hiding places. Kill them at the rate of one a day. Prevent them joining up. . . . Always aim for surprise. Maintain secrecy. Be cunning. Remember that we are involved in a real guerilla war in which we can only succeed by doing exactly what I have said. The mobile troops must never rest. They must forget defence works. Live constantly under canvas. Scour the country in sun and rain, at every season and at every moment. Measures that may have seemed unlikely to be introduced have been taken decisively in four months so as to clarify the situation politically and free the troops from all obstacles. From today I expect rather more of the troops than they have so far given, because I can really say to them: *it's up to you!* Everyone can understand this battlecry and respond to it with honour[105].

Badoglio was also very keen on keeping up constant pressure on the Gebel and followed operations in hand very closely, as is evident from his cables:

From the weekly report I see that the Bedouin hunt continues with significant results and that outside supplies are becoming increasingly difficult. So our policy is working. We need everyone to be convinced that our present motto should be not to slacken. It is just a matter of time before this rebellion is exhausted. Bravo Graziani. Carry on[106].

Express my warm congratulations to officers and troops for their last military action and repeat to them the motto not to slacken. Carry on the attack and we shall successfully resolve the problem that weighs so heavily on our country[107].

On 1 October Graziani returned to the subject with a detailed circular to all officers and officials in which he summarized the measures taken in six months of government, the results achieved and the plans for the future. The

---

[105] Graziani circular dated 16 August 1930, mentioned in *Dieci anni di storia cirenaica*.

[106] Badoglio to Graziani, 9 September 1930, in ACS-FG, 1/2/2.

[107] Badoglio to Graziani, 9 October 1930, in ACS-FG, 1/2/2.

mobile groups in the Gebel, he wrote, provide protection for road works and traffic, but above all:

They are the rebel *duar's* mastiffs. They snap at them and pursue them everywhere when the opportunity permits, and they destroy them daily, man by man, as has to be done in accordance with the tough guerilla war they are fighting, being content with partial but continual successes. They must not allow themselves ever to be surprised because only in that way can they be defeated. They have to forget about defences, living under canvas no matter what the weather or the terrain. They fight offensively, firing only occasionally and making much use of the bayonet, thus attacking frequently and everywhere. They know neither rest nor respite. They oppose the enemy as equals; and they are superior in mobility and speed[108].

In the same circular Graziani outlined as well the colony's new military organization and the division of mobile troops in accordance with the following scheme: (1) Marmarica military zone, with one Eritrean battalion (XIII), one tank squadron and 50 irregular horsemen; (2) Gebel command, with four Eritrean battalions (XVI, centred in Gubbia; XVIII, at Belghes; XV, at Maraua; XXII, at Gerdes Abid) and four Savari squadrons, plus irregular groups at Derna (110 men), Cyrene (110 men, partly mounted) and Barce (275 men); (3) Benghazi sector, with two Eritrean battalions (XVI at El Abiar, II at Soluk), one tank squadron and two groups of 100 irregular horsemen; (4) Agedabia military zone, with one tank squadron and two Saharan groups[109].

The command directly responsible for the fight against the forces of Omar al-Mukhtar was that of the Gebel, held from early July by Lieutenant

---

[108] Graziani circular dated 1 October 1930, in ASMAI, 150/22/98. We also transcribe the list given by Graziani of the measures taken: 'a) general disarmament, which since 1 April has yielded these results: 5218 rifles, 153 pistols, 208,562 cartridges; b) reduction of armed irregulars from 2500 armed with 1891 (rifles) to 900 armed with 70–87 (rifles), carefully selected and controlled; c) abolition of the Libyan battalions which still appear to be organisms tainted by sectarian and rebellious influence; d) ratification of the death penalty for anyone found guilty of connivance and thus of rebellion, and for deserters; e) joining together of the camps, as a first step, of the Gebel, and along the coast of the Marmarica and Sirtica zones f) closure of the Senusi *zavie*, and open combat against Senusi influence wherever exercised; g) absolute cessation of frontier land traffic and strictest control over maritime traffic for Egypt.'

[109] Graziani circular 1 October 1930, *cit*. In December an 8th Eritrean battalion was set up with elements taken from other battalions and with reserves still to arrive, destined for the Agedabia zone to replace Saharan groups which were taking part in the conquest of Cufra. At that time the Akif group was one of the mobile troop units, being composed of several hundred horsemen from Tripolitania, whom Graziani had brought with him for hunting the *duar* in the Gebel; in spite of high hopes that it aroused, the Akif group met with little success and was first reduced in size and then repatriated. Finally, it is worth noting that both the infantry and cavalry of the mobile forces were made up exclusively of Eritrean and Libyan *ascari* (except, of course, the commanders), while the garrison troops (not listed here) and naturally the technical corps (aviation, tank and motor transport) were all Italian.

Colonel (later Colonel) Giuseppe Malta, one of the finest officers in Tripolitania. In his brilliant account of operations in the Gebel from July 1930 to December 1931, Malta first of all gave an estimate of the number of troops available to Omar al-Mukhtar in the summer of 1930, according to the information of the Italian high command: the Baragit *dor* (Abid and Auaghir), commanded by Abd el-Hamid el-Habbar, with 300 men; the Brahasa-Dorsa *dor*, commanded by Osman Sciami, with 380 men; the Hasa-Abeidat *dor*, commanded by Fadil Bu Omar, with 380 men; and the Brahasa Ariff (50 men) and Dorsa (40 men) groups[110].

As we have already noted, the deportation of the peoples of the Gebel greatly facilitated Malta's task, and he was able to concentrate solely on wearing down the elusive *duar*, until such time as lack of new supplies caused their collapse[111]. Malta therefore proposed two objectives: more efficient use of the mobile groups and the creation of an information service. To achieve the former objective he first had to improve the training of the troops and then get them accustomed to coordinating their action at all times: no more large-scale, centrally organized operations based on information that was always incomplete and late, but an incessant series of strikes, swift attacks every time contact was made, with the non-engaged mobile groups seizing the initiative to cut off all the enemy's possible escape routes. During the summer Malta's forces were busy protecting the population transfers; but between October and December they engaged the *duar* on some ten occasions, following fairly important successes during September in the Cyrene region (about 60 dead, including Fadil Bu Omar, one of Omar al-Mukhtar's best lieutenants) and in October at Wadi es-Sania (some 70 dead and Omar al-Mukhtar himself forced to beat such a hasty retreat that he left his spectacles to be recovered by his pursuers). In all other instances the *duar* managed to disengage with light losses, 10–15 men and a few rifles, demonstrating that on the tactical level the guerillas were still in good shape; but by now the initiative had passed to the Italians (from September to December the rebels took the offensive only once, raiding a caravan of camels near Derna) and the losses of the *duar* were only with difficulty made good. By now all links between the concentration camps and the rebels had been cut, and Omar al-Mukhtar's forces had to rely for all their provisions on the assistance that

[110] *Gebel cirenaico. Operazioni conclusive 1930–31*, report by Colonel Giuseppe Malta, s.d., 80 typewritten pages, in AUSE-FL, 158/14; this is a detailed and interesting report, even if it tends to isolate the Gebel from the wider theatre of war, and from now on it is referred to as *Relazione Malta*.

[111] For operations in the Gebel in 1930–1, see above all *Dieci anni di storia cirenaicia, cit.*, and *Relazione Malta, cit.* Graziani's book relies largely on these two sources but is altogether less reliable.

the Senusi organization managed to obtain from Egypt—a long, slow and dangerous journey[112].

Malta's second objective, the creation of an efficient information service, was, on the other hand, only partially realized, even though daily experience showed that in order to destroy the *duar* it was necessary to locate them and then pursue them as precisely and continuously as was possible for aircraft. The deportation of the population had already drastically altered the nature of the problem, because it had deprived the rebellion of its own most efficient means of information: without the vigilance and protection of the people, the *duar* were starved of information concerning the movements of the Italian troops and, in general, what was happening in the Gebel, something that explains their difficulty in regaining the initiative. In this novel situation, the Italian commands were finally able to attempt to organize their own information service (which under normal conditions would quickly have been surprised and wiped out) and to discover more easily people who were prepared to collaborate in the hunt for the Senusi forces. In autumn 1930 Malta, in fact, managed to obtain the services of several loyal informers whom the Gebel civilian commissioner, Daodiace, had selected from small groups of collaborators; these informers were, indeed, responsible in October for the success at Wadi es-Sania, by locating the *duar* and guiding the Italian mobile groups. However, the rebels, having identified the new threat, hunted down the informers and eliminated them. The right way had been found, wrote Malta, but it was necessary to strengthen the service by no longer entrusting it to individuals but to groups of scouts capable of giving warning of attacks[113].

4. The exhaustion of the Gebel guerillas

In winter attention shifted from the Gebel to the desert for the conquest of Cufra, which used up most of the resources available, especially aircraft, motor vehicles, camels and materials. The Cufra oasis, formerly a Senusi base, was the only place in Libya not yet reached by the Italian forces, protected as it was by 800 km of desert; some hundreds of rebels from Tripolitania and Fezzan had sought refuge there, and the Senusi flag still waved. Now, however, the desert was dominated by the superior Italian technical and organizational capacity; and indeed all attempted forays from Cufra were

---

[112] In the latter half of 1930 the *duar* lost about 250 men and 140 rifles (*Dieci anni di storia cirenaica*, cit.), less than in most of the preceding half-year periods; however, it is possible that after the deportation of the population the dead mentioned by Italian sources were all authentic guerillas, whereas in the previous periods they had also included women and shepherds killed by the troops during operations or machine-gunned from the air in searches for terrorists.

[113] *Relazione Malta*, cit.

easily repelled by the troops of Lieutenant Colonel Maletti, another experienced colonial officer who commanded the Agedabia military zone. The oasis itself did not pose a direct threat, therefore, to Italian military supremacy, but its conquest was dictated by considerations of prestige. Badoglio entrusted the task to Graziani, who, after minute preparation, in December 1930 and January 1931 led a powerful column, composed of Saharan units (Libyan *meharists*), tanks, motor vehicles, spotter planes and thousands of camels, into the oasis and occupied it, though not without violence and reprisals against the population. Graziani wrote that 'the occupation of Cufra struck an important blow at Senusi prestige and deeply demoralized the rebels who were still fighting in the Gebel'; yet he immediately contradicted himself by saying: 'the fall of Cufra had no repercussions, not even logistical, on the situation in the Gebel, which was something quite separate, living its own life'[114]. This second judgment seems to have accorded more with reality.

On the other hand, the measures taken to stem all traffic from Egypt had a direct impact on the guerilla war in the Gebel. As already mentioned, Senusiya had traditionally been engaged in two-way commerce between the Gebel and Egypt (livestock, skins, butter for cereal, tea, sugar and industrial products), which Italian surveillance along the frontier had never been able to interrupt, partly because of the hidden protection that the English authorities gave the Egyptians by allowing them to organize contraband traffic. In this area, too, the deportation of the Gebel tribes radically changed the situation, partly by automatically bringing the exchanges to an end, and partly by giving decisive importance to the supplies that the forces of Omar al-Mukhtar were able to obtain from Egypt, the only ones still available to the *duar*. Interrupting this flow of supplies now became one of Graziani's priority objectives, and he tried in vain to achieve this end by bringing pressure to bear on the Italian representative in Cairo, Cantalupo, to get the Egyptian government to strangle the contraband traffic. Cantalupo replied, boasting the results obtained by diplomatic action but reminding Graziani that the rebellion could only be quelled by force, as in his telegram of February 1931:

I agree that the occupation of Cufra will not induce Omar al-Mukhtar to surrender right away. But I do not share the view that Egypt constitutes the exclusive factor of resistance. Indeed, frontier contraband is already certainly down to a minimum. That Omar al-Mukhtar is receiving arms from here has been assumed but never proved. In speaking of contraband arms it is necessary to furnish precise details: until now I have not been able to do this because that government (of Cyrenaica) has never given me concrete facts. Even the

---

[114] GRAZIANI, *op. cit.*, pp. 219–20. We revert to this book for a fuller description of the Cufra enterprise.

recent advice of an arms caravan which is presumed to have reached Cyrenaica is far from proven, and this government (the Egyptian) states that it is unfounded, as explained in my separate communication.

Although I have no right or authority to express opinions on the internal situation in Cyrenaica . . . I would definitely clarify my thinking, until new facts intervene, thus: I am perfectly aware that the Cyrenaican situation is not subject to miracles and that it has to be resolved gradually. Yet whereas, on the one hand, I do not think that pessimism is justified, given the patently continuous improvement on our side and the ever-increasing and proven precarious rebel situation, it does not seem to me, on the other hand, that one should wait for Egyptian measures at the frontier to bring about Omar al-Mukhtar's defeat. The rebels in Cyrenaica must, as always, be fought in Cyrenaica.

Apart from that, I can show to the Foreign Ministry that in five months of diplomatic activity, in perfect harmony with the military authorities of this government, the legation in Cairo has seen frontier contraband reduced to a minimum—I repeat, to a minimum; this proves that my confidence in the ready collaboration between Cairo and Benghazi, i.e. between foreign powers and the colonies, is well founded, inasmuch as the frontier situation, which has formerly been so harmful to Cyrenaican policy, has now improved to such an extent that we cannot ourselves expect more[115].

The total elimination of the contraband traffic had, however, assumed such importance for Graziani that at the end of January, after the successful conclusion of the Cufra action, he suggested a sensational new measure to Badoglio: the construction of a network of barbed wire extending 270 km along the Egyptian border, so as to cut off completely any possible flow of

---

[115] Cantalupo to Graziani, 9 February 1931, in ACS-FG, 2/3/9. Cantalupo had been colonial under-secretary and enjoyed the confidence of colonial circles. Graziani replied on 10 March (*ibidem*): 'No pessimism on my part but realism to the point of exasperation. No claim that the complete defeat of Omar al-Mukhtar may, at least for the moment, depend on Egyptian clampdowns, but no longer any faith in them. . . . In any case, the Bardia-Giarabub network will clarify the situation better than any other argument. Not bearing these factors in mind, it would be quite simple to say that the Cyrenaican rebels can go on fighting for ever in Cyrenaica, where they may well be killed one by one but where no pitched battle will ever be possible. The contraband traffic has not, in fact, stopped, but from pure commercial speculation has been transformed into an excellent means of supplying war materials, with a power base in a foreign country that I cannot invade. Two essential and cardinal factors are thus lacking in the conduct of the campaign: firstly, the guarantee of frontiers, which a government, in bad faith, either cannot, will not or, even if it wishes, is incapable of arranging; secondly, the possibility of striking at the heart and very base of the adversary, as I have indicated. These are the fixed principles and immutable laws of war, which no oriental diplomat has ever been able to destroy with his wiles. Omar al-Mukhtar and his protectors will therefore wait in vain to find me an ass camouflaged as a lion. I will strangle them sooner or later with a sword fiercer than the fiercest western reality—if it were possible, I would say pagan. . . . This is my sincere Fascist word and certainly you will understand it as such.'

supplies to the guerillas. With the full support of Badoglio, De Bono and Guariglia (representing the Foreign Ministry), the construction of the barbed wire entanglement was decided upon in February, and completed in six months, from April to September 1931, overcoming numerous local difficulties. It was a barrier of wire several metres wide and 270 km long, running from the port of Bardia to the Giarabub oasis, supervised by the air force and by armoured patrols, which could not prevent the infiltrations of well organized groups but which slowed them down and exposed them to pursuit by modern methods or obliged them to take very long detours to the south across the desert[116]. The guarding of the most direct route between the frontier and the Gebel was entrusted to the Marmarica troops; and to survey the desert strip from the 29th to the 32nd parallel the Wadi Mra sector was established, patrolled by three Saharan groups, a tank squadron and air force units. This created virtually insurmountable difficulties for the passage of supplies to the Gebel, even if small groups of men and camels succeeded, right to the end, in getting through the tight network of the Italian deployment.

There was a pause in operations in the Gebel during January and February because the action in Cufra involved much manpower and because Malta's mobile groups were busy surveying the forced transfer of almost 10,000 Abeidat from the camps in Marmarica (from which they had tried to organize a mass escape with the support of the *duar*) to the much tougher and safer camps in Sirtica. The march of 1100 km across the steep southern slope of the Gebel, chosen for safety reasons, was completed without incident (though probably with a high cost in human lives, seeing that Graziani himself wrote that the Abeidat paid dearly for their attempted revolt); and in mid-February the mobile groups returned to the Gebel, while Omar al-Mukhtar, who had taken advantage of the pause in patrolling to reorganize his forces, tried to regain the initiative with a raid in the Apollonia zone. Thus the final phase of the war in the Gebel opened, with the imbalance of forces destined to increase rapidly as a result of the growing efficiency in blocking the enemy supplies and in the new reconnaissance activities of the Italian troops.

The latter, as Malta wrote in his report, entailed the replacement of the first informers, who in the now-lifeless Gebel could not long escape being hunted down by the rebels, by groups of scouts, well armed and used to combat, and thus capable of shadowing the *duar* without risking being easily surprised and eliminated. The necessary men were found in the concentration camps, among those who had for years collaborated with the resistance or even served directly as soldiers in the *duar*: the moment the Senusi organization crumbled and guerilla resistance proved clearly to be in difficulties, the extraordinary solidity hitherto displayed by the semi-nomad society of the Gebel cracked,

[116] GRAZIANI, *op. cit.*, pp. 219 *et seq.*

and personal interests and traditional hatreds re-emerged[117]. The political authorities resisted, for a considerable time, the arming of indigenous groups, particularly of ex-rebels, so much so that until spring 1931 only one mobile group had its own scouts; and certainly the problem of loyalty among the new recruits was a real one, after so many disappointments in previous years with informers who had not managed to free themselves from subjection to Omar al-Mukhtar. The new enlisted men were therefore carefully selected and vetted (the leader of the scouts, for example, personally hated Omar al-Mukhtar for ancient family reasons), until such time that they came to be identified by the rebels and were thus wholly compromised. As Malta wrote, 'the command sought this very thing: compromising the scout with the enemy in order to bind him inextricably to our cause, stimulated not only the desire for gain but also the thirst for revenge'[118].

The scouts were offered payments, rewards and even participation in raids (but principally the chance to get out of the concentration camps and be active once more in the Gebel). Divided into well armed and equipped small units, they fought in the Gebel, following the indications of aerial reconnaissance or the information they had gleaned; when they sighted a group of rebels they set off in pursuit, sending a warning to the Italian command, and then guided the troops to the attack, while other groups of scouts spread out along the likely escape routes. Even if the trap did not always close on the vigilant *duar*, the presence of these scout units made it possible for the Italian troops to move about the Gebel, no longer blindly but ever more often after due deliberation; thus the opposition of the political authorities was surmounted and during the spring of 1931 all mobile groups were provided with their own scout units. During the entire spring and summer of 1931 there were no major clashes

---

[117] It is impossible to analyze Cyrenaican society from the outside, on the basis of sources that are as untrustworthy as the Italian colonial ones. So we will not go more deeply into the problem, but confine ourselves to saying that the resistance of the peoples of the Gebel was actually never as tightly knit as is suggested in studies of the guerilla war. A proportion of *sottomessi*, especially among those more fully integrated into the urban economy, sided openly and loyally with the Italians, while the Libyan battalions, Savari squadrons and *meharist* groups had always found all the volunteers they needed (and if the Libyan battalions were to be broken up because they were suspected of connivance, the others gave indisputable proofs of loyalty and efficiency in fighting against Senusi resistance forces). Up to 1930, however, the people of the Gebel as a whole had shown extraordinary solidarity with the rebellion, rising above internal disagreements and disputes, because the Senusi had managed to display a capacity for political and religious hegemony based on particular environmental and economic-social conditions. The deportation of the population brought about a crisis in the Senusi hegemony and in the traditional mechanisms of social control, opening the way to an explosion of forces that centred on survival and on affirmation of personal and sectorial rights; this explains the relative ease with which the Italians found the scouts they needed in the concentration camps, whereas in the Gebel the *duar*, which continued to feel themselves part of an organic (though by now vanished) society, steadfastly resisted.

[118] *Relazione Malta, cit.*, which we refer to for the overall problem.

in the Gebel but dozens of skirmishes, almost all along the same lines: sighting of groups of rebels by aircraft or by scouts, approach marches by one or more mobile groups, attempts at surprise or encirclement, scattering of rebels into small patrols which filtered through enemy lines, and pursuit by cavalry, aircraft or reserve troops. Graziani wrote in a summary of a year and a half's fighting:

Hemmed in ever more closely and battered continuously, (the rebels) have suffered incessant spiritual torment which has resulted in their having to change tactics: whereas before they had retained some vestige of initiative and were still attempting large-scale forays and ambushes, offering stubborn resistance if attacked, by the end of the spring (1931) operations they had given up any initiative and kept most of their forces hidden in the Gebel, being reduced to the occasional raid with groups of 50 or at most 100 men, always on horseback.

A first tangible result had therefore been achieved: initiative in operations had by this time passed completely into our hands; not only that, but the so-called nuclei employed new tactics, for when attacked they never engaged us but immediately withdrew from combat, breaking up into small groups who resolved matters by fleeing in every direction, cleverly managing in this way to avoid any prearranged concentric action by our troops. Not possessing equal mobility, our men had to watch the escape of their prey, who, being thus split up and moving swiftly, gave no chance of being caught and destroyed[119].

In spite of their superiority in numbers and methods, and their excellent organization by Malta, the mobile groups had no easy task. As Malta himself wrote: 'to pretend that in a territory as big as Sicily, five or more manoeuvring units launched from different points can cover large distances without any wear and tear, and converge punctually at dead of night on a point marked by a rough sketch at a scale of 400,000/1, thus suddenly closing the broad net thrown by the high command around a highly manoeuvrable enemy, all this merely represented an ideal, which could only be attained as a result of errors[120].

Yet however much effort was required to maintain constant pressure, the Italian troops had an abundance of supplies, the chance of rest periods, high morale deriving from an uninterrupted sequence of successes, and the awareness that they already had the situation well in hand. We have no direct accounts of conditions in the *duar* of Omar al-Mukhtar, but everything points to the fact that they must have been very serious because of lack of supplies and the impossibility of withstanding continuous mopping-up operations

---

[119] Graziani to De Bono, 18 September 1931, in ACS-FG, 2/3/11.
[120] *Relazione Malta, cit.*

except by keeping constantly on the move. On the tactical level the guerilla leader was still well in control, managing to avoid the destruction of his forces by extreme vigilance and flexibility[121]; the 200 killed from April to September (according to Italian sources) were few considering the disparity of forces and means in the field, and compared to the greater losses sustained in the more fortunate years of major encounters and successes[122]. The light Italian losses during the same period (20–25 men) demonstrate, nevertheless, that the *duar* were in no position to launch an attack but only to escape enemy pressure by movement and systematic flight. The greatest demonstration of the strength of the Senusi rebellion and the ascendancy of Omar al-Mukhtar is furnished by the incredible firmness with which the *duar* were to resist in such adverse conditions almost until the end of 1931.

In the summer the Italian commands had the feeling that resistance in the Gebel had almost reached its limits. Cantalupo wrote from Cairo:

. . . One has the feeling that traffic in contraband is diminishing and tapering off increasingly, and that the resumption noted during the winter is happily on the decline. In my view, this very evident diminution has been due to two factors: one extremely important reason has been the barbed wire and the more active military surveillance by General Graziani at the frontier, and a secondary one has been the financial straits of the Senusi organizers living on Egyptian territory on the proceeds of contraband speculation. The latter seem neither willing nor able to risk their cash to the dangers represented by the barbed wire and the more frequent encounters with our troops, and therefore take far fewer pains to send off caravans, and in any case in much smaller numbers. Not only that, but the few that do dare face the danger are immediately identified at the exact point where they cross through the barbed wire and set foot on Marmarican territory by our motorized forces, and are invariably wiped out. This policy has good results: the smugglers seem very discouraged, and one can even foresee the coincidence—without wishing to

---

[121] For example, in May Omar al-Mukhtar assembled all his horsemen in a single *dor*, giving it the job of carrying the heaviest weight of the fighting, while the infantry were divided into small groups, so that they could more easily escape mopping-up operations. When the Italians realized this, they combined their own Savari squadrons into one mounted group, but thanks to better facilities they were able to provide supplies of fresh horses which gave the Savari greater mobility and striking power.

[122] In *Dieci anni di storia cirenaica, cit.*, the following figures are given for losses from April to September 1931, pointing out that two-thirds of these applied to the Gebel and the remainder to the semi-desert regions crossed by supply caravans: 267 rebels killed, 146 rifles taken, 44 horses killed, 51 horses captured, 166 camels killed, 689 camels captured and 561 sheep captured. Italian losses: 23 *ascari* and 5 Italians. The most striking fact is the very low number of sheep captured in a region which, until the year before, numbered them in hundreds of thousands—a demonstration of the frightening effectiveness of destruction of life in the Gebel. The comparatively high number of camels killed and captured is due to losses sustained by the supply caravans between the Gebel and the frontier.

be too optimistic—between the completion of the construction of the barbed wire barrier and the cessation of the phenomenon of contraband[123].

Graziani echoed this opinion in a circular of mid-August:

The measures taken for the complete isolation of the rebels can be said to have ended, since by the end of the month the barbed wire network will be finished. Broadly considered, they have completely overturned the political and military situation in our favour, and reduced the rebels to an even more tragic state of desperation[124].

Nevertheless, concluded Graziani, the rebellion continues because Omar al-Mukhtar has never surrendered.

5. *Capture and death of Omar al-Mukhtar*

In the early days of September the Italian command in the Gebel received news that the Brahasa-Dorsa *dor*, perhaps reinforced by the Abeidat *dor* with Omar al-Mukhtar, was concentrating to the south of el-Beda to carry out a raid, around Cyrene, on the livestock necessary for its survival. The mobile groups were put on alarm and available scouts were despatched into the zone; on the afternoon of 9 September they sighted the *dor* near Slonta (i.e. not far from an Italian garrison—a fact demonstrating how the guerillas continued to be active throughout the Gebel). On the following day Malta positioned three Eritrean battalions and the group of Savari squadrons in the zone, attacking the *dor* (a hundred or so horsemen) at dawn on 11 September in the Wadi Bu Taga. The *dor*, however, was already on the move, according to Omar al-Mukhtar's shrewd habit of making an early departure to avoid being surprised; it therefore split up rapidly into small groups which made their way through the Italian lines. One of these small formations was nevertheless sighted by the aircraft patrolling the area and a signal was sent to the closest Savari squadron, which set off in pursuit; hampered by the poor condition of their horses, too much time without any rest and lack of food, eleven rebels were overtaken one after another and killed, while the twelfth was recognized as Omar al-Mukhtar and spared. The action (which we have described in detail because of its exemplary development) was broken off and the important prisoner taken under heavy escort to Apollonia[125]. On 12 September Omar al-Mukhtar was transported to Benghazi in a destroyer and

[123] Cantalupo to the Foreign Ministry, 24 July 1931, in ACS-FG, 2/3/9.

[124] Graziani circular to all dependent authorities, dated 17 August 1931, in ASMAI, 150/22/98. In another circular of the same day (*ibidem*) Graziani called on the leading colonial authorities not to enter into negotiations or agreements with the Senusi, deriving from 'rumours coming from all over the place about the very serious conditions which the rebels were enduring and the desire of many of them to give themselves up rather than risk being executed'. Any negotiations, warned Graziani, could only be carried out under his personal responsibility.

[125] The accounts from the Italian commands that took part in the Bu Taga action are kept in ACS-FG, 2/3/11; for all these events, cf. ROCHAT, *cit.*, pp. 25–9.

formally identified by Italian officials who knew him; in any event he had made no attempt to conceal his identity nor his role.

The news of his capture was announced on 12 September in Tripoli and in Italy. Badoglio lost no time in demanding the elderly leader's head:

Should the captured man really be Omar al-Mukhtar, I think it would be opportune to hold the trial and carry out the sentence, which will undoubtedly be the death penalty, in one of the big native concentration camps[126].

Graziani, who was in Rome on his way to Paris, hurried back to Benghazi. He arrived on 14 September, finding a telegram from De Bono: 'Good. We shall hold a trial and then unfailingly a sensational execution'[127]. There was another from Badoglio, who had flown to Rome:

Have conferred with the Colonial Ministry. Make immediate arrangements for criminal trial which can only end with the death sentence according to local customs. Have sentence carried out in most important native concentration camp[128].

Given such premises, the trial before a special tribunal, formally held on the afternoon of 15 September, could only be a tragic farce, highlighted solely by the extreme dignity and restraint of Omar al-Mukhtar. It is enough to note that counsel for the defence, Captain Lontano, was punished by Graziani with ten days of close arrest for the following reason:

Appointed counsel for the defence of a rebel leader confessedly guilty of every charge with which he was accused, he pronounced the defence in an apologetic tone, in contrast to the guilty man and the special conditions of the place and surroundings in which the case was held[129].

Omar al-Mukhtar was executed on 16 September at Soluk, in front of some 20,000 deportees and prominent men assembled for the occasion: 'The impression produced was enormous,' wrote Graziani, not in the least racked by doubts over his action[130]. The deed set a suitable seal on a policy of brutal

[126] Badoglio to De Bono, 12 September 1931, in ACS-FG, 2/3/2. This and subsequent telegrams appear in ROCHAT, cit., pp. 25–6.

[127] De Bono to Graziani, 14 September 1931, in ACS-FG, 2/3/2.

[128] Badoglio to Graziani, 14 September 1931, in ACS-FG, 2/3/2. We mention all these telegrams to make clear that responsibility for Omar al-Mukhtar's execution cannot be attributed only to Graziani (even though he, as usual, took all the credit), but has to be shared among the highest competent authorities.

[129] The punishment resulted from a circular by Colonel Nasi, Graziani's second-in-command in Cyrenaica, which on 12 November 1931 informed the officers of a series of measures taken against their colleagues, as a warning. The circular (now in ACF-FG, 6/11/1) does not mention the name of the officer punished with ten days of close arrest, but it seems certain that the man must have been Captain Lontano, defending counsel of Omar al-Mukhtar, since there was no other trial of a Senusi leader during that period (cf. ROCHAT, cit., p. 26). The episode is in keeping with the general absence of morality displayed throughout the Omar al-Mukhtar proceedings, as recounted by Graziani in his book.

[130] GRAZIANI, op. cit., p. 273.

repression. France, a more shrewd colonial power, had chosen to commute the death penalties of celebrated military leaders like Abd el-Krim and Abd el-Kader; but Fascist Italy did not refrain from taking revenge, not even for the advantages that might accrue from an act of apparent generosity which would have avoided transforming the legendary seventy-year-old head of Cyrenaican resistance into a martyr of Arab independence and the Islamic faith[131].

The disappearance of Omar al-Mukhtar undoubtedly worsened the situation of the guerillas, now deprived of their unquestioned leader at the very moment when the completion of the frontier network of barbed wire decisively put an end to all traffic between the Gebel and Egypt. As an example, let us follow the movements of a caravan consisting of 50 camels and 25 men on foot which was sighted on 11 October by a patrol of *meharists* between Gialo and Agedabia, south-west of the Gebel; eluding the convergent manoeuvres of the *meharists*, a tank squadron and an Eritrean motorized unit, the caravan plunged into the desert about 400 km south of the Gebel, but after days of intensive search by all available aircraft was spotted again on 15 October still 200 km short of the border. Pursued, bombed and machine-gunned by the planes for three days, the caravan was finally intercepted and destroyed on 17 October by Saharan units 100 km from the border. The efficiency of the surveillance deployment, with its modern organization and equipment, was thus able to seal the frontier hermetically to flocks and caravans; even single horsemen were only able to break through the barbed wire at the cost of many lives[132].

To exploit the confusion caused by the death of Omar al-Mukhtar, on 17 September Graziani issued a proclamation that promised pardon to any rebels who would surrender. The proclamation, strongly criticized by Badoglio[133], met with no success: in a month and a half there were only about ten surrenders. The collapse of the resistance stemmed from the complete absence of fresh supplies and of any future prospects: on 9 December an assembly of

---

[131] Note that the sentence lacked any legal basis: since he had never offered submission, Omar al-Mukhtar could not be accused of treason, but should have been considered a prisoner-of-war (cf. also DE LEONE, *op. cit.*, p. 559). There was, however, no reason to expect that the Fascist authorities would abide by the law; and, in fact, Omar al-Mukhtar, who did not deny having led the rebellion, but regarded it as his bounden duty to his legitimate lord, was presented as confessedly guilty by Fascist propaganda and colonial historians.

[132] GRAZIANI, *op. cit.*, pp. 285–7.

[133] On 17 September Badoglio cabled Graziani: 'Decisions such as those taken . . . imply a change in the line of conduct so far laid down. It would have been opportune for you to have sought my approval beforehand. It is still understood that there will be no delay in the operations and that we shall continue to strike hard.' (ACS-FG, 1/2/2) The proclamation in GRAZIANI, *op. cit.*, p. 278; in it, on p. 279, is a message from Badoglio to the troops in which he again urges them to 'strike hard' and 'not let up'.

sixty or so guerilla representatives (who clearly still enjoyed freedom of movement in the Gebel) decided to end the struggle, leaving to individuals the choice between crossing the frontier into Egypt and surrender[134]. During the next few days the *duar* that had held out dispersed for the last time; the majority of the men gave themselves up to the Italians, while the most notable leaders sought refuge over the border.

This new turn of events did not wholly meet with the approval of Badoglio, fearful lest the resistance should still have a chance of flaring up again. 'These last rebels, who have proved the most inflexible,' wrote the marshal, 'I would prefer to have seen eliminated rather than allowed to surrender, since they will always constitute a disorderly element. In any event, now that the proclamation has been made we shall have to keep our word'[135]. And right after the death in fighting of Jusuf Bu Rahil, Omar al-Mukhtar's successor as guerilla leader, Badoglio declared: 'The rebellion can only be said to be over a month after the last rebel has been killed'[136]. Actually all organized resistance was by now at an end, and the Italian patrols were merely killing individual men exhausted by their privations[137]. Even Badoglio was eventually convinced and, so as not to lose pride of place in the victory celebration, on 7 January sent Graziani the text of an order of the day to broadcast officially on 24 January, the first anniversary of the occupation of Cufra:

I can state that the rebellion in Cyrenaica has been completely and definitely crushed.

We are grateful to his excellency the head of government and to his excellency the minister of the colonies who have firmly approved and in every way supported our action.

I commend for recognition of all Italians resident in Tripolitania and Cyrenaica the name of General Rodolfo Graziani, who, with intelligence, energy and constancy, has followed the instructions I have given him and has fully succeeded in the mission entrusted to him.

---

[134] GRAZIANI, *op. cit.*, pp. 291–2.

[135] Badoglio to Graziani, 21 December 1931, in ACS–FG, 1/2/2.

[136] Badoglio to Graziani, 22 December 1931, in ACS–FG, 1/2/2. Jusuf bu Rahil was killed on 19 December near the frontier barbed wire network; of Omar al-Mukhtar's other lieutenants, Abd el-Hamid el-Habbar managed to get through to Egypt and Osman Sciami surrendered to the Italians.

[137] According to the *Relazione Malta, cit.*, losses in the Gebel from July 1930 to December 1931 were as follows: Italians, 3 dead, 6 wounded; *ascari*, 45 dead, 117 wounded; rebels, 624 killed, 234 taken prisoner, 95 *sottomessi*, 338 horses killed and captured, 342 rifles captured in the fighting, 54 rifles surrendered. According to Graziani, from March to December 1931, throughout Cyrenaica, the Italians had 138 killed and 270 wounded, the rebels 1641 men killed and 541 surrendering (*op. cit.*, p. 297).

For the first time, after twenty years from landing in these countries, the two colonies are completely occupied and pacified. This fact should not only be a source of legitimate satisfaction for us all but also the point of departure for a stronger impetus towards civil progress in the two colonies[138].

Badoglio was right in claiming that Cyrenaican resistance was completely crushed, nor was there any possibility of its revival, because the situation that had generated and sustained the guerilla war had radically changed. The deportation of the people of the Gebel, the havoc wrought in the concentration camps, and the planned elimination of the flocks and herds that constituted the principal resource of a population of semi-nomad shepherds, had logically resulted in the destruction of the foundations of the existing society in the Gebel. The decisive moment in the repression, it is important to repeat, was the removal of the people and animals of the tableland: when this was completed, Omar al-Mukhtar and his followers were still living and fighting on familiar terrain, but which had become alien because empty of life, where they no longer had roots and from which they could now derive nothing. Deprived of its popular base, the Senusi guerilla war was destined to end rapidly.

V. *The consolidation of Italian occupation.*

1. *The concentration camps*

We know very little about the concentration camps in which the peoples of the Gebel and the semi-desert zones were confined because writers of memoirs and of colonial history have wholly ignored the problem (with the exception of a few defensive allusions by Graziani). Even our own searches through the archives of the Ministry of Italian Africa, of the army and of Graziani himself have until now proved insufficient, leading to the conclusion that as little as possible has been said, and above all written, about the subject[139]. Just the same, we have collected together what fragmentary

---

[138] Badoglio to Graziani, 7 January 1932, in ACS-FG, 1/2/2. The text of the order of the day was attached to the letter. Cf. GRAZIANI, *op. cit.*, p. 307.

[139] As we have already indicated, our researches in the official archives cannot be regarded as complete because of the lack of order and difficulty in consulting the archives in question. It is to be hoped that systematic researches and, above all, better organization of the archives will enable more complete results to be achieved in the future.

information exists, to emphasize the gravity of this feature of the repression and the urgent need for systematic research on the matter[140].

The first and most obvious problem is the difficulty in obtaining full information concerning the overall Cyrenaican population and its losses during the years of the Italian conquest. According to the Turkish census of 1911, just prior to the Italian invasion, there were 198,300 inhabitants of Cyrenaica (excluding Cufra), which rose to 180,000–200,000 in an Italian estimate of 1921[141]. In 1922–3 the first thorough study was carried out, entrusted to an expert, Colonel Enrico De Agostini, who calculated the indigenous population of the country to be 185,400 (181,750 Arabs and 3650 Jews)[142]. The English scholar Evans-Pritchard, however, spoke of an overall population of 200,000, a quarter of whom lived in the towns[143]. According to an official Italian count at the end of 1928, the indigenous population had, however, leapt to 225,000[144]. The census of 21 April 1931, the first carried out by modern techniques and complete investigation of the entire territory, brought the indigenous numbers down to 142,000 (plus 16,000 Italians and 2400 foreigners), a total largely confirmed by the census of 21 April 1936, which gave the figure of 142,500 inhabitants[145].

On the basis of these figures, there was a drop in numbers of the Cyrenaican population during the years of undeniable repression, but this drop is difficult to quantify. If we start with the estimate by De Agostini and the census of 1931, we get a sharp decrease of 40,000–45,000 inhabitants, which rises to about 60,000 if we accept Evans-Pritchard's figure, and to 80,000 on the basis of the 1928 estimate. The decline is partly due to the emigration to Egypt in 1930–1, which diverse sources like Graziani and Evans-Pritchard reckoned at

---

[140] This chapter restates and develops, with better documentation, the pages we wrote in 1973 (ROCHAT, *op. cit.*, pp. 29–39). In a note on *Il genocidio delle genti cirenaiche secondo G. Rochat*, which appeared in 1979 in the journal 'Intervento', nos. 38–39, De Leone challenged the contents, sources and statistics of our 1973 article, claiming that to accuse Fascist policy in Cyrenaica of genocide was possible only in an atmosphere of anti-Italian factionalism and prejudice. However, De Leone laced his arguments with complaints of personal slights, nondescript digressions, distortions and falsification of facts and documents. Cf. Giorgio ROCHAT, *Il genocidio cirenaico e la storiografia coloniale*, in 'Belfagor', 1980, no. 4, pp. 449–55.

[141] Elio MIGLIORINI, *Il territorio*, in AA. VV., *Il territorio e le popolazioni*, Rome, 1955, edited by the committee for documenting the work of Italy in Africa, p. 98. This book, the mouthpiece of official colonial culture, is nevertheless full of gaps and contradictions; Migliorini, for example, quite ignores De Agostini's work of 1922–3, which is the most detailed and reliable of the entire Italian period.

[142] Enrico DE AGOSTINI, *Le popolazioni della Cirenaica*, Benghazi, 1923, published by the government of Cyrenaica.

[143] EVANS-PRITCHARD, *op. cit.*, pp. 39–41.

[144] *Annuario statistico italiano 1928, ad vocem*. It should be remembered that these are still estimates susceptible to a certain margin of error, though accepted by the leading colonial historians.

[145] *Annuario statistico italiano* of the relative years, *ad vocem*; E. MIGLIORINI, *art. cit.*, pp. 98–9.

20,000 people[146]; but this still does not explain a decrease in the population of some tens of thousands, nor do Italian sources provide any direct information regarding it. It must be remembered, however, that the 1931 census was, to all appearances, carried out in accordance with political opportunism rather than scientific precision, to the point of not recording the deportation to camps in Sirtica of a large part of the Cyrenaican population, said to be still living in their traditional regions; it is probable that, by the same standards, at least some of the Egyptian emigrants were registered as still in the country[147]. More reliability can perhaps be attributed to the census of 1936, which gave a total of 142,500 inhabitants; but this does not corroborate the 1931 results because in the 1936 census some thousands of repatriates from Egypt were also included. A comparison between the figures of different years must also take into account the natural population increase; between the census of 1931 and that of 1936, for example, the population of Tripolitania jumped from 512,000 to around 600,000, while that of Cyrenaica remained stationary.

In conclusion, one has to calculate a minimal decrease in the population of Cyrenaica (excluding Italians and foreigners) from 185,000 in 1923 to the 142,500 of 1936; if we then accept that in addition to the latter figure some 10,000–15,000 of the 1930–1 fugitives had remained in Egypt, we arrive at a minimum figure of 30,000 dead in the years of the Italian conquest, which does not take count of the omitted natural growth of the population, and which rises to 45,000 or even 70,000 depending on whether we accept the estimate of Evans-Pritchard or the Italian one of 1928[148]. According to Italian sources, the operations affecting the ranks of the rebels (and, we should add, the people at large who were directly involved in the mopping-up activities) caused 6500 deaths from 1923 to 1931[149]. We deduce from this that the fall in population must be in small part attributed to war operations and, to a greater extent, to the conditions created by the Italian repression (hunger, poverty and epidemics) and to the deportation of the people (transfer marches, death through malnutrition in the camps, epidemics, and the inability to adapt to the terrible new surroundings); but our information is not sufficient to

[146] Graziani memorandum for De Bono, 1 April 1932, in ACS-FG, 6/11/1; EVANS-PRITCHARD, *op. cit.*, p. 197.

[147] It is worth mentioning that the aforesaid book by the committee for documenting the work of Italy in Africa, AA. VV., *Territorio e popolazioni*, threw no doubts on the validity of the census of 1931, nor did it try to explain the heavy drop in population as shown by the figures quoted.

[148] We have no information which either confirms or casts doubt on the accuracy of the 1928 estimate. Even if this were to prove too high, it could still be shown that until 1928–9 the Cyrenaican population was on the increase and therefore that the drop must be attributed to the harshest years of the repression under Graziani.

[149] *Dieci anni di storia cirenaica, cit.*

enable us to distinguish between these diverse causes, nor to analyze methods and incidents of this massacre, which, we should not forget, spared the towns and only hit the people of the Gebel and the semi-desert regions.

Another set of parallel facts shows the decisive manner in which the repression of the rebellion in 1930–1 was handled: this relates to the systematic destruction of livestock, about which we have only incomplete, approximate and partly contradictory information, but enough to emphasize Italian policy and its harsh effects. The Turkish census of 1910 indicated the presence in Cyrenaica of 1,260,000 sheep and goats, 83,300 camels, 27,000 horses and 23,600 cattle[150]. The operations in the Gebel brought about a progressive diminution of this animal population (from 1923 to 1928 the Italian forces killed or confiscated as booty about 170,000 animals)[151], but in 1928 there were still estimated to be at least one million sheep and goats[152]. The clearance of the Gebel caused a drastic decline: apparently the number of animals left after the mass deportation was around 600,000[153], but these were rapidly decimated as a result of lack of pasture and the measures taken by the Italian high command to prevent provisions reaching the guerillas. In this area, too, it is impossible to follow the various phases of the livestock destruction in detail, but its consequences are vividly conveyed by these statistics, emanating from a report by Graziani:

	1930	1931	1932	1933
Sheep and goats	270,000	67,000	105,000	222,000
Cattle	4,700	1,800	2,000	3,000
Camels	39,000	16,000	11,000	11,500[154]

[150] EVANS-PRITCHARD, op. cit., p. 37. Obviously these are approximate figures, but neither Italian nor English scholars dispute them.

[151] Dieci anni di storia cirenaica, cit. The report provides overall figures, without distinguishing between sheep, horses and camels, nor between animals killed and captured; all the evidence shows that these are the totals provided by the commanders of single operations, hence to be treated with much caution, yet useful as indications. They are as follows: 1923, 24,000 head; 1924, 25,000; 1926, 37,000; 1927, 26,000; 1928, 20,000; 1929, 2500; 1930, 26,000; 1931, 2500.

[152] According to Jean DÉSPOIS, La colonisation italienne de Lybie, Paris, 1935 (which, however, we know through MIÈGE, op. cit., p. 180) in 1926 there were in Cyrenaica 800,000 sheep, 75,000 camels, 14,000 horses and 9000 asses. According to CIASCA (op. cit., p. 551), on 30 April 1928 there were a million sheep, 100,000 goats, 10,000–15,000 cattle and 40,000 camels. Although they partly contradict each other, the two sets of figures agree in showing a decrease compared with 1910, which was fairly sharp for camels, horses and cattle, less so for sheep. It is worth noting that Déspois, the famous French geographer, had direct knowledge of Italian Libya, whereas Ciasca was the most authoritative colonial historian of the time.

[153] GIGLIO, La confraternita senussita, cit., p. 114; EVANS-PRITCHARD, op. cit., p. 189.

[154] Graziani to Balbo (with copies to De Bono and Badoglio), 26 April 1934, in ACS-FG, 5/9/6. This is a report on the 'general situation in the colony at the present date', written by Graziani when about to give up the vice-governorship. Compare the figures given by Déspois (in MIÈGE, op. cit., p. 180, and in EVANS-PRITCHARD, op. cit., p. 37) relating to 1933: 98,000 sheep, 25,000 goats, 2600 camels, 8700 cattle, 1000 horses and 5000 asses. There are large contradictions here as well, which do not, however, affect the overall trend of the phenomenon.

These figures, despite gaps and partial contradictions, demonstrate clearly that 90–95% of the sheep, goats and horses, and possibly 80% of the cattle and camels died. Graziani himself, in 1934, boasted that the colony's livestock resources had partly been replenished 'in comparison with the few thousand (animals) that had remained at the beginning of 1932'. And he continued, justifying the slaughter of the livestock:

Where, in the face of all this, are those Cassandras who prophesied the end of the Cyrenaican economy because of the losses in livestock which occurred while the people were being rounded up? Were we perhaps expected to stake our reputation on saving some sheep? The people represent the inalienable heritage of a ruling nation; so, of course, do the livestock, but they fluctuate and can be replaced within a short time[155].

We come now to the available statistics—as usual few and far between— relating to the actual deportations. We know that, on the whole, reckonings have to exclude the urban populations (about 50,000 people), those of the inland oases (5000–10,000) and the people who already had solid connections with the towns or who were politically trustworthy (according to Graziani, these included 540 Orfa tents around Barce, 1350 Hasa tents around Apollonia, 140 Abeidat tents around Derna and 1200 more around Ain Gazala, giving a total of 10,000 to 20,000 persons, based on the fact that the number of individuals per tent, i.e. per family, depended on variable factors such as wealth, tradition and losses in the war). The deportees, on the other hand, were nomad and semi-nomad populations, namely those principally engaged in livestock rearing and extensive agriculture in the Gebel, in Marmarica, in the Benghazi region and in Sirtica. Different reports mention 80,000 deportees, without further amplification[156]: this is probably too low a figure because, if we add the 70,000 to 80,000 exempted from the measure and the 20,000 or so who fled to Egypt, we arrive at a total valid only if we accept the lowest of all the estimates of the Cyrenaican population.

A more reliable and detailed point of reference is furnished by a report on the specific subject of the concentration camps which Graziani sent to De Bono on 2 May 1931. For the time being, we give only the actual numbers:

[155] Speech by Graziani to a group of colonists in Benghazi, 25 February 1934, in ACS-FG, 4/8/11.
[156] Cf. GIGLIO, La confraternita senussita, cit., p. 144; GRAZIANI, op. cit., p. 115; EVANS PRITCHARD, op. cit., p. 189; Atti del parlamento italiano, legislatura 1929–34, Atti della camera, doc. 80/A, Relazione della giunta generale del bilancio sullo stato di previsione della spesa del ministero delle colonie per il 1931–32, p. 15. All the facts mentioned by Graziani concerning the deportations, which we have used (in particular the list of exempted groups and the distribution in the various camps in July 1931) come from GRAZIANI, op. cit., p. 104.

	Approx. number of people
El-Abiar camp	3,123
Soluk camp	20,123
Sidi Ahmed el-Magrun camp	13,050
Marsa Brega camp	21,117
El-Agheila camp	10,900
Agedabia camp	10,000[157]

This gives a total of 78,300 deportees (79,800 if we include the 1500 Mogarba who, according to the report, had just been transferred from el-Agheila to Nufilia); but this is certainly below the real total, firstly because the report does not take into account the series of smaller camps, the existence of which is verified in Graziani's book, such as Driana, Sidi Chalifa, Benghazi itself and Suani Terria, secondly because these figures relate to May 1931 and thus do not include those who died during the transfer marches and in the first eight to ten months of imprisonment. It appears, therefore, that the total number of deportees must go up to about 100,000; this figure, taking account of the emigrants to Egypt and those exempt from deportation, brings the total Cyrenaican population before Graziani to close on 200,000—the middle estimated figure—and to around 50,000 dead during the period of repression.

The total figure of deportees provided by Graziani in his book, relating to July-August 1931, is lower, although a direct comparison is difficult. Graziani, in fact, mentions 15,200 tents, plus 7000 people in the el-Agheila punishment camp: altogether 60,000–70,000 people, though we have no way of knowing whether this drop is due to differences in calculating or to the high mortality rate which was a feature of all the camps. We have no direct information on this latter point, but merely a series of sparse yet eloquent facts, admittedly insufficient to authorize peremptory estimates and conclusions.

We begin with the details furnished by Graziani in the aforementioned report of May 1931, bearing in mind that by this time the camps already consisted of neat, closely packed rows of tents set up in the sand along the coast, surrounded by double barbed wire, and with strict surveillance of the deportees' movements and of the collective services, which were as a rule tragically inadequate. Of the camps mentioned in the report, two were medium-small—el-Abiar, with 3100 people, and Suani Terria, with an

---

[157] Graziani to De Bono, 2 May 1931, in ASMAI, 150/22/98. This list causes some puzzlement, because it does not include the Suani Terria camp, which is mentioned in the report, and gives instead the total of the Agedabia camp, which the report does not dwell upon. For the camp of el-Agheila the report gives a total of 3000 Mogarba and 7900 relatives of rebels in the punishment camp, adding that 1500 Mogarba had been transferred to Nufilia.

imprecise number of inmates but certainly fewer than the other[158]; living conditions in both these camps were relatively acceptable. The internees at el-Abiar had almost 1500 sheep, a sufficient supply of cereals and foodstuffs, and had already sown adequate quantities of barley and wheat: 'the local agricultural-pastoral organization is sufficient to provide work and earnings,' concluded Graziani. At Suani Terria, too, there were good work possibilities, again according to the Italian authorities:

With the shifting of groups traditionally engaged in agriculture, it has been possible to put back in use many gardens of the zone which had long been abandoned and which now provide a livelihood for a number of families. In any case, there is no need to worry about the economic conditions of the people transferred to this camp because the numbers of livestock provide sufficient farm products for their needs[159].

Communal facilities, however, were scarce: one Italian and one Arab teacher, a first-aid station and a medical tent at el-Abiar, nothing at Suani Terria. In both camps work was in progress for setting up a station for the carabinieri, plus an entomological hut at el-Abiar and a first-aid post at Suani Terria.

Conditions at the large camps of Soluk, Sidi Ahmed el-Magrun, Marsa Brega and el-Agheila, which contained overall some 65,000 people, were very different. In all four camps arrangements were strictly minimal: access roads, wells for people and animals, essential hygienic provisions and barbed wire. However, the prerequisites for self-sufficiency in food were lacking, since both the existing livestock and the sowings of cereal were wholly inadequate for the minimal necessities of survival. Because it was not part of the Italian programme to supply food at government expense (even though this was to happen later), the authorities busied themselves with road-building schemes (branches between el-Agheila and Benghazi) capable of furnishing the internees with minimal earnings. Here is the report:

This plan of works, therefore, will enable us to take a confident view of conditions for all the people in the (Soluk) camp. . . .

The work in progress at the camp (of Sidi Ahmed el-Magrun) and on the road to Ghemines has greatly helped to improve the economic conditions of the people; we are likewise considering an organic work plan for this place, so that there will be plenty of work, with payment, for the population, until such time as an economic organization is developed which will be sufficient for the needs of the inhabitants. . . .

---

[158] In the map of the positioning of camps on 1 July 1931, on p. 104 of Graziani's book, Suani Terria has 100 tents and el-Abiar 924; from the overall correspondence this gives an average of three-four people per tent.

[159] Graziani to De Bono, 2 May 1931, cit.

Many individuals at Abeidat and Marmarici are presently engaged in construction work on the Agedabia-Benghazi branch road, and this will continue until the organization of the people transferred to the new centre (of Marsa Brega) makes it possible for us to create an active, self-sufficient economy[160].

Attaining self-sufficiency in feeding the camps therefore remains a fundamental objective starting with the establishment of market gardens: 20 hectares planned at Soluk, 20 planned at el-Agheila and 15 at Marsa Brega. 'In this way it will be possible to rebuild in that place (Marsa Brega) the economy of many farming families, encouraging the development of agriculture in places where, previously, nothing like it had been attempted[161]. Furthermore, it was hoped to transform the semi-nomads into fishermen (two boats had been sent to Marsa Brega and two promised: the internees, Graziani was sure, would enjoy fish, especially when salted), and looms and wool were distributed to the poorer women so that they could make tents and carpets. The authorities then endeavoured to set up shops of various kinds in the camps; at Sidi Ahmed el-Magrun, for instance, 'the local government office is trying to get shopkeepers to take the initiative in constructing buildings for their own shops, so that a number of such places will take on the guise of a small centre, which will certainly develop in the future'[162]. Such shops were for the time being the only services available in the camps, although provision was being made everywhere for barracks for carabinieri, offices for administration, casualty stations and schools (only Soluk already had a hospital with thirteen beds and a school with accommodation for the teacher). The health organization could count, in all, upon two doctors (each of whom was responsible for two camps and over 30,000 people), on a few first-aid tents and several sick-bays, which were equipped for the vaccination of all inmates against smallpox. The Soluk camp also had a veterinary surgeon and a post office.

The picture that emerges from the report is truly depressing: tens of thousands of people huddled up against one another (as is evident even from the photographs that Graziani published in his book), practically without the means of subsistence, compelled to await a meagre salary for desultory road works[163], with a few shops as the only meeting place, an almost non-existent health service, and that at the very time when the traditional semi-nomad way of life and diet rich in meat and milk gave way forcibly to life at sea-level

---

[160] Graziani to De Bono, 2 May 1931, cit.

[161] Graziani to De Bono, 2 May 1931, cit.

[162] Graziani to De Bono, 2 May 1931, cit.

[163] In 1934 Graziani stated that for all the road works carried out in four years 45 million lire had been spent on 1,516,000 working days for Italian labourers (average pay 30 lire a day) and

in overcrowded camps, with a different diet (inevitably so, once livestock had disappeared) which was not only quite inadequate but which also produced an explosion of the region's traditional diseases. Italian sources nevertheless remain silent on conditions in the camps and on their mortality rate, which, judging from notes and scattered statistics, must have been very high. Instead, colonial propaganda painted idyllic pictures, like the one described by Graziani in a press conference of June 1931:

No radical change of life style has been imposed on the people, no disturbance has been caused by their transfer to the plain south of Benghazi. As they formerly lived in their tents and with their herds, so they live now in their new encampments, and in this respect I insist in pointing out that these are not concentration camps true and proper, as might be supposed, because concentration camps come into being when stable populations are assembled in determined places, living in inhabited centres, whereas here it is simply a matter of moving nomad populations, who retain in their new home their life habits, albeit circumscribed and controlled. Thus in the localities of southern Benghazi and Sirtica, to which they have been transferred, the nomad peoples can better benefit from relief, economic and hygienic measures than could ever have been adopted previously, by reason of their continual travels[164].

2. The dissolution of the concentration camps

Everything points to the fact that Graziani and Badoglio intended to keep the concentration camps going for an indeterminate period, definitively transplanting the deported populations in Sirtica, so as to leave the Gebel

---

57 million lire on 5,694,000 working days for Libyan labourers (average pay 10 lire a day). (Graziani speech of 25 February 1934, *cit.*). As an indication, calculating that half of these working days must have been effected by the men of the concentration camps during 1931–3, we arrive at 200 working days and 2000 lire in pay for each family over three years. In the afore-mentioned speech Graziani also said that the overall expenditure on grain, barley, flour, work tools and the like for the people during 1930–3 amounted to 12,688,100 lire; assuming, as a guideline, that two-thirds of this sum was distributed in the concentration camps, we get an average of 500 lire per family over three years. These estimates are certainly not of great use in assessing the living conditions of the deported populations, but serve to give an idea of the very modest efforts made by the Italian authorities to ensure their survival; indeed, it would appear that the authorities provided nothing for their needs apart from the above-mentioned donations and their employment on road works.

[164] From a speech by Graziani to a group of journalists in Benghazi, 9 June 1931, reported in *Dieci anni di storia cirenaica*, *cit*. One of the favourite themes of colonial propaganda was the great effectiveness of the hygienic arrangements in the concentration camps; see the report of Professor Tedeschi, director of the Derna hospital (GRAZIANI, *op. cit.*, pp. 111–18), who introduced the sterilization of syphilitics among his modern systems of disease prevention.

103

available for Italian immigration. In May 1931 Graziani concluded the aforementioned report to De Bono with these words:

As your excellency will see, the organization of the former nomadic peoples and their transference to the southern Benghazi area and to the western part of the colony can now be said to be an accomplished fact. The camps are by now well on the way to being set finally in order and, although I am sure any connivance with the rebels has been eliminated, I am making sure that tomorrow's population is more docile and accustomed to work; this will certainly attach them, for reasons of self-interest, to the new lands where they have been transferred, losing the habit of nomadism and acquiring the tastes and needs of sedentary populations; for it is upon these that we must necessarily found and develop our programme of pacifying and exploiting Cyrenaica[165].

At the end of 1931, when resistance was by now broken, Graziani again insisted on the need to maintain a strict watch on the Egyptian border and to keep the people far from the Gebel, to avoid a resumption of the rebellion. Law and order in Sirtica was, even in the long term, guaranteed:

The organization of the camps of the *sottomessi* improves by leaps and bounds. . . . If the harvest is good, we shall be able to say we have solved the economic crisis by next spring, together with that of the pastures, which are steadily expanding, with an associated build-up of livestock resources[166].

Badoglio fully agreed with the need to pursue a harsh policy against the people and the Senusi, as is clear from his letter of instructions dated July 1932:

I want to clarify, without further discussions on them, the following points:

(1) So long as any member of the Senusi is alive we shall always have in him a sworn enemy who will try by all available means (a) to keep alive the Senusi idea with propaganda; (b) do us harm by all open or covert means, using all the arts in which the oriental mind is so fertile.

(2) The Egyptian government will *never on any account* fight on our side and against the Senusi.

(3) The English leadership will not lift a finger to help us if such an action were to displease the Egyptians.

---

[165] Graziani to De Bono, 2 May 1931, *cit.*

[166] Graziani to Badoglio and De Bono, 22 December 1931, in ASMAI, 150/22/98. Graziani also requested a renewal of the Italian colonial personnel: 'It will therefore happen that some of the old officials will be replaced by others who have never known and do not know a single one of the major or minor leaders presently interned (and who may in due course be freed and reappear on the scene), thus avoiding the possibility of their still being influenced. In no colony have I ever come across men who have so easily allowed themselves to become susceptible to the oriental virus and to the various ideologies relating to colonization, juxtaposition of races, collaboration and so forth. The term *absolute rule*, which simply presupposes the obedience of the native inhabitants and their full accountability to our laws, is still unknown to almost all the various men who have lived here for years.'

(4) The Egyptian government will put every obstacle in the way and even prevent the return of refugees, in exactly the same way as the Tunisian and Algerian governments have done with the return of the Tripolitanians.

(5) We have to rely exclusively on our own forces and the ill-feeling of our neighbours.

Having thus outlined the conditions of the question, which, I repeat, by now we have to accept as indisputable truths, we need to adopt the following lines of conduct:

(1) To regard any representative of the Senusi leadership as a very dangerous enemy who must always be fought by every possible means until he is destroyed. Therefore, avoid any contact with such people; prevent them entering the colony; and do not, for any reason, engage in discussion with them through intermediaries.

(2) Do not try to get the refugees to return. It is better to lose them for ever.

(3) We must not on any account dismantle the framework of our command, based as it is upon the barbed wire network and the concentration camps. Only time and continual surveillance, as well as the diligent examination of the situation, will teach us how to broaden the scope of our organization. But it is as well to remind ourselves that this is not a matter of months but of years. After a twenty-year illness convalescence must needs take a long time.

(4) The Gebel must be controlled mainly by Italian colonists.

(5) To continue the search for arms with the conviction that they are still hidden from us, just as happened in Tripolitania.

(6) Give active attention to the running of the concentration camps so that they can continue to be managed without any inconvenience and the local people are convinced, or better still grow accustomed to thinking, that they are their permanent destination. Facilitate settlement by giving priority to house-building and land assignation.

(7) Take great care with the organization of youth and their instruction and education. From their ranks we will draw the men for our battalions.

These are the directive lines to follow, which we have already laid down for some time. Everything that arises, I am certain, can be (*illegible word*) in the afore-mentioned cases and handled as foreseen. I repeat that we should not allow ourselves to be alarmed by any information and any proposition. Our line is traced out and it is essential, as before, *not to soften*[167].

These directives from Badoglio were already superseded as far as the concentration camps were concerned, for they were by this time in course of being dismantled. The punishment camp for the relatives of rebels at

[167] Badoglio to Graziani, 29 July 1932, in ACS-FG, 1/2/2.

105

el-Agheila had, in fact, already been dissolved since 1 April 1932, because, wrote Graziani, there was no sense in continuing to be harsh on relatives after having reprieved the surviving rebels themselves: they and their relations were therefore to be sent to the camps of their respective tribes at Marsa Brega, Soluk and Sidi Ahmed el-Magrun, or permitted to stay at el-Agheila in a 'normal' camp, while the Hasa were to return to Apollonia and the Orfa to Barce[168]. De Bono approved, but criticized the importance attached to the measure before the press:

It does not seem to me wise to give too much publicity to such information and, in general, to measures adopted by this government in respect of indigenous people once they have been pacified, which will simply result in their true significance being exaggerated in Italy and abroad[169].

The dissolution of the el-Agheila punishment camp was an exceptional step; but already by the end of June 1932 Daodiace, commissioner of the Gebel, suggested to Graziani, apparently at the latter's explicit request, a plan for the return of the population to the Gebel, but not to their traditional homes, seeing that the needs of the Italian settlement had to be given priority. Daodiace, with great optimism, wrote:

Your excellency (Graziani) knows very well to what miserable conditions the peoples of Cyrenaica have been reduced, but your excellency must also be persuaded that a rapid and almost immediate alleviation of their economic conditions is possible. To restore their prosperity all that is needed is an abundant harvest this year and two or three years of good grazing, in peace and quiet, for the livestock[170].

The reasons that lay behind the decision to break up the camps and return the populations to the Gebel do not emerge explicitly from the documents, but from all this paper work two main motives can be detected: the failure of the plan to convert the Sirtica concentration camps into permanent places of settlement because of the impossibility of guaranteeing sufficient food and adequate hygienic and sanitary conditions for sheer survival, and the need for

---

[168] Graziani to Badoglio and De Bono, 29 March 1932, in ASMAI, R50/22/98. On 11 February Graziani had granted an amnesty to political prisoners.

[169] De Bono to Graziani, 6 April 1932, in ASMAI, 150/22/98. The censorship demanded by De Bono helps to explain the silence of the Italian press on the concentration camps.

[170] Notes for Governor Graziani, prepared by the commissariat for the Gebel, dated 27 June 1932, in ACS-FG, 4/8/8. Daodiace proposed that the Orfa (most of whom had escaped deportation) should remain around Barce or be transferred along the coast, from Tocra to Tolmeta; that the Abid, by now much reduced in numbers, should be settled at Om-Giuabi, where a silted-up Roman well could be reopened; that the Dorsa, by now having dwindled to fewer than 5000, should be sent to the outskirts of Tolmeta and Hania; that the Hasa should stay around Cyrene; that the Brahasa, greatly reduced in number because they had suffered the greatest losses, should be settled at Maraua and Gerdes Gerrari; and finally that the Abeidat should be sent to Om-er-Zem, Marthuna and Chaulan.

cheap manpower to develop the Gebel. Daodiace insisted again on the people's quick return in a document that is additionally interesting in that it underlines local opposition:

I tell you, excellency (Graziani), that this return of the people will come up against veiled hostility, both on the part of the carabinieri service (and by this I mean not so much the officers themselves as the circle of non-commissioned officers and *zapatie*, i.e. the mass of subordinates) and also groups of the Italian population, especially the more ignorant or less intelligent elements and those who have just arrived in the colony. This hostility does not have clear and determined motives but stems from a certain vague worry that the return of the population to this territory will either threaten their standard of living or rather prevent them from quickly gaining control of it.

I do not in any way share this worry, for I consider that both in the Gebel and its southern extensions there is room for everyone, compatriots and natives alike. I regard it as unlikely, excellency, that in the short term there will be any renewal of the type of plundering which we have recently wiped out. Plundering activities in Cyrenaica were politically organized, and it was able to persist for so many years because it enjoyed this kind of support. Today this political organization, this juncture of interests between the organizers of the rebellion and the heads of the population is finished, finished for ever. The former have disappeared, the latter have lost all forms of prestige, since in the various kabyles there is a feeling of bitter resentment towards them, insofar as they are held responsible for the disaster. The people are reduced to obedience and do not nor cannot have any inclination to offer resistance or rebel against our government[171].

The return of the Gebel populations was nevertheless deferred, very probably for security reasons; in the second half of 1932 freedom was given to the Abeidat of Marmarica and (probably) to the Morgaba, who had played a secondary part in the rebellion, living in semi-desert regions which were of no interest to the colonial planners[172]. At the beginning of 1933, when the general situation in the country had returned to normal[173], the people of the

---

[171] Daodiace to Graziani, 5 July 1932, in ACS-FG, 4/8/8.

[172] The release of the Abeidat of Marmarica is documented in Graziani's correspondence (his letters to the ministry, 2 August 1932, and to Badoglio, 2 October 1932, in ASMAI, 150/22/98); the release of the Mogarba, however, is not mentioned, but seems certainly to have taken place in the second half of 1932, if not before (for these peoples, who lived in Sirtica, deportation must have been less hard). The Abeidat of the Gebel, who had been in the forefront of the rebellion, were, on the other hand, kept confined until the following year (but we do not know the date of their release).

[173] On 28 January 1933 Graziani told the ministry he had freed another eleven political internees; there were only three more remaining in Cyrenaica, plus those from Ustica (ASMAI, 150/22/98).

Gebel and the Auaghir were still being held in the camps at Soluk, Sidi Ahmed el-Magrun, Marsa Brega and probably other smaller camps around Benghazi. We have no general information about conditions in these camps, but can furnish a few figures on the Soluk and Sidi Ahmed el-Magrun camps in the spring of 1933[174]. Soluk then contained about 13,000 Auaghir, Abid, Orfa and associated tribespeople, showing a significant drop on the 20,000 deportees of two years previously, which is not explained (but probably due to mortality in the camps)[175]. Sidi Ahmed had 8400 people from the Brahasa, Dorsa and associated tribes, again a notable decrease compared with the 13,000 of 1931. All of them were without means of subsistence, for they had lost practically all their livestock (3400 Abid and Orfa had in all 220 head of livestock, 8400 Brahasa and Dorsa 1000 head, and 6200 Auaghir 6800 sheep, 126 camels, 7 cows, 18 horses and 176 asses) and all their belongings (in respect of tents, clothing, implements and baggage in general the reckoning was an average weight of 30–40 kg per person). In the Soluk camp there was at the time a new outbreak of exanthematous typhus, which the authorities, in a report of 18 February tried to pretend was nothing to be alarmed about, but then admitted, on 6 March, was a serious epidemic:

The situation in the Soluk centre is slowly worsening without any sign of becoming stabilized. . . . Within a month the number of infected tents has risen by 70. . . . It seems to me and to the director of health that the waiting period recommended by the board is now over; petechial typhus subsists and is spreading. I request the honourable board to let me issue the instructions and furnish the necessary means to tackle the epidemic[176].

The health organization in the camp, of which Italian propaganda boasted so loudly, was in fact in a disastrous state: there were no tents or clothes for isolating the victims of typhus, and not even a stove for disinfecting the clothing of those who were eventually cured. While waiting for the camp to be eased of congestion, demanded as an essential prophylactic measure, the authorities had done nothing but resort to repressive acts, isolating with

---

[174] All the following information comes from two documents; Egidi, regional commissioner of Benghazi, to Graziani, 18 February 1933; and Egidi to the civil and political affairs department of the Cyrenaican government, 6 March 1933 (both in ACS-FG, 4/8/8).

[175] On 2 August 1932 Graziani had given orders for the Auaghir to be transferred from Soluk to camps 'offering better living conditions' (letter cit.), but this measure was never taken because in 1933 the Auaghir still made up three-quarters of the camp population. It should be noted that the number of deportees in the individual camps must have increased rather than diminished, because in 1932 the reprieved ex-rebels and their relations from the dismantled el-Agheila punishment camp were put in these camps. So there were no measures taken to free individuals on anything like a regular basis. It does not appear to us, therefore, that there can be any doubts that the marked drop in camp population numbers was due to the high mortality rate among the detainees, with an explosion of epidemic diseases, old and new, as a result of environmental conditions and scarcity of food.

[176] Egidi to the department of civil and political affairs, 6 March 1933, cit.

barbed wire and stepping up surveillance of the most severely stricken camp of the Abid and Orfa; yet as the board admitted, the efficacy of such measures was a sheer illusion, because typhus was also raging in the three Auaghir camps[177]. The situation was grave enough for Graziani to intervene with all haste, ordering the Soluk camp to be cleared:

I have for some time been persuaded of the need and opportunity to proceed without any further uncertainties on the clearance of the Soluk camp. It is now necessary to adopt, from every point of view, the logistical principle of 'dividing in order to eat and live', just as the other principle of 'joining in order to fight' was strictly applied in its time; I am sure that the slight risks and consequences entailed will always be handled with your customary foresight and energy. I give authorization, therefore, for the Soluk camp to be cleared, in the manner deemed most consonant to its varied needs, as far as concerns the Auaghir. Only the Abid-Orfa, who can be better looked after, must stay there. As regards them and the Magrun camp, I will make further arrangements. . . . I wish this to be carried out with the greatest urgency[178].

In the following weeks it was decided to break up all the concentration camps within a year and to return the people to their original homes, with restrictions dictated by the recognized priority given to the requirements of the Italian settlers and of public order. In May the Abid were transferred from Soluk to the Barce camp where, wrote Graziani:

They went through a second process of being rounded up and concentrated before they were finally transferred to Gerdes el-Abid, their natural home, which in the meantime had been fitted out on the model of the centres of Sirtica and southern Benghazi, already accommodating the massed populations[179].

Simultaneously, Graziani gave orders to arrange the transfer of the Brahasa to Gerdes Gerrari and the Dorsa to Tolmeta, creating a minimum of infrastructure in these areas: barracks for the carabinieri, administrative offices, first-aid post, school, mosque and the like[180]. These transfers (and those of other peoples, of which we have no direct information) took place between August and September, so that by the beginning of autumn Graziani was able to announce that the dissolution of the concentration camps had been terminated without causing any obstacles to the Italian settlement of the

---

[177] Our documentation, however, does not give any direct figure relating to deaths in the concentration camps.

[178] Graziani to the commissioner for the Auaghir, 6 March 1933, in ACS-FG, 4/8/8.

[179] Graziani to Badoglio, 29 May 1933, in ASMAI, 150/22/98.

[180] Graziani to the secretary general of the government of Cyrenaica, 16 May 1933, in ACS-FG, 4/8/8. In the Sidi Ahmed el-Magrun camp there must still have been Brahasa and Dorsa, practising horticulture, as well as the more troublesome Auaghir; a sign that the concentration camps were still being used, at least for the time being, as an instrument of selective repression.

Gebel, now made easier by the availability of manpower[181]. As Graziani explained to the Italian colonists in February 1934:

The indigenous populations have all been taken back to the regions adapted to their form of life, *firmly based on the principle that the Gebel, backbone of the colony's farming economy, must remain free of them and earmarked for mainland colonization;* that innumerable provisions have been made for the people so sorely tested by the rebellion; and that the generosity of the Fascist government, truly Roman, has been bestowed on them with the closure of the concentration camps and the almost total freeing of internees and those imprisoned for minor political crimes, so that today there are only fifteen of the former interned in Italy and throughout Cyrenaica less than 400 detainees, most of them having committed common crimes, still in prison[182].

A month later the situation in Cyrenaica had become sufficiently normal to take another step:

On the occasion of the Greater Bairam, the last Ustica internees have been freed and at the same time the Abid people have been transferred from Barce to Gerdes Abid, their natural homeland. By these two acts the ethnic reconstruction of the colony has been completed and the total pacification of all its inhabitants achieved. Cyrenaica now sets out, fully confident in word and deed, towards its certain goal of economic prosperity and civil development[183].

As he was about to leave Cyrenaica, in April 1934, Graziani summarized the results achieved as follows:

With the settlement of the Brahasa tribe in the Gerdes Gerrari region, all the ethnic groups of Cyrenaica have been redistributed in the territories formerly occupied by them prior to their concentration in Sirtica and southern Benghazi, taking into account, of course, the Gebel tableland zone, destined to be organized for colonization and thus to be left free of indigenous

---

[181] Graziani to Badoglio and De Bono, 22 September 1933, in ASMAI, 150/22/98. To quote the only case where we have available figures, the Dorsa tribe, which in June 1932 had between 4000 and 5000 members (notes from Daodiace to Graziani, 27 June 1932, *cit.*), dwindled to 2600 when it was allowed to return to the Gebel (Graziani to Balbo, 26 April 1934, *cit.*).

[182] Graziani speech, 25 February 1934, *cit.*

[183] Graziani to Badoglio, 26 March 1934, in ACS-FG, 1/2/2. The situation of the Egyptian exiles was also returning to normal, according to the 'Bollettino informazioni del comando delle truppe della Cirenaica', in AUSE-FL, 177/1. After an initial very hard period, when many of the emigrants died from malnutrition ('Bollettino' no. 7, December 1932–March 1933), at the end of 1934 there still remained in Egypt some 12,000 Cyrenaican and 4000 Tripolitanian refugees, while 2250 had already returned to Cyrenaica ('Bollettino' no. 11, August–November 1934). According to the Italian vice-consul at Sollum, two thousand of these Cyrenaican exiles were sworn enemies of Italy, another two thousand had been satisfactorily settled with relatives, but the majority, approximately eight thousand, were seeking repatriation, especially since the demand for manpower in the Gebel guaranteed them a higher standard of living than the miserable one they had to endure as a result of the crisis in the Egyptian economy.

peoples. The only exceptions are a few Abeidat groups, specifically the Faiza and Abd el-Gader branches of the Mansur kabyle, totalling about 2000 people, formerly living in the Gebel between Gubba and Slonta, who have been transferred to Zavia Omm Rocha in Marmarica, between Marsa Luch and Bardia, where they enjoy excellent living conditions. Since they constitute a factious unit by reason of solidarity, homogeneity and historical tradition, they are to be allowed to stay there, not only for reasons of the Gebel's security but also, and above all, because their ancient land is now part and parcel of the zone reserved for colonization.

The map enclosed with the present report (*word missing*) gives the general picture of the current ethnic reconstruction of the colony, which corresponds exactly, apart from the exception mentioned above, to the distribution of the Cyrenaican tribes, namely:

The Mogarba—between el-Agheila, Marsa Brega and Agedabia

The Fuacher—along the line bounding the regions of Agedabia and of the Auaghir

The Auaghir—in the territory of that name (Benghazi region)

The Abid—in the Gerdes Abid zone

The Orfa—on the Barce plain

The Dorsa—at Tolmeta

The Hasa—around Apollonia, from where they have never been moved

The Brahasa—in the Gerdes Gerrari zone

The Abeidat—from Derna to Tobruk

The Marmarici, i.e. the Ghetan, Meriam, Sciuaer, Mnefa, Habbun, etc. groups—between Tobruk and Bardia.

The distribution, as can be seen, corresponds to the original territory. That does not mean that the ethnic groups have gone back to their former free, nomadic life. On the contrary, the present distribution, though offering ample scope for pasturage and sowing requirements, conforms to the strictest criteria of political control and vigilance of the population, which only now has the feeling of being well and truly governed and administered.

At one time the people of Cyrenaica were left free to move around the territories belonging to them, so much so that it was difficult for the regional commissioners to know where they were at any given moment. Today that does not happen and cannot be allowed to happen. There are no more 'pertinent zones', and the demarcation lines of the territories assigned to the various ethnic groups, as shown on the map here enclosed (*word missing*), only indicate the limits within which the camps of the nomadic peoples of the various administrative localities are set up, and not the whole territory where the various groups are permitted freedom of movement.

In fact, the tribes have been settled in prearranged encampments, situated in places where the best opportunities exist for agricultural and pastoral activities. Group freedom of movement is permitted, subject to proper methods of control, only to camps of shepherds, but the carabinieri are constantly in touch with the people, whether in an encamped or shifting group. Broadly speaking, it is a genuine organization of mobile police, which must be retained until the new indigenous generation, having grown up and been educated in the new political atmosphere, has replaced those of the present generation whose livelihood is based solely on nomadism, who are impatient of any kind of discipline and who rebel against any form of sound political and social order. . . .

Formerly the nomads knew no other authority than their chiefs. Today these no longer exist. The people's leaders are now either our officials or the *mudir* assisted by the *muktaz*. The *mudir* are no longer easily manipulated by the plots of the old chiefs, but can be relied upon as active, honest and trustworthy collaborators because they have been chosen from the ranks of local people who, through culture, attitude, loyalty and political background, offer the best guarantee in keeping with their delicate functions and their position as government officials. . . . All today's *mudir* speak and write Arabic and Italian, and most of them have come out of our schools. They are directly accountable to our regional authorities for order and discipline in the camps, and possess those powers that were formerly recognized as those of the chiefs[184].

This policy should not be seen merely as an excuse for driving the semi-nomadic tribes from the most fertile lands of the Gebel and subjecting them to strict military and political control, but as part of a broader design to destroy the traditional Gebel society of livestock breeders so as to transform it into a reservoir of low-cost, constantly available manpower. Graziani had publicly expressed a pathological inability to understand the Arabic civilization of Cyrenaica: 'Nomadism,' he wrote in 1932, 'must be regarded as an immanent danger, and must therefore be strictly, and permanently, controlled and checked' for political and economic reasons, the nomads being by nature enemies of farming and progress, and potentially rebels[185]. In apparent contradiction to these premises, Graziani intended to banish a large part of the population expelled from the best land of the Gebel 'to the territories of the pre-desert boundaries', namely that arid belt of steppe between tableland

---

[184] Graziani to Balbo, 26 April 1934, *cit.* Graziani continued to demand the maintenance of a military organization along the frontier with Egypt until such time as Italian control over the Gebel had been assured. In fact, he feared the possible effects of a surprise attack by Senusi raiders: 'A group of four or five such marauders which manages to get into Cyrenaica and carry out an act of brigandry against a single colonist family in the Gebel would be enough to create panic among all the settlers and thus seriously compromise the development of our work of colonization, already so ripe with promise.'

[185] GRAZIANI, *op. cit.*, pp. 122–3.

and desert where nomadic livestock raising was the sole resource; instead of being encouraged to strike roots in the soil, the surviving members of the proudest Gebel tribes would thus be condemned to a nomadic life on the very brink of subsistence, which would have kept them permanently in a state of absolute inferiority, in veritable 'native reserves'. In fact, in the ensuing years the reconstitution of the Cyrenaican livestock resources proceeded very slowly indeed[186], because Fascist colonial policy chose to concentrate on the agricultural development of the Gebel and on large-scale Italian immigration. In this context traditional livestock breeding became a secondary economic activity, the principal purpose being to maintain, without any burden on the state, a supply of under-employed manpower, which could be called on for any subordinate and risky jobs in the economic sector.

According to Graziani, in the spring of 1934 some 20–25% of the people expelled from the good lands of the Gebel were employed in government road and building work. For example, 3800 Abid (men, women, elderly people and children—all that remained of one of the proudest Gebel tribes) provided 800 workers, and 2600 Dorsa a further 680[187]. Such high percentages suggest forced recruitment, which meant good business for the contracting firms: according to the facts provided by Graziani himself, the daily pay of an Italian labourer averaged 30 lire, and that of an Arab worker only 10 lire. Out of this salary, too, came ingenious deductions, like that described by Graziani:

In what we might well call such happy economic conditions, confronted by the present world crisis, it was necessary for the government to intervene in order to get the people to make economies for their own benefit and for the reconstruction of the fund of livestock. To this end, a daily sum of two lire was held back from every worker's pay, which was paid into the postal savings book of each registered worker. The saving thus realized is now in the order of a million and a half lire, and will go to the acquisition of animals, which will naturally remain the property of the individual savers[188].

The crown of this policy, which aimed at drawing a disposable and depersonalized lumpen proletariat from the ruins of a secular civilization, was represented by the boys' camps, which in 1934 had 2800 members.

---

[186] In 1933 there were 222,000 sheep and goats, 3000 cattle and 11,500 camels (Graziani to Balbo, 26 April 1934, *cit.*); some years later there were 210,000 sheep, 70,000 goats, 1000 horses, 550 asses, 9000 camels and 9500 cattle, the last being on the increase because of the needs of the Italian colonists (Touring Club Italiano, *Libia*, *cit.*, p. 121). If we bear in mind that in 1933–4 160,000 head of livestock had been imported from Tripolitania, the results do not appear very brilliant, but prove the lack of care and the poverty of the pastures reserved for livestock raising.

[187] Graziani to Balbo, 26 April 1934, *cit.*

[188] Graziani to Balbo, 26 April 1934, *cit.*

The first of these (wrote Graziani), that of Sidi Ahmed el-Magrun, was created at the end of 1931 with the aim of providing a more direct form of assistance to Libyan children who had been orphaned or abandoned between the age of 6 to 15 years. The swift and brilliant results obtained from the first group of 60 boys placed in a suitable camp decided the government to extend the institution to other centres in the colony.

Today there are youth camps organized on this model at Sidi Ahmed el-Magrun and at Soluk, these being the best, and at Tobruk, Agedabia, Barce, Cyrene and even Cufra, plus sports camps at Ghemines, Suani Terria, Giardina, Carcura, Guarschia and in virtually all the encampments of the various ethnic groups of the colony[189].

The boys' camp of Sidi Ahmed el-Magrun, continued Graziani, accepted 539 Brahasa and Dorsa children (it seems from the report that these had not followed their tribes to the Gebel) and 120 Auaghir.

The establishment is run on military lines, according to the rules in force for indigenous troops, suitably adapted. The boys are divided into centuries, and these in turn into maniples and squads. The graduates are selected from the ranks of the boys themselves, notably those who have demonstrated special aptitudes and passed an appropriate theoretical and practical examination. Command of the centuries and discipline in the camp are entrusted to a national non-commissioned officer of the royal corps of colonial troops. Each day the boys receive an hour of military instruction (identical to that of regular local soldiers) and an hour of sports and gymnastics instruction. Most of the boys in the camp (the best physically and intellectually) are taught a trade. For this purpose there is in the camp a craft school run by national personnel and divided into departments of carpenters, fitters, forgers . . . , tinsmiths, shoemakers . . . , tailors . . . , and a first-aid unit[190].

Other camps were organized along the same lines:

From these training grounds of Italian culture and civil, professional and military education, will emerge the first groups of the new Libyan generation (concluded Graziani). From them the colony will be able to obtain the individuals best suited to the needs of agriculture, civil administration (local white-collar personnel) and especially the Libyan units of the royal corps of colonial troops, into which the first recruits have already entered from Marmarica, with about a hundred boys from the Magrun and Soluk camps due next July; when these reach the maximum age limit (18 years), they will be enrolled in the VII and IX battalions of the new force[191].

[189] Graziani to Balbo, 26 April 1934, cit.

[190] Graziani to Balbo, 26 April 1934, cit. The overall costs of the seven boys' camps was around two million lire, which give an annual average of 700 lire per boy. It is worth noting that the Soluk camp also included 34 boys, the only ones out of a total of 2800 inmates.

[191] Graziani to Balbo, 26 April 1934, cit.

Actually, the major result of these camps was to furnish recruits for the reconstituted Libyan battalions, which very shortly, still under the orders of Badoglio and Graziani, were to help bring the sorrows of Fascist 'civilization' to Ethiopia.

Romain Rainero

The capture, trial and death of Omar al-Mukhtar in the context of the Fascist policy for the 'reconquest' of Libya

The episode which certainly dominated and virtually concluded the entire campaign of 'pacification' imposed by the Fascist government on the colony of Libya, culminating in the elimination of the rebel leader Omar al-Mukhtar, cannot be completely isolated from the overall Fascist policy for the colonies and its own imperial dreams which, from the 1930s, was proclaimed as the primary objective of the regime. The superseding of Liberal policy, denounced for years as having failed completely to cope with the colonial situation now inflamed by rising nationalistic fervour, had been urged repeatedly, together with the need to disavow and hence throw out the whole package of pre-Fascist agreements concluded with local leaders by Bertolini and Colosimo. While the liberalism of this 'old' policy should not be exaggerated, and although Italian policy in Libya was still marked by many contradictions between 1915 and 1922, the breaking off of any dialogue with the 'rebels' emerged as the government's declared criterion after the March on Rome. Colonial authoritarianism, which had been in evidence even during the Liberal period, now became the uncontested doctrine; and the campaign of 'pacification' inaugurated the era of systematic violence against the indigenous peoples. This short-sighted policy frequently drove the victims to resistance, which was eventually concentrated in Cyrenaica; and after the initial Fascist military endeavours of the early period, such resistance found its inspiration in the rebel stronghold of the Gebel region. The chauvinist, nationalistic climate fostered by the government in Rome, with its extravagant claims overseas, was bound to bring the whole question of relations with the Libyans to the point of open crisis, highlighted on the one hand by the exhortation of violence as government doctrine and on the other by vain reminders of agreements which Fascist Italy had fully decided to renege.

119

Against this background, rendered more precarious by the intransigent declarations of the Senusi and the sworn intention of the Fascists to 'liquidate' the entire political problem by military means, the crisis was inevitably steered into a blind alley of military reactions and the intransigence of those very Italian authorities whom the Fascists expected to come up with an urgent solution of the problem, not least because of the unconcealed policy of mass demographic settlement of the Fourth Shore.

The years between the coming to power of Fascism in Italy and the arrival in Tripoli (21 January 1929) of Marshal Badoglio as governor had not, paradoxically, been marked by the resounding success that Fascism had for years demanded of its proconsuls, and which, by crushing rebellion, had displayed its determination and strength to the world. Having forgotten and denounced the agreements of Er Regima (25 October 1920) and of Bu Mariam (20 October 1921), Fascism had not managed, in almost seven years of government, to get the better, once and for all, of the Senusi 'rebels'. After the conclusion of the Garian meeting (18 November 1920), matters took a more 'national' turn than before when, under the guidance of Senusiya itself, the much-feared integration of the people of Tripolitania, Fezzan and Cyrenaica occurred, with the view of defending the 'Libyan homeland'. Seven years of war achieved a few results territorially, with the obvious expansion of the Italian perimeter, but the region of the Gebel Akhdar (Green Mountain), which agricultural studies and plans for demographic colonization showed to be the only possible site for a genuine programme of Italian farm settlement, remained totally insecure. In this context, the visit that Mussolini paid to Libya in April 1926 seems rather significant, not so much for the 'violent shake' he proposed giving to the whole Libyan question, nor even because he wanted 'to carry the triumphant and immortal Roman lictor to the shores of the African sea', as for his 'unwavering desire' to bring the people of Rome to that land[1]. There were no bounds to the excitement of colonial extremists at this kind of talk. And Graziani, African general and proconsul *in fieri*, was to accord it solemn recognition in his *Verso il Fezzan*: 'His (Mussolini's) landing could be likened to the new baptismal chrism of our great Mediterranean destiny, reddened by the blood spilled in the Campidoglio (Gibson's attempt on Mussolini's life just prior to his departure) . . .' In general political terms, it was not merely a matter of repeating that the agreements with the local leaders were no longer valid, but, above all, of emphasizing officially the 'Roman' continuity of this policy. The Fascist

---

[1] Mussolini's speech is in *Opera Omnia*, Vol. XXII, p. 115. The most interesting document concerning the trip and its 'imperial and Roman' phases is still the special number of the journal *Costruire*, no. 5, May 1926, *In Africa con Mussolini*, from which the quotation by Dario Lischi is taken (p. 1).

journalist D. Lischi was to put it well when he underlined 'the importance of the presidential gesture, which was a bold and firm reaffirmation of Italy's destiny and a classic evocation of a past which, although separated by centuries, had nonetheless never ceased to tower in the background of world history . . .'

Thus the role of Libya, in Mussolini's ambitious project of solving the problems of unemployment and over-population in country districts, assumed ever greater importance. The government could no longer go back on its plan to recover the best lands of the Gebel Akhdar, still under the control of the Senusi 'rebels'. There were no further doubts as to the links between the two poles of Fascist policy, and the more recent studies in this field have highlighted their ruling criteria with an abundance of detail. They are, on the one hand, 'ruralization' and, on the other, the demographic policy. The demographic campaign began in 1926, and the launching of the campaign to colonize Libya was an inevitable consequence of this. However, there still remained the problem of 'pacification': despite all efforts, the Cyrenaican crisis showed no signs of being resolved, and three years after Mussolini's appearance in Tripoli there was still no progress towards realizing the colonization of the Cyrenaican tableland, which the offices responsible for land division regarded as the only possible site for any serious Italian agricultural settlement. The political situation only assumed important new dimensions with the appointment on 21 January 1929 of Marshal Badoglio as 'single governor of Tripolitania and Cyrenaica', having been named a few days previously (18 December 1928) as governor of the two regions separately. In this new post, which the word 'single' indicated as ranking higher than the equivalent previous position, Badoglio, who counted upon putting down the rebellion within five years, tried to apply a new look to his African proconsulship, with sights fixed on inevitable 'military goals'. Particularly interesting in this context, it appears to us, was the proclamation on the occasion of assuming power, which has become famous both for its authoritarian 'Roman' form and for its repeated use of a pseudo-Moslem type of military prose. It has to be said, nevertheless, that the proclamation 'Udite! Udite! . . .', though hailed by a part of the official press as 'an act of pride and loyalty rather than of strength'[2], caused not a few reservations among experts on oriental affairs. Professor Nallino, for example, in the authoritative journal of the Oriental Institute, had no hesitation in writing: 'I do not know whether it is a good idea to continue circulating the text of this proclamation, which, notwithstanding the respect and recognition due to the illustrious marshal of Italy, will, in the opinion of some people, not seem altogether happy because

[2] These are the words of G. MACALUSO ALEO, *Lo stroncamento della ribellione in Cirenaica*, in 'L'Illustrazione coloniale', 1 December 1930, p. 25.

of some rather immoderate expressions and certain formal details . . .'[3]. The comment evidently had political repercussions, partly because it presumed to imply that the policy towards the Senusi would be more in line with their national aspirations than a slavish imitation of the 'direct' policy adopted in Eritrea. Nallino made no secret of this, underlining that 'among other things, this three times repeated Udite! Udite! would seem more suitable for some of the peoples of Eritrea and Somalia than for the inhabitants of Libya . . .' The matter did not pass unobserved. Firstly, the 'scholar' Macaluso Aleo, among other things accused the review *Oriente Moderno* of 'being written in a peculiar language that is neither Italian nor oriental', which could 'only be wholly understood perhaps by a few dozen scholars' and which therefore was not in keeping with the new times. Another person to get involved was the standard-bearer of those new times in Libya, General Graziani, who was angry with Nallino not only for having criticized Badoglio's proclamation but also a speech by Graziani himself in which the latter had referred to Senusiya as a 'sect' and not a brotherhood. Speaking on 23 November 1930 at the Fascist Institute of Culture at Benghazi, he declared: 'When a brotherhood starts dabbling in politics, I do not for one moment hesitate in calling it a sect. When Professor Nallino, arguing with Macaluso, says: Is a sect perhaps tentacular because it seeks to make proselytes and tries to expand? Well, then, Fascist Italy is tentacular, too; I denounce it, as I have denounced it to the higher authorities . . . It is plain to see that Professor Nallino has never seen and examined a Bedouin encampment'[4].

This outburst of polemics is additionally interesting because it reveals something that is a constant factor in Graziani's behaviour, namely the wish to be seen as a 'new man' and to pursue, without reference to any kind of precedents, a policy of absolute victory, ruling out any diplomatic settlements with the 'rebels'. This attitude is in striking contrast to the policy of open diplomacy adopted by Marshal Badoglio, at least at the start of his mandate, in choosing to negotiate with the 'rebels'. Possibly in order to gain time and thus enable the Italian armed forces in Cyrenaica to be reorganized, and meanwhile permit the arrival of powerful 'new' military means (aircraft and tanks in particular) which had been requested and promised by Rome for such actions, Badoglio appeared to be indulging in a phase of dialogue with the rebels, mainly through the intervention of the Cyrenaican vice-governor, Colonel Domenico Siciliani. Negotiations and meetings took place during May and June 1929, but because of their equivocal and uncertain nature they resulted in nothing but a subsequent period of misunderstanding and crisis.

[3] C. A. NALLINO, review of the book by G. MACALUSO ALEO, *Turchi, Senussi e Italiani in Libia*, Benghazi, Vitali, 1930, in 'Oriente Moderno', October 1930, p. 518.
[4] R. GRAZIANI, *La situazione cirenaica*, Benghazi, Cyrenaica, 1930, p. 27.

In this context, the meeting which was held at Sidi-Rahuma on 19 June 1929 between Badoglio and Siciliani on the one side and the leader of the Cyrenaican rebellion, Omar al-Mukhtar, on the other, assumes capital importance.

The misunderstandings about this meeting are such that we have two quite contradictory versions of the event and its motives, which are worth considering. According to Graziani's evidence, the meeting of 13 June was simply a repetition, in the presence of the highest Italian authority in Italy, Marshal Badoglio, of the surrender ceremony which Omar al-Mukhtar had already performed at Barce on that same day (13 June) before Colonel Siciliani. Graziani's version, mentioned in his memoirs, leaves no doubts: '. . . At this meeting (13 June) Omar al-Mukhtar made the following declaration: "Do not call me a rebel because never before today have I submitted to the government, which therefore I have always fought because religion enjoined me to do so. Today I submit with all my men: from today absolute and complete peace will reign in Cyrenaica. Everyone must obey the legitimate government of Italy. Move about as you wish, do away with convoys, do away with redoubts—in Cyrenaica none of these things are of further use because in Cyrenaica there is no longer any war"'[5]. At the conclusion of the Barce meeting, according to Italian sources, Omar al-Mukhtar's position was precisely as stated in that declaration; and it received full news coverage, including a special communiqué from the Agencia Stefani, which left no doubt as to the event and its significance: 'An event of singular political importance has taken place in Cyrenaica. The leading members of the rebellion have made their act of submission. On the day of 13 June, at a place near Barce (El-Merg), the rebel chiefs, including Omar al-Mukhtar, leading representative of the rebellion which he has headed with grim determination from 1923 until today, Sidi Hasan ben Mohammed Ridà es-Senusi, son of the famous er-Ridà who defected to us last year, and Fadil bu Homar, leading representative of the Brahasa tribe, appeared before

---

[5] The statement attributed to Omar al-Mukhtar was repeated twice, in the terms here mentioned, by Graziani (*Cirenaica pacificata*, Milan, Mondadori, 1932, p. 30, and *Libia redenta*, Naples, Torella, 1948, p. 46), but underwent some variation both in the almost contemporary version of C. GIGLIO (*La confraternita senussita*, Padua, Cedam, 1932, p. 136) and in that of E. DE LEONE (*La colonizzazione dell'Africa del Nord*, Vol. II, Padua, Cedam, 1960, p. 551), which sounds rather different: '. . . today I give myself up; for me General Badoglio is the first Italian governor whom Cyrenaica has ever had. From today there is a government, the Italian, in Cyrenaica, from today there are in Cyrenaica soldiers of the government. From today Cyrenaica enters a new era, that of peace. I am at the government's disposal. But give me time to calm and persuade all those who were with me and all those to the east and the west, because I want there to be not a single dissident. Peace, however, is absolute and complete from this moment. Move about as you wish, do away with convoys, do away with redoubts. In Cyrenaica none of these things are of further use because in Cyrenaica from now on there are no more rebels.'

vice-governor Siciliani saying that they were placing themselves uncon-
ditionally in the hands of the Italian authorities, pledging themselves to
observe the conditions laid down in the celebrated proclamation issued by
Marshal Badoglio when he assumed the governorship of Tripolitania and
Cyrenaica. . . . ' And even the fact that Omar al-Mukhtar had accepted a clock
as a gift from vice-governor Siciliani, intended to 'mark the hour of peace',
was quoted as proof of 'the submission that had taken place'.

According to the Arab version, however, such a 'solemn submission' had
not occurred; the meeting had served only to inform the Italian delegates of
the conditions laid down by the Senusi in order to reach a new *modus vivendi*,
and it was in expectation of this that the Senusi had offered a truce.

There were thus a number of serious contradictions. One person who had
no doubts about the substance of the 'surrender' of the rebel leader and his
men was Governor Badoglio, who, preparing to go to Sidi Rahuma, sent a
triumphal telegram to the Duce which was certainly imprudent in form and
solemn content. Indeed, to say, as did Badoglio, that 'I leave tomorrow for
Benghazi to receive the formal act of submission. With joyful heart I send
this telegram to your excellency since I am sure that a new life is beginning
for Cyrenaica,' simply showed that his assessment was either rash in the
extreme or quite unjustified, given the complexity of the Cyrenaican crisis[6].

After Sidi Rahuma the situation became no clearer, nor did the two
versions come closer together: Badoglio's interpretation, whereby the surrender had been ratified by Omar al-Mukhtar and his aides, clashed head-on with
the one issuing from Senusi sources, according to which the negotiations
aimed, unsuccessfully, at working out a new formula of autonomy which
would recognize Senusi authority in the country. The flimsiness of the former
version is demonstrated by the fact that the negotiations, still on the same
subject, were to continue on 28 June at Bir Gandula with vice-governor
Siciliani. The hoped-for agreement did not come about, but events as they
developed cast grave doubts as to the credibility of the Badoglio interpretation. It is worth noting that even the semi-official book by Carlo Giglio,
published in 1932 with a preface by Rodolfo Graziani, did not trouble to
conceal the flimsiness of Marshal Badoglio's version, adding: 'There are two
versions of this remarkable event, the one from Arab sources and the official
one from our own government: it is hard to establish the degree of truth in
both versions and to know what really happened. It appears from Arab
sources that in the spring of 1929 conversations were begun between the
governor of Benghazi and Sidi Idris to persuade the latter to instruct Omar
al-Mukhtar to give up the rebellion. Because he expected negotiations to go
on for a long time, Omar al-Mukhtar, together with Sidi Idris, pledged

<hr>

[6] Highly confidential telegram no. 6459 of 14 June 1929, ASMAI, 150/21/90.

himself to keep the peace for as long as they continued: thus at the Sidi Rahuma meeting the old man did not offer to submit but promised a cease-fire. That there was no question of submission can be proved by the fact that he was not disarmed, which would certainly have been a *sine qua non* condition for surrender. Consequently, according to Arab sources, it was General (*sic*) Badoglio who wrongly interpreted the action of the elderly rebel, who had undertaken only to observe a truce; this is in keeping with his word when, after the negotiations failed, he resumed his freedom of action. According to this version, again, the Colonial Ministry had suddenly disowned the Benghazi government and given orders for the negotiations to be suspended and for fighting to start again with the Senusi: as a result, Omar al-Mukhtar had resumed guerilla warfare against us. The official version of the government, on the other hand, explains matters quite differently[7].

Apparently there was quite a lot of perplexity in the Fascist camp, too, as Giglio persisted in accusing Badoglio of foolishness, especially after Omar al-Mukhtar's account of events, written on 20 October 1929 and published by the two Cairo Arab newspapers ('El-Ahdar' and 'El-Mohattam'). In it the Senusi leader gave his own rather more credible version of the negotiations, which were intended to be in various phases and did not involve, either at Sidi Rahuma nor elsewhere, any discussions whatsoever about a rebel 'surrender'. The conditional four-point armistice suggested by Omar al-Mukhtar was accepted by Marshal Badoglio as it had been by Colonel Siciliani[8]. According to this Arabic document, negotiations appeared promising, but a successful outcome was prevented by a clear desire on the Italian side to see the incipient agreement come to nothing, since its provisions certainly could never be reconciled with the repeated pronouncements of the Fascist government at home concerning the 'total reconquest of the Cyrenaican region, without any concessions to the rebels', and regarding the use, for demographic colonization, of the best area in Cyrenaica, namely the Gebel Akhdar itself.

The breakdown in negotiations for the 'surrender' was inevitably recognized by Omar al-Mukhtar as soon as it became clear that the truce was not being accompanied by any real progress in the interrupted dialogue, and hence was being utilized by the Italians to build up the logistical and strategic strength of the armed forces, as demanded by Badoglio. Disappointment and

---

[7] C. GIGLIO, *op. cit.*, p. 136. There is no explanation as to why Giglio continued to call Badoglio general and not marshal.

[8] The four points were: '1. General amnesty for all those guilty of political crimes, both those within the country and those outside it, and freeing of prisoners for political reasons. 2. Withdrawal of all the garrisons set up during the 1341 war (1922–1923), including those of Giarabub and Gialo. 3. The right on my part to collect legal tithes from Arab residents around the Italian coastal garrisons. 4. Duration of the armistice, two months, renewable.'

protest were loudly voiced by the Arabs: 'Let every fighter know, therefore,' wrote Omar al-Mukhtar, 'that the sole aim of the Italian government is to stir up discords and plots among us in order to destroy our bonds and break up our union, and to be able to prise away and snatch from us all our legitimate rights, as has already happened many times. But, thanks to God, they have not managed to do any of this.

'Let the whole world bear witness that our intentions towards the Italian government are noble, that we have no other aim than to claim our freedom and that the objective of the Italians is to repress any national movement which aims at the reawakening and progress of the Tripolitan people. . . .

'Nevertheless we cannot say that all the Italian people approve of the idea of war, especially at a time when other nations are showing themselves agreeable to the peoples of the East; on the contrary, there are politicians inclined towards peace who take into account their country's interests, and know that ruin and loss is caused by war—just as there are a few individuals who desire the destruction by any means of the Tripolitan people. May God not permit the latter to have their way.

'There is no nation that does not know that in order to gain freedom it is necessary to deploy every effort, whether easy or hard.

'We are now defending our very existence and are sacrificing our blood in order to redeem our country and to achieve the ends that we have mentioned. Nevertheless, we undertake that such a situation will only last until the individuals who are set upon using violence against us change their ways, start out on the right path and treat us with fairness rather than with flattery and deceit.'

It is interesting in this context of the Sidi Rahuma meeting and the failure of the peace discussions to examine what may be regarded as the last version of Graziani, the one published in 1948, arising from his ancient rivalry with Marshal Badoglio, particularly in the light of the subsequent careers of the two men, one in favour of the armistice and the downfall of the Fascist regime, the other a steadfast Fascist and responsible for the military destinies of the ephemeral Italian Socialist Republic. Reproducing in his book *Libia redenta* part of the version of events previously narrated in the triumphant climate of *Cirenaica pacificata* sixteen years beforehand, Graziani referred to the journalistic mishaps of the meeting, which had been magnified so disproportionately by the Fascist press as to engender a political inquiry: 'The Colonial Ministry was so bothered by all this rumpus that it immediately had the editor of the Tripoli newspaper ('L'Avvenire di Tripoli') recalled by the director of the Press Office in Rome. . . . But from the inquiry that was held concerning the matter, it emerged that the author of the panegyric to Badoglio and of the account of the 'triumph' of Sidi Rahuma was Badoglio himself: from the first to the last word, he had written it all in his own hand on paper headed 'The Governor-General of Libya'. Naturally, Rome's irritation was transformed into uncontrollable mirth'[9].

What happened in Cyrenaica after the cease-fire is well known. The political and military events have at least some connection with the change in direction sanctioned by Badoglio, who abandoned the clumsily trodden path of negotiation and saw himself forced to sacrifice, in this sudden alteration of policy course, vice-governor Siciliani. For the latter, the sentence of liquidation was not, it is true, so much due to Badoglio alone as to the central authorities via the Colonial Minister De Bono, who always claimed that Mussolini himself had intervened. Fundamental to all this is the programme cabled on 10 November 1929 by De Bono to Badoglio, in which the pronouncement of the 'new' Fascist policy for Cyrenaica is exhibited in the most blatantly violent terms.

'Unfortunately, what I foresaw and pointed out in my various communications has now come to pass. The head of government, being acquainted with the situation, approves my proposals, as follows: (1) break off any form of negotiation with, and toleration for, the rebels, attacking them and giving no quarter; (2) all Senusi persons in our hands to be strictly and manifestly supervised, without any considerate treatment; (3) no more talk of submissions if they have not already happened; (4) captured leaders to be hanged. . . .

Vice-governor Siciliani has by now demonstrated all too clearly that he is not equal to his position. He must be replaced as soon as possible, without giving the impression that we have suffered a setback'[10].

At this point the entire Cyrenaican problem seems to have slipped back into the usual path of military repression: the rebellion, which after the end of the truce sprang up again almost everywhere, destroyed the last hope of a negotiated settlement. Minister of the Colonies De Bono delivered a cutting reply to Badoglio when the latter attempted with difficulty to explain the results of his irresponsibility at Sidi Rahuma, still hoping for dissension among the Senusi forces: 'It is my opinion that we should not wait to see if other ex-rebels follow the example set by the adherents of Omar al-Mukhtar, but that we must absolutely prevent such an example being followed at all. I believe, after what has happened, that we should force his hand so that the *dor* that is still armed definitely gives up its weapons, especially as your excellency told me verbally that we could have taken these *dor* (sic) whenever

---

[9] The episode is found in the note to p. 58 of the *op. cit.*, as is that of the famous clock that was supposed to 'strike the hours of peace', which Omar al-Mukhtar flung to the ground, breaking it, in fury at the governor who was responsible for the famous proclamation 'Udite! Udite! . . .', the 'lion' to whom Omar al-Mukhtar instead attributed 'asses' ears'.

[10] Telegram no. 7325 of 10 November 1929, in ASMAI, 150/21/90.

we wanted. In fact, I am not alarmed at the situation, but it is undeniable that we have not cut a very fine figure because the entire Cyrenaican policy was based upon the proclaimed pacification, from which Omar al-Mukhtar has emerged as the principal actor and exponent'[11]. The severest accusations were hurled at Siciliani himself, who suddenly became the man principally responsible for Badoglio's errors, and De Bono did not spare him prior to getting rid of him: 'Months ago I warned you not to trust anyone. I have insisted at least five times that steps should be taken to disarm the *dor*, but your excellency has always nourished illusions. Your excellency will agree that we have not cut a very fine figure. I tried to make clear in every possible way that any concession would be taken as weakness by the rebels'[12].

Clearly at this point it seems opportune to examine the question more closely to find out whether Siciliani was really 'nourishing illusions' or whether rather it was the policy of the Italian government itself in not being clear either as to its true intentions or its plans concerning relationships with the local people. It appears absurd to us to accuse Siciliani, as De Leone then did, of being 'devoid of Volpi's keen political sensibility and of the good sense that had induced De Bono not to draw back from the path outlined by his predecessor' or of being preoccupied ever since his arrival with 'associating his name, above all, with some sensational turn of events'; these views do not seem in any way justifiable[13].

What seems mainly clear is that the Fascist government deliberately prevaricated with the 'rebels' and played for time so as to allow military reinforcements to reach Cyrenaica and so as to perfect new tactical measures that would give the Italians the opportunity to achieve their only goal, namely the physical destruction of the rebellion.

In this context the appointment of General Graziani and the dismissal of Siciliani (15 March 1930) were determinant factors in the political sphere. Graziani's reputation for severity and intransigence during his Libyan career made him a ravager in the Gallieni style and certainly not a man of tact and diplomacy such as Siciliani had appeared to be. The hallowed tones employed by one of his admirers, Giglio, are an interesting reminder of how Graziani's strategy was judged at the time: 'He was the man best suited for the job, an authority on the mentality of the Libyan people, a brave general, whose intuition and shrewdness were combined with the sound judgment of our countrymen, accustomed to every exertion but above all not subject to preconceptions of any kind'[14]. And that he did not hold any preconceived

---

[11] Telegram no. 7335 of 11 November 1929, in ASMAI, *ibid.*
[12] Telegram no 132 of 10 January 1930, in ASMAI, see note 10.
[13] E. DE LEONE, *op. cit.*, p. 550.
[14] G. GIGLIO, *op. cit.*, p. 141.

ideas was evident when on 5 April 1930, in his first important report to Badoglio, he declared his intention to dissociate himself 'in the most absolute manner from what had happened before', meaning that he was announcing in the most explicit fashion that he was abandoning the diplomatic manoeuvres previously practised by Badoglio himself, relying henceforth on arms alone to wipe out the 'revolt'. The political analysis of the Cyrenaican situation was fairly clear, but it is important to examine with some care the individual elements which combined to make the report of 5 April a document of such capital importance. Graziani's overriding concern, politically motivated, was to express, very prudently, a viewpoint that aimed firstly at destroying the myth of pursuing a solution entailing the submission of various indigenous groups, and secondly at exaggerating the efficiency of the enemy, painting in darkest terms the dire situation handed down by the previous Italian authorities in Benghazi. It is worth looking closely at the three parts of the document. The statement that 'Senusi activities have an impact everywhere' did not imply that the Senusi were recognized as having some political right to 'sovereignty' but rather that a certain form of colonial policy was being accused of the more serious responsibility of preparing Italy's 'surrender'. The argument becomes clear from careful reading of the two following paragraphs:

'*They all* hope that if they do not manage to establish peace by force the government will be induced to yield, making a variety of concessions.

'*All of them*, be they important or ordinary people, *sottomessi* or not, are doing everything possible to keep the rebellion alive, thus disturbing public tranquillity.

'This is an absolute reality, and to deny it is a refusal to see matters clearly'[15].

This was not so much a matter of 'absolute reality', as Graziani maintained in his attempt to denigrate the fighting quality of Omar al-Mukhtar's Arab soldiers, as his own desire to stress the proven inefficacy of the idea of submission, until now assumed by the Italian colonial authorities as being the consequence of their repressive activities. According to Graziani's analysis, which likened the situation of Cyrenaica 'to a poisoned organism which produces, in one part of the body, a festering bubo', it became clear that 'the acts of brigandry' committed by Omar al-Mukhtar's men were due to shortcomings of the Italian armed forces, despite a superiority in numbers and weapons, to the policies of 'wait and see' and conciliation thus far adopted, and to the absence of extreme severity towards all the local people, guilty of assistance to, or of direct or indirect connivance with, the rebels. Basically, Graziani's programme of reorganization was not a plan which 'was to restrict

---

[15] The complete text of Graziani's report to Badoglio and the Colonial Minister of 5 April 1930 is in ASMAI, pos. 150/22, fasc. 98.

itself to these aspects' so much as one that entailed an extreme stiffening of repressive measures and (why not?) collective responsibility of the local community which, from now on, would permit, or indeed necessitate, total Italian control being exercised with the utmost harshness. Graziani's military and political proposals involved him in a series of measures designed 'to bring about a more homogeneous territorial organization, with the creation of a Gebel Commissariat which will be better able to put this awkward territory in order; to establish an atmosphere of unyielding rigour, immediately bringing back the penalties for deserters; to treat the crime of connivance as the same as that of treason against the state and hence punishable by death; and to institute, as the absolute cornerstone of any pacification, complete disarmament of the people, outside and inside.'

The report of 5 April posed the simplest of equations: the anti-Italian resistance movement is supported by all the Arabs and there can thus be no discrimination among them; all of them are enemies of Italy, at least potentially, and should be treated as such. And with a similar conclusion Graziani even went counter to the directives previously communicated to him by the Duce in the eight-point programme outlined by Minister De Bono following his nomination as vice-governor and the tribute to him in the Chamber of Deputies (21 March 1930), i.e.: (1) Clear and effective distinction between those who had, and those who had not, offered submission, in their homes, their places of work and their dealings. (2) Give safety and protection to the *sottomessi*, but keep a watch on their every activity'[16].

Graziani's overall policy and his aim to transform his own proconsulship into a privileged platform for airing his personal views against, and to the detriment of, his natural superior, the 'sole' governor, Marshal Badoglio, had the effect of ensuring that every consideration of the problem was henceforth seen in the light of the extremism and 'new' style that he preached. The arrival of powerful aerial reinforcements reflected the recognition of a mobile enemy in a contest of geographical complexity, but also the need to use them in a wholly new way. Thus the 'flying tribunals' cut short the legal procedures and made sure that military justice need not be delayed. These measures entailed summary trials by special courts flown in by air, to the evident satisfaction of Graziani and of the president of the tribunal itself, General Olivieri: '. . . In this way judicial action proceeds rapidly and smoothly. As soon as information is received of the red-handed arrest of a criminal, the tribunal and Justice descend from the sky. And this has become so normal that when an aeroplane lands on the spot where a crime has been committed you

---

[16] R. GRAZIANI, *Cirenaica pacificata, cit.*, p. 49 and De Bono to Badoglio and Graziani, 24 March 1930, in ASMAI, pos. 150/22, fasc. 98.

hear murmurs of the word 'tribunal' going round the encampments'[17]. There was no possibility of recourse against such decisions because the appeal procedure was not even provided for in the setting up of the Special Tribunal. It was, by and large, a form of justice that often dispensed with the proper rules, even if the accusations levelled against its actions and circulating for some time in the Arab world (such as throwing the condemned men out of the aeroplane) appear frequently to have been unfounded.

All these measures were accompanied by a threefold series of corresponding tactical decisions, i.e. the reorganization of the troops, the concentration of the entire nomadic population of the region and, finally, the construction of the 'frontier network of wire' along the border with Egypt. Briefly, these three steps were taken in the expectation that they would, in conjunction with one another, eventually lead to the final episode of the capture and death of Omar al-Mukhtar, and hence persuade his followers to give up the fight. The efficacy of Graziani's measures was not so much evident in the logistical reorganization as in the decisions that were taken to organize and deploy the troops. The guiding principle of the troop reorganization begun in May 1930 (circular of 6 May) was to disarm and demobilize a large part of the Libyan mercenary forces, which were held to be of little value against the rebels. In the meantime measures were taken to reinforce special troops, mainly Eritreans attached to 'mobile groups', assigned to the four major sectors where the rebels were notably active: Marmarica, the Gebel, the Auaghir (Benghazi) territory, and the territory of Sirtica. Graziani's definition of the mobile groups, assisted by an equivalent number of air squadrons, is clearly stated in the circular of 1 October 1930:

'The *mobile groups*, free of the political superstructure that previously hampered or compromised the operation, are the rebel *duar's* mastiffs.

'They snap at them and pursue them everywhere when the opportunity permits, and they destroy them daily, *man by man*, as has to be done in accordance with the tough guerilla war they are fighting, being content with partial but continual successes.

'*They must not allow themselves ever to be surprised because only in that way can they be defeated.*

'They have to forget about defences, living under canvas no matter what the weather or the terrain.

'They fight offensively, firing only occasionally and making much use of the bayonet, thus attacking frequently and everywhere.

'They know neither rest nor respite.'

---

[17] Report from General Olivieri in R. GRAZIANI, *Cirenaica pacificata, cit.*, p. 141.

'They oppose the enemy as equals; and they are superior in mobility and speed'[18].

Along with this process of reorganization, which was the prelude to the large-scale mopping-up operations in coordinated sectors, the Italian authorities launched their plan to concentrate the entire population of the Gebel—a decision dating from more or less the same period of May–June 1930. The gravity of the decision to set up 'concentration camps' should not be underestimated; this was a completely new departure in the treatment of colonial peoples, who never, in the entire history of Italian colonialism, had undergone such an experience. Official history writers kept the facts concealed for a considerable time of what was virtually the genocide of the Cyrenaican people, or passed it off, as did Pace, in terms of a 'far-sighted system . . . a real act of charity', a basis of life for the Cyrenaican people, who would thus be assured of new and more secure economic activity, 'with agricultural and pastoral employment freely available to the population'[19].

The reality, as we now know from documents, of the forced exodus of the people from the Gebel was quite different, much more painful and far more costly in human lives and suffering. The objective pursued by the Italian authorities in this operation was to break once and for all the territorial links of assistance and support that the people of the Gebel were giving to the meagre but effective force of guerillas. The five ordinary camps, with some 80,000 people, which were set up from the second half of 1930 to the early months of 1931, emptied an immense territory which could from then on be quite easily surveyed from above by aircraft and on the ground by mobile columns, any person being found within the perimeter being defined as a rebel. According to the report of 2 May 1931 sanctioning the conclusion of the concentration camp operation, the number of indigenous inmates of the ordinary camps and the special camps designed for suspects and relations of rebels totalled 78,313[20]. Isolated from the rest of the world by barbed wire and under military surveillance, these camps undoubtedly represented a worsening of living conditions for people who until then had seen the comings and goings of the war without taking any decisive part in it. The laborious and painful work of transferring the people from their native regions to the camps was fraught with economic, social and political consequences; those involved lived out this their Calvary without finding

---

[18] Circular from R. Graziani no. 3500 of 1 October 1930, p. 3.

[19] B. PACE, *I campi di concentramento*, in L'Azione coloniale', Rome, 25 April 1933, p. 2.

[20] According to the report of vice-governor Graziani, Benghazi, 2 May 1931 (*Sistemazione delle populazioni nomadi trasferite*), the ordinary camps were: El Abiar (3123 inmates); Soluk (20,123); Sidi Ahmed el-Magrun (13,050); Marsa Brega (21,117); Agedabia (10,000): the special camp was at El-Agheila and contained 10,900 suspects (ASMAI, pos. 150/22, p. 98, fasc. 7).

anywhere in the world that measure of solid support and those repercussions that such a policy might have been expected to arouse.

'Colonial solidarity' paralyzed many reactions in the principal capitals of Europe, Africa and Asia, which only too often were inclined to accept passively what the Fascist propaganda machine, with undeniable skill, said about the matter, namely that these changes were due exclusively to the need for eliminating endemic forms of traditional resistance to law and order on the part of nomadic people who had always been given to violence, rape and plunder. Yet, few though they may have been, the protests that did result have been recorded. The most eloquently tragic of the comments on the exodus and on Italian policy in Libya came from the socialist Yves Farge: 'Eighty thousand Arabs have been uprooted from the Mont-Vert, in Cyrenaica, where they have lived for centuries. This region, one of the easiest places to cultivate, was ideally suited to the European type of agricultural working, and because of this was understandably coveted by the Italian settlers. Families, tribes and entire communities have been uprooted from their country. They were given five days to pack whatever they could carry. Then, escorted by carabinieri, the native caravans laboriously moved off. Did they know where they were being taken? After several terrible days on the move they realized they were being driven towards the Sirte desert'[21].

Not so outspoken, perhaps in deference to a certain colonial 'front', but nonetheless interesting was the reaction of the semi-official journal L'Afrique Française of Paris, which did not denounce Graziani's entire policy in so many words but expressed serious reserves about the validity of these decisions[22]. For a colonial publication this was already clear proof of passion and perplexity. In any event, the idea of concentration by deporting the population of the Gebel caused a stir, especially after the repeated declarations by the Fascists when the rebellion was over that had it been real, there would not have been any justification for such a distressing 'necessity'.

It is worth reflecting on the question of exactly who was responsible for taking the initiative in setting up the concentration camps. Was it the 'sole' governor, Badoglio, or was it his restless vice-governor, Graziani? Was it Colonial Minister De Bono or someone else? According to the text of the messages from Badoglio to Graziani on 20 June 1930 and from Badoglio to De Bono on 1 July, 'credit' for the initiative should go to Governor Badoglio, even if Graziani's memoirs conveniently overlook this fact in claiming the idea to have been his alone. This probably constitutes yet another chapter in

[21] Quoted by P. MARION, L'Islam accuse . . ., in 'Le Quotidien', Paris, 22 September 1931.
[22] There are not many articles in the journal 'Afrique Française' for the year 1930, but all are deprecatory in tone and emphasize the merits of France's native policy 'à la Lyautey', very different from that of Italy, typified by the concentration camps.

the long story of rivalry between the two, exemplifying Graziani's constant endeavour to bypass his superior and enter into a dialogue with the highest authorities in Rome, whether De Bono or Mussolini himself. It is interesting, in any event, to examine the two most important documents, namely the instructions from Badoglio to Graziani of 20 June and Badoglio's memorandum to De Bono of 1 July. The former effectively embodies, for the first time, the idea of concentrating the peoples of the Gebel outside the Gebel itself: 'What path should we follow? We must, above all, create a large and well defined territorial gap between the rebels and the subject population. But from now on the path has been traced out for us and we have to follow it to the end *even if the entire population of Cyrenaica has to perish*. It is therefore urgent that the entire subject population should be herded into a restricted space, in such a way that we can keep suitable watch over the people and maintain an absolute gap between them and the rebels. Having done that, we can then go on to direct action against the rebels.'

A few days later, Badoglio himself repeated these ideas to Colonial Minister De Bono, insisting on the concentration and deportation of the populations: 'The only course to pursue is, first of all, to isolate the *dor* from the rest of the people and cut the organizational link between them and the *dor*. It cannot be denied that this procedure is grave, complex and certainly not immediately effective. But it is the only one that I judge possible. It is already being set in motion. All the tribes will be removed from the tableland and concentrated in the foothills, between the slopes and the sea. . . .' The extreme cruelty of the plan is even foreseen and demonstrated without any sense of shame: '. . . even the whole population' may perish as a result of it, but this policy must not be changed. The initiative was thus Badoglio's, yet no less Graziani's; his Latin quotation in this context: 'salus publica suprema lex' shows his support of the policy even through the habitual liturgy of Latin quotations, designed to emphasize the classical and imperial Roman theme.

The second aspect of the 'new' policy of Badoglio and Graziani was the setting up, as already mentioned, of the barbed wire frontier entanglement which was intended to act as a death trap for all those who had found a refuge or a supply base in neighbouring Egypt.

It was a guarantee that nobody could get away and that there would be no support from Egypt to resistance in the Gebel. The fact that a strong group of Cyrenaicans, with the Grand Senusi at their head, had taken refuge on Egyptian territory had always led Omar al-Mukhtar's followers to expect Egypt to lend its weight to guerilla strategy as a whole, often relying on the theoretical frontier line as a certain escape from pursuit and attack. Traffic in arms and movements of troops had always threatened the successful outcome of the Italian army's eastern operations. The barbed wire network caught the rebels in a 'mousetrap', as *L'Afrique Française* put it, and made quite clear, given its extreme technical difficulty and very high cost, that the Fascist government was firmly determined to go to any lengths to pursue victory by physically wiping out Omar al-Mukhtar and his followers.

The final phase of the military 'pacification', viewed against this background of relentless Fascist policy and last-ditch resistance by the 'rebels', was preceded by an event that has often been veiled in silence but which is, in our opinion, important, namely the clandestine celebration by the Libyans of the nineteenth anniversary of the Italian landing in Tripoli and of the colonial conquest. Indeed, until now there has been no record of this quite lengthy document which, emanating from Syria, Egypt and Tunisia, circulated through the colony of Libya, and which is not even known in precise detail by modern Libyan historians. We found it in the archives of the Colonial Ministry, and its text appears to us as significant as the one, dear to Mustafa Lacheraf, on the 'permanent resistance' of the North African peoples. In celebrating the 'black day' of 19 years previously, namely the day the Italians landed at Tripoli, the authors of the pamphlet launched bitter accusations against the conduct of the war as dictated by Graziani. 'If the Italians had waged the war as men and as heroes,' stated the document, 'it would have been easy to tolerate them; instead, despite their strength and our weakness, they knew no other way than to inflict terrorism, cruelty, torture, destruction and tyranny, to convert the *sottomessi* to Christianity, outrage honour, slaughter old people and children, despise the people, ridicule their faith and religion, corrupt the character and customs of the land, suppress the Arabic language and replace it with their own, trample on the country's interests, wipe out its culture, and rob the native inhabitants of their possessions and their camps in order to send them to their colonies, until the impoverished Tripolitans were transformed into day-labourers suffering humiliation and penury. Today the prisons are full of innocent people, and in these gaols torture has gone to incredible extremes, without comparison in the whole of history. Today the courts savagely and cruelly condemn Moslems. Religious missions are established far and wide throughout the land. Blood flows everywhere; corpses are abandoned and bones are scattered.

Despite all these ferocious acts, which are contrary to every human law, the Italians are not ashamed to boast to their people that the region of Tripoli and Barce enjoys complete tranquillity and peace, that the inhabitants of the country love the Fascist government (yes indeed!) very much, that calm reigns everywhere, that there is no longer any war nor any crisis, but simply the normal kind of events that are happening in all the more civilized regions of Europe. Fascist government! Why all these lies? What is to be gained by distorting the truth and coming out with these falsehoods? How much longer is this arrogant policy and this obstinacy likely to continue? How long can you go on concealing the truth of the situation to your own countrymen?

Why not recognize the errors of the past, the seriousness of the present situation and the bleakness of the future? From whom can you conceal your cruelty which is being committed in our country at a time when it is quite impossible to hide what is going on, no matter what methods are being employed? Have these twenty years not been sufficient to make you change your policy, seeing that during that entire period you have not enjoyed one day of respite? Are you not happy to have tried in vain to reduce the people of Tripoli and Barce to a state of humiliation and shame? What have you gained from a regime of terrorism and cruelty? Have you not understood the error of your policy even after having changed fourteen governors up to this day? . . .' The document concluded with an appeal to all the Libyan people, reminding them of the violence they had undergone and pointing out that unflagging struggle was the only salvation against the spread of Fascist colonialism.

Having completed the frontier entanglement in record time and introduced new rules for 'hunting' the rebels, the history of the Fascist 'reconquest' of Libya entered a new phase of extreme harshness on the one hand and of operations to occupy the peripheral regions on the other. There was no concealing the gravity of the situation for the rebels, who were thus trapped in a vice of sword and fire, roaming a land now emptied by virtue of the deportations to concentration camps, and isolated by the barbed wire and the steady build-up of Italian military preparations. From his exile in Geneva, the spokesman for the Arab peoples' liberation movement, Chehik Arslan, hurled his dramatic accusations against Italian imperialism: '. . . We ask the Italians, who, after boasting of having concentrated eighty thousand civilian and long-since disarmed Arabs, with their livestock, into a confined space on the plain of Sirte, the aim being to wipe them out and hand over their Cyrenaican lands to Italian colonists, are now priding themselves in having captured 100 women and children and several hundred poorly armed inhabitants of Cufra who resisted the column of occupation: 'What has this got to do with civilization?' In modern times these rehashed methods of the Middle Ages cannot be allowed, and they will not enhance the prestige of Fascism or of Italy in the world's eyes. And the new Italy says that it aspires to an extraordinary political and economic expansion in the Orient! Does it really believe it can achieve its aim with such procedures?'[23].

There were a number of similar calls in the Arab world, and the news, albeit grave, of further Italian military successes also helped to prolong desperate resistance almost everywhere; but this was doomed in time to peter

[23] C. ARSLAN, *L'impérialisme italien en Tripolitaine*, in 'La Nation Arabe', Geneva, February 1931, p. 15.

136

out, trapped as it was in the relentless enemy vice, with no hinterland any more to furnish reinforcements.

The operations in the Fayed zone and the lightning-swift repression in Marmarica had set the tone of grim resolution and extreme rigour which General Graziani was determined to employ in order to 'liquidate' the Omar al-Mukhtar problem. The occupation of Cufra, carried out on a large scale with transport methods both traditional (over 5000 camels) and modern (20 aircraft, more than 300 trucks and a large number of tanks), was concluded on 19 January 1931 with the total taking over of the oasis region; it marked the death throes of the rebellion, by now entrapped in the Gebel without any passage in or out to provide hope either of escape or fresh supplies.

The Cufra operation had been a victory but as usual there was always the risk that such a success would remain isolated and not have an effect on the main body of resistance, namely in the Gebel. Graziani's old circular returned to haunt the Italian army commanders: Why were the rebels still resisting after the initial successes, asked Graziani, and answered: 'Above all because Omar al-Mukhtar will never submit, and because he always has the chance (*the old hero a fugitive everywhere*) of a final escape to Egypt, abandoning his flocks to their fate (*as is the old custom of all the native chiefs*), he will resist as long as possible in the hope, no longer of a success that will somehow resolve his situation materially and morally, but of God's intervention, staunch in his Moslem fatalism. He hopes, furthermore, as do all, both *sottomessi* and rebels, hope with him, that a sudden change in government instructions may lead the conflict back to the area of old and by now superseded agreements.

'And finally because the disruption that his wretched men brought to the peaceful life of Cyrenaica may give him the remote hope that the government will go back on the measures *adopted* to bring the present abnormal situation to an end'[24].

The question of the rebellion and its continuation seemed to depend on the problems connected with the security of the frontiers, which the barbed wire had perhaps not wholly resolved. With this in mind, Graziani, in a telegram to the Italian ambassador in Cairo, Roberto Cantalupo, emphasized that 'the fall of Cufra will certainly not induce Omar al-Mukhtar to clear out of the Gébel as long as the frontier furnishes him with the means to fight and the provisions which the people are now unable to supply him with'. But Cantalupo soon came back on this, pointing out that Graziani could not presume that there had been Egyptian connivance or clandestine traffic

---

[24] Circular no. 1890 from vice-governor Graziani of 17 August 1930, p. 11 (politico–military directives).

through the frontier network, stressing rather that 'the rebels in Cyrenaica must, as always, be fought *in* Cyrenaica'[25].

Although this was the climate in the Italian camp, it cannot be claimed that the situation of Omar al-Mukhtar and his supporters was good: on the Cyrenaican side one has to take account of a negative factor, namely the increasing tendency of some of the local people to become informers, for cash, on behalf of the Italian army command, in the certainty of imminent Italian victory. Their role should not be under-estimated, and Graziani himself mentions in his memoirs how they were used, particularly in this phase:

'The informers' job was to keep at the rebels' heels without ever losing touch with them. Being extremely knowledgeable about the terrain, the habits and needs of the rebels themselves, the most frequented watering places and pastures, the stores of barley, they generally knew—almost unhesitatingly—where to concentrate their searches within a given zone. Having sighted the *dor* or a part of it, while some dogged its heels and kept it permanently in view, others returned to base to give news of it, returning to the spot with the troops. On other occasions it happened that the air force, in its almost daily reconnaissance flights, would notice something suspicious in a particular area: on the basis of reports provided by the observer, the Gebel army command then sent out the informers who scoured the ground minutely. All actions in the Gebel up to the capture of Omar al-Mukhtar (11 September) were conducted along similar lines: it was the only method, given the situation as it then was, which allowed units to be deployed in a sensible and economic fashion, and which at the same time offered the chance of concrete results'[26].

But apart from the problem of informers, it was the gravity of the overall situation which appeared to rule out any likelihood of further resistance. And this fact certainly could not be overlooked by Omar al-Mukhtar. Italian archives still contain several letters written by him on various occasions to the Cyrenaican leaders who had taken refuge in Egypt, and from their tone it is quite evident that the dominant theme of his correspondence was his clear judgment concerning the current crisis. Among the 41 documents that were captured on 25 August 1931 in an Italian action at Bir Hamerin against a caravan of five camels there is abundant proof of the fears and uncertainties affecting the Cyrenaican resistance movement during that period[27]. Furthermore, the items of correspondence found in Omar al-Mukhtar's bag at the

[25] Telegram no. 300 of 4 February 1931 from Graziano to Cantalupo and telegram no. 453 of 9 February from Cantalupo to Graziani in AMAE, *cit.*
[26] R. GRAZIANI, *op. cit.*, p. 233.
[27] These complete letters are now in AMAE, 1931, B 1, fasc. 5, pos. 1/3; the letter of 5 September 1931 is in the Colonial Ministry.

time he was captured, as well as the documents taken from a rebel courier killed on 27 September 1931 at Wadi Maaten, are illuminating on the subject of the last phase of resistance. Some of the group of 41 documents mentioned above are worth studying in order to understand better the problems and crises of the resistance movement. On 22 August 1931, for example, Omar al-Mukhtar underlined to a prince of the ruling house of Egypt 'the unbelievable atrocities committed against the exhausted Moslem brothers of Libya', 'the harm done to men, women and children, let alone to property', and how 'a group of Moslems, for about twenty years, has lived at the mercy of hunger, thirst and other similar privations, without being heard by anyone, finding no compassion except from God, neither from people of the Moslem faith, from members of the Egyptian government or from Arab leaders in Egypt full of enthusiasm for the great cause of Islam. . . .'. In another letter addressed to a certain Raa el Ureidi, his bitterness about the measure of solidarity for the Cyrenaican cause is freely expressed: 'You tell me that some people who have gone there (to Egypt?) regret the times that are past: regret is inadequate to describe the situation; indeed, anyone who is really aware of what is going on ought rather to weep because our situation has never been (so serious) at any time in human history. . . .' And on the same day he informed another Senusi leader: 'I see no harm, and in fact it is a duty to reveal, in all its truth, the situation in which we find ourselves, a situation never experienced in many centuries of human affairs; we suffer all this in the name of Islam and for love and devotion to the most renowned name (of Mohammed). However, our sufferings have reached their limit and we have now done our duty in full measure. It is up to others, too, to do the same, even at the cost of selling all they have . . . Against overwhelming forces the vanquished may be forgiven . . .' And in reference to two of his chiefs in the Gebel, he recalled the Bedouin song: 'Their cruel fate puts them at the mercy of their slave; but do nothing, for that is destiny and our faith is never weakened, our hope remains ever strong. . . .' The difficulties being encountered by the Cyrenaican resistance and Omar al-Mukhtar's men are evidenced too by a valuable eye-witness account of someone who actually met him after the fall of Cufra, namely Mohammed Asad, who left the description of his mission to the Gebel Akhdar in his memoirs. The meeting took place after a series of arduous détours caused by the Italian military threat, during which Omar al-Mukhtar gave the Grand Senusi's envoy sad information, though this did not seem to have affected his fighting plans: 'There was deep seriousness but no despondency in Omar al-Mukhtar's voice as he described for me the inevitable outcome of his long struggle for freedom; he knew that the only thing he could expect for himself was death, but that he had no fear of death. He did not pursue it, yet he did not attempt to escape it. And I am sure that even if he had known what kind of death was in store for him, he would not have tried to avoid it. He seemed conscious, with every fibre of his being and in every action he took, that each man bears within himself his own destiny wherever he goes and whatever he does'[28].

The situation in early September thus appeared desperate for the men of the Gebel, gripped as they were by hunger, short of weapons, and having to contend with the egotism of the Egyptian Grand Senusi, the aggressive operations of the Italian army, the frontier network of barbed wire, and the air force which observed and controlled everything. So in this context the news of the capture of Omar al-Mukhtar on the morning of 11 September in the Slonta region had an impact like an exploding bomb; and there was a feeling that this must be the last major event before the whole Cyrenaican rebellion was brought to an end. The sequence of events leading to the capture of the rebel leader unfolded quite simply; and examination of the Italian archives has provided no substantial confirmation of a version relating, according to some rumours, to a presumed act of treachery on the part of another rebel leader, a certain Hamrusc. To set in perspective the entire event that was to culminate in the trial and execution of Omar al-Mukhtar, we have to resort once more to the detailed account which General Graziani wrote in a special secret file, summarizing and describing the activities of the various groups involved in the episode[29]. In this collection of documents the information does not appear to be very different from many other documents related to other, less sensational events. Graziani, prefacing his account, does not confirm the rumours of treason, but speaks instead of the 'surprise' in the list of normal operations: 'In the early days of the month of September, information assembled from various sources reached the Gebel command that the Brahasa Dorsa *dor*, with Omar al-Mukhtar, was concentrated in the southern Beda zone, intending to carry out a raid on the livestock of Cyrene . . .' (p. 6). Then the phonogram of 9 September from the commander of the Slonta garrison recounts the episode in terms of a purely accidental encounter: 'At 24.00 hours three scouts of the Ragazzi group having left Belghes 8 this evening with five other scouts arrived stop having taken the following route: Gsur el Sahar Talgasa—Got Setlun near Maten Arus at Gifas two rebel lookouts sighted stop halted Gifas until 17.00 hours to watch movements having noted presence *dor* stop due nature terrain many gardens and caves unable ascertain size rebel forces but noises and voices women and children and noise horses believe many people involved stop five scouts

---

[28] MOHAMMED ASAD, *Le Chemin de la Mecque*, Paris, Fayard, 1979, p. 309. They are, as is mentioned, the memoirs of the Austrian Leopold Weiss, converted to Islam, and involved during that period in almost all Arab events.

[29] *Relazione sugli avvenimenti che condussero alla cattura di Omar al-Mukhtar*, letter 16972 of 18 September 1931 from Graziani to De Bono, in ASMAI, Fondo Volpi, pos. 5/2.

remained near *dor* to watch its movements stop request orders for scouts who already arrived Slonta.'

As a result of similar information Colonel Malta set in motion an encircling operation with four mobile columns, the Ragazzi, Sqadroni, Piatti and Marone groups, calling in the two air operational centres at Benghazi and Apollonia, the XV Eritrean battalion, the Seventh Savari Cyrenaican squadron and the tanks that were already in the area. The three Italian planes employed were responsible for the success of the encircling movement around the rebel group already sighted and cut off all chances of escape southwards. The short pursuit ended with the skirmishes at Wadi bu Taga, where the Seventh Savari squadron, commanded by Captain R. Bertè, carried out the most important feat, that of arresting Omar al-Mukhtar. The report tells of the last stages of the episode: 'Soon after 8 o'clock (6–7 kilometres south-west of Slonta), the group was less tightly knit and I got the impression that it was trying to break up by making for the adjacent thick wood. One Savari killed the horse of a rebel (firing from horseback): the rider fell and got up again, trying to get away by walking rather slowly and heavily. Two other Savari overtook him on horseback, disarmed him (he had made no effort to defend himself, having kept his musket over his shoulder) and one was about to kill him when the other stopped him in the act, recognizing the rebel as Omar al-Mukhtar. This identification was immediately and definitely confirmed by four other Savari. I placed Omar al-Mukhtar, who was wounded in the left arm, on one of the squadron's horses, made the men fall in, and having called off the pursuit, had the few Savari present form a semi-circle round the prisoner and returned swiftly along the road to Slonta, reaching it at 9 o'clock . . .'

We also possess the surviving rebels' version of the episode, which informed the Senusi leaders in Egypt of the capture of Omar al-Mukhtar, this account not differing very much from the one put out by the Italians: '. . . On the day of Friday 12 September 1931 the Saied Omar al-Mukhtar went to pay a visit to the tomb of Sidi Ràfa, companion of the Prophet, near Zavia Beda, accompanied by sixty horsemen as escort; having reached the place called Gebobia, some distance from the *dor*, information was picked up by the Italians who barred his way with some 5000 infantry and cavalry, and attacked him and his companions. The action lasted eight hours, and included the use of vehicles and armoured cars. Alongside the Saied some fifty horsemen died the death of martyrs'[30]. From these and from other documents of the same origin, including the account of Omar al-Mukhtar's death, about which we shall speak later, there appears to be no confirmation of the rumours of an

---

[30] Letter from two rebel *camaican* to the Grand Senusi, 14 September 1931, doc. no. 6 of those captured on 27 September from the courier Mohammed Mumen near Wadi Maaten, in AMAE, *ibid.*, Libya, pos. 1–3.

alleged act of treachery which might have led to the encounter at Wadi bu Taga.

As soon as the news of the Senusi leader's capture was confirmed, the Italian authorities were carried away by the importance of the event. Initially they feared that the information might not be true, and thus after the Cyrenaican regent Moretti had relayed the news to Graziani there were insistent calls for an 'exemplary' retaliation. As soon as Badoglio, sole governor of Libya, told Colonial Minister De Bono of the capture, the latter promptly expressed his scepticism: '. . . I do not believe that Omar al-Mukhtar would have been so idiotic as to get himself captured stop his identity must therefore be confirmed beyond all doubt . . . But if this happy event should be true, the first thing we must do is not to rely on anything and not to alter our political and military line of action . . . Make the arrangements that seem best suited to circumstances stop'[31]. This telegram of 12 September crossed the many others that were flying around that day between Benghazi, Tripoli and Rome where Rodolfo Graziani learned the news as he was about to board his train for Paris on a visit to the Colonial Exhibition. Graziani returned post-haste to Benghazi where in the meantime the identity of the celebrated prisoner had also been confirmed by vice-governor Daodiace, who had met Omar al-Mukhtar on various occasions, the last time being during the negotiations of 1929 which had culminated in the meeting at Sidi Rahuma. Taken under escort to the port of Apollonia, Omar al-Mukhtar was put aboard the destroyer *Orsini*, which took him to the prison in Benghazi. From that moment on, the triumphal announcements from the various colonial authorities came fast and furious, all of them more or less repeating the text of the 'highly confidential' telegram which regent Moretti had sent to De Bono, to Badoglio and to Graziani, which described how Omar al-Mukhtar appeared to be 'resigned and calm at his fate', replying 'concisely to all the questions put to him'[32].

At Benghazi Omar al-Mukhtar was joined by Graziani, who was to give a complete account in his memoirs of the discussion he had with the prisoner: from this Omar al-Mukhtar emerges with even more dignity and serenity in

[31] De Bono to Badoglio, 12 September 1931, ACS, Fondo Graziani 2/3/2.
[32] The telegram no. 2058 of 12 September 1931 would be the outline of the official communiqué which was given soon afterwards to the press: 'Omar al-Mukhtar was captured in an action undertaken by the Gebel command to surround the *dor* sighted at Wadi Bu Taga south of Beda which probably intended to carry out a raid in the Cyrene-Apollonia territory. Action completely successful with rebel encirclement. Seventh Savari squadron launched in hard pursuit of group of fifty horsemen succeeded in capturing aforesaid *achuan* who had been separated from group itself and had tried to hide in woods. He was taken to Apollonia yesterday evening. Comm. Daodiace, who recognized him, says that he appears resigned and calm at his fate and replies concisely to all questions put to him. Other losses suffered by rebels in the operation are confirmed as twelve killed, four muskets taken, fourteen horses killed, seven captured with harness. Our losses one horse killed, one wounded', AMAE, *ibid*.

his attitude towards his conqueror, refusing to intervene personally in order to get the rebels of the Gebel to surrender ('. . . we have sworn that we will all die, one by one, but not to give ourselves up, and I *would never* have done so. That is certain.').

The drama of the Cyrenaican leader was drawing to its conclusion as frantic meetings and discussions between the various Fascist authorities were held to decide his fate. The plan of action proposed by Governor Badoglio to Minister De Bono was simple and stark: '. . . Should the captured man really be Omar al-Mukhtar, I think it would be opportune to hold the trial and carry out the sentence, which will undoubtedly be the death penalty, in one of the big native concentration camps'[33]. Whereupon Badoglio promptly passed on to Graziani his plans, which had been accepted by De Bono, issuing detailed instructions: '. . . Make immediate arrangements for criminal trial which can only end with the death sentence according to local customs. Have sentence carried out in most important native concentration camp . . .' Meanwhile, on the same day, the governor's office confirmed the arrangements, announcing with 'absolute secrecy' what the ministry had by now decided should be done: '. . . there will be a trial and subsequently an unfailing public execution . . .'

One could criticize and question interminably this decision to hold a 'regular' trial that would be guaranteed to end 'unfailingly' with Omar al-Mukhtar being condemned to death, especially if it is remembered that the basis of the whole proceedings, as foreseen in those few days, was essentially the charge of treason and hence of rebellion. The treason, according to Fascist definition, followed upon the agreement of Sidi Rahuma and the unconditional surrender which had been underwritten by the Cyrenaican leader: resumption of hostilities in the early part of 1930 was proof of the blackest perfidy of Omar al-Mukhtar and thus the breaking of the word he had given and of the pact he had made with Badoglio. But we now know that there are serious doubts concerning the Sidi Rahuma episode and the validity of the announcements regarding the 'surrender' of Omar al-Mukhtar; it seems clear that this point of view was circulated by Fascist journalists and propaganda sources without any foundation. This controversial state of affairs thus cast doubt on the very basis of the trial itself—a trial which certainly ranked alongside those of other great resistance leaders in the history of North Africa, from Abd el-Kader onwards, but with a very different outcome. In those other circumstances the political aspect of the facts associated with the resistance persuaded the French authorities to resort to political solutions such as banning and exile rather than the legalistic solutions which the Italian authorities decided were opportune for the 'Omar al-Mukhtar problem'. It

---

[33] Badoglio to De Bono, 12 September, ACS, *cit.*

is worth noting, in this respect, that during the few days that elapsed between the capture and the execution things underwent a marked change, which is important to stress. The press only put out the defamatory version, reminding the public of 'the perfidy and duplicity which manifested themselves most strikingly in the vilest treachery . . . with which he repaid the tolerance and generosity shown to him by the colonial government, when he had offered submission on behalf of himself and his men'[34]. But during the actual trial (the records of which had until now been kept secret but are now in our possession) there was no reference to such features in the counts of indictment: among the 26 charges of the official *Elenco dei capi di imputazione*, there was no mention of this aspect, the actions of the prisoner being vilified with accusations of livestock theft, hold-ups, violence and raids against civilians and military personnel, homicide and attempted homicide; but of pacts of submission, violated or otherwise, not a hint.

Another problem for the Fascist authorities was that each of them sought to extol their own handiwork and thus claim the merit for having been the one and only conqueror of the rebel leader: far from strengthening their reciprocal relationships, the fate of Omar al-Mukhtar merely revealed deep schisms and led subsequently to political complications for the regime, both in the colony and elsewhere.

For the record, after an initial interrogation aboard the *Orsini* by Daodiace, of which no documentary traces have so far appeared, the official questioning of Omar al-Mukhtar took place on the premises of the Investigative Office of the Benghazi Regional Prison. Examining judge Giuseppe Franceschino, assisted by military lawyer Giuseppe Bedendo, had no difficulty in getting the prisoner to admit numerous attacks and guerilla activities under his command, out of hatred for the Italian presence in Cyrenaica. What is most striking in Omar al-Mukhtar's replies is the quiet confident concerning the resumption of hostilities after the violation of the Bu Regima pact and after the results of the meetings in 1929. Regarding the former, his declaration is peremptory: 'It was not I who gave the order for resuming hostilities. . . . In my opinion, it was the Italians who started hostilities again because . . . they captured and shot our men who by order of Idriss had gone out to collect provisions . . . ' As for the meetings of 1929, the version maintained by Omar al-Mukhtar is the same as the one that nowadays appears to be the most likely: ' . . . In 1929, too, the breakdown in negotiations was in my view the fault of the Italian government. . . I also wrote to Marshal Badoglio, and having obtained no answer I went away and resumed guerilla warfare. . . ' These are specific declarations, but it is worth emphasizing, too, what Omar al-Mukhtar

---

[34] Similar statements appeared throughout the Italian press. The quotation is taken from *La cattura di Omar al-Mukhtar*, in 'Il Messaggero', 16 September 1931.

said on the same occasion of his interrogation in Benghazi prison about his 'treason': 'I never submitted to the Italian government: I only had conversations with it.' And that this declaration was fundamentally sound and recognized as such can be argued from the address of the Public Prosecutor, which, although contentious and biased, did not pursue this theme but dodged the issue by merely stating: '... Today Omar seeks to excuse himself by saying that he wrote to his excellency Badoglio and that he did not receive a proper reply. The Italian government does not traffic its own sovereignty: it makes as many concessions as possible. So much the worse for those who do not appreciate such a gesture ...' Defending counsel Captain Roberto Lontano, who perhaps took his responsibility more seriously than his superiors hoped, vainly obtained from the accused a formal declaration of 'never having received payment from the Italian government'; in this declaration, never denied by the prosecution, perhaps lies the nub of the 'treason' charge—a charge which, with all these definitions, is not conducive to a calm analysis of the case. But there was nothing calm about the proceedings in the trial which was held later the same day at 5 o'clock in the afternoon of 15 September, with great ceremony, in the Palazzo del Littorio. It was, in fact, a mock-trial which began with an extempore contribution by Public Prosecutor Giuseppe Bedendo concerning the coincidence on that very day of the birthday of the Prince of Piedmont, which gave him the opportunity to appoint himself spokesman 'for the feeling of the people' and give vent to 'his most heartfelt alala'. Much could be said about the significance of this absurd interlude which, moreover, was faithfully reported in the proceedings of the trial, and the fact that in another instance, during a court sitting with Lt. Col. Umberto Marinoni presiding, a similar outburst was made by Bedendo, who was to emerge as chief advocate in the trial; as the mouthpiece of Graziani, he was to write of the latter soon afterwards in a poem composed in Roman dialect which hailed the trial and the fate of Omar al-Mukhtar[35].

After such an introduction, the climate of the trial was predictably impassioned. The Italian soldiers and local *sottomessi* who crowded the hall of the court, formerly seat of the regional parliament set up under the 1914 statutes, had been assembled by order of the colonial authorities to be made aware, as Bedendo immediately pointed out, that the 'policy of former times was now on the wane' and that 'Omar al-Mukhtar's fate should point the direction of this new imperial change of course'. The list of crimes officially charged against the Senusi leader was the object of sarcastic sallies by the

[35] This is the famous book by R. BEDENDO, *Le gesta e la politica del generale Graziani*, Rome, CESA, 1936. Note the abundance of insulting epithets hurled at Omar al-Mukhtar, described as an 'animal', and concerning his death: '.... morí siccome n'topo' (p. 202).

prosecutor, who proceeded to rage against the defendant to his heart's content. Clearly the ground had been well prepared for the ritual of a 'regular' trial and a 'regular' death sentence: only once during this phase did defending counsel Captain Lontano manage to focus attention on the controversial question of the surrender agreed with the Italian authorities and patently give the lie to those who supported the 'treason' argument. Since submission was directly connected, in its practical effects, with the monthly clerical payment, the question 'Have you ever received payment from the Italian government?', which received the reply, not contradicted by the prosecution, of 'No, never!' from Omar al-Mukhtar, appears to have been decisive even for purposes of the trial, which, after this episode, once more sank to the level of the mock- or farce-trial that was to be recorded in the history books.

In this situation the address of the public prosecutor can be read as a revealing document that typifies the Fascist 'colonial spirit', now, ten years after the March on Rome, emerging as the gospel of Italian overseas policy. First of all comes the systematic denigration of the defeated enemy in a trial viewed as putting an end to 'the fame of a legendary hero who always takes flight in times of danger'; then there is the insult, to the effect that 'you are not a soldier but a bandit who has always lived underground . . .'; and finally the sneering gibe that 'you have said God has this time abandoned you, but if he has failed you, human justice has caught up with you. . .' The entire trial is in fact summed up in that address, which consisted of a long polemic that was accepted without question by the court, and disputed only by defending counsel Lontano, who requested that attenuating circumstances should be taken into account, 'considering the age of the defendant and his religious fanaticism'; but it availed him nothing, for not only did he fail to avoid the death penalty being pronounced on his client but he himself was involved in a Fascist reaction that was to accuse him of having argued 'the defence in an apologetic tone, in contrast to the guilty man and the special conditions of the place and surroundings in which the case was held'[36].

Given all this, the death sentence which was pronounced on Omar al-Mukhtar after half an hour was the logical conclusion to a judicial process that was certainly neither fair nor farsighted. The very indifference of the condemned man, who merely observed: 'From God we have come and to God we must return', when sentence was passed on him, was surely not the reaction that the colonial authorities had hoped for. Furthermore, the haste with which they proceeded to carry out the sentence was in itself significant: cheated of a desperate outburst or public act of repentance by their victim,

---

[36] Captain Lontano's punishment was ten days of close arrest, as appears from a circular from Graziani which does not mention his name but for various reasons certainly relates to him. ACS, Fondo Graziani, 6/11/1.

they used the episode as a scenario for the regime. In front of 20,000 inmates of the Soluk concentration camp, all from the Gebel, Omar al-Mukhtar was executed at 9 o'clock on 16 September; his death, which according to the statements of Graziani himself, he faced with 'a composed, firm and decisive bearing', concluded an affair which Fascist Italy staged as a calculated act of ferocity against its adversary. And in this context the Fascist authorities declined to pay heed to pleas for clemency, as had previously been exercised by the French towards other defeated leaders (for example, Abd el-Kader and Abd el-Krim), or to recognize the political disadvantage of transforming the head of resistance into a martyr of the 'Libyan nation'; and indeed the Arab policy that Mussolini repeatedly stated he wished to initiate was to be impeded for many years by the Soluk execution.

In fact, the conclusion of the Omar al-Mukhtar affair, though depriving the resistance of a leader who was undoubtedly important for the movement as a whole (which, after his death, struggled to recover but never succeeded, completely dying out), nevertheless failed to create political harmony in the Fascist seats of power, especially between Governor Badoglio and his recalcitrant aide Graziani. Mutual suspicion arose over the question of who was entitled to claim credit for getting rid of the resistance leader, and this was to poison the relationship of the two in years to come. Graziani's reluctance to accept any checks or controls over his actions was abundantly evident, too, in the instance of the Soluk execution, when he sent an account of it directly to Colonial Minister De Bono, as if to claim an autonomy which was disputed by the authorities in Tripoli. The very tone of the proconsul's telegram ('. . . with the disappearance of Omar al-Mukhtar a new life is certainly beginning for Cyrenaica, which ardently hopes for peace . . .') was hardly calculated to dissipate the old rancours which were to become even more bitter in innumerable arguments behind the scenes, as revealed, in various aspects, by the archives[37]. The precise and detailed correspondence of the Italian ambassador in Egypt, Roberto Cantalupo, also focuses attention on Graziani's military achievements and his reiterated claim of exclusive credit for the success, though still complaining, even after the Soluk incident, that diplomatic efforts to control war contraband from Egypt, and thus from the whole region, in support of the Senusi 'pacification' policy were dubious and inconsistent. In this context it is worth referring as well to the telegraphed report on the action at Wadi Bu Taga by Colonel Malta, who attributes its success solely to the military organization and the brilliance of the operational plans as conceived by Graziani. It reads as follows: 'Wadi Bu Taga action in accordance with orders given this command namely to repel with cavalry

---

[37]Telegram 2098 from Graziani to De Bono, in AMAE *cit.*, 16–9–1931.

groups rebels where squadron group able to operate stop objectives have been achieved by magnificent attack of closest squadron and by action of all units and air force which cooperated most effectively stop special praise for 22 Eritreans who with brilliant march took part from Abid zone for Piazzi and Ragazzi groups who by their previous movements furnished facts useful for hunting *dor* and for all groups on foot and on horseback and their brilliant commanders for converging action that finally led to capture rebel chief stop may I express to all warmest congratulations and those of army command and government'[38].

The whole question is raised again in the memoirs of Graziani, who quotes profusely from his own writings and orders, leaving out anything Badoglio or the Tripoli authorities in general might have done to end the rebellion. In his famous order of the day of 24 January 1932 ('I can state that the rebellion in Cyrenaica has been completely and definitely crushed...'), Badoglio tried in vain to apportion the various degrees of merit, pointing out that General Graziani deserved the recognition of all and sundry for having 'with intelligence, energy and constancy, followed the instructions I have given him' and so succeeded in the mission entrusted to him. The role attributed to Graziani was certainly not the one that Graziani himself had in mind. He made this clear in the course of an argument with ambassador Cantalupo concerning a publication which the Army High Command circulated during the early part of 1932 entitled *Il reticolato confinario*. In this the Cyrenaican commander summarized again the story of the rebel defeat and the arrival of a Fascist peace in Cyrenaica, listing in 'logical succession' the measures taken to destroy the rebellion once and for all, namely:

—*movements* of people from their traditional homes and their concentration in coastal zones, placed under proper guard;

—complete *disarmament* of the people themselves, and finally

—*closure* of the frontier with Egypt.

It was over this last point that Cantalupo felt bound to argue, challenging the assertion that the closure of the frontier with Egypt, decided upon by the military authorities in Benghazi (namely Graziani), and designed to deny the rebels supplies of provisions and weapons that they were obtaining from Egypt, was the final, decisive measure: 'The truth is that the predecessors of General Graziani and myself, in Cyrenaica and in Egypt, had to put up with large-scale contraband activity to and from Egypt which continued virtually unhindered until 1928 or 1929; this contraband trade was in fact gradually reduced and then curtailed altogether by measures taken simultaneously to control it more strictly, General Graziani's decision to post troops along the

---

[38] Radio-telegram no. 14322 of 14 September 1931 from the commander of the Gebel Col. Malta, in AMAE, *ibid*.

frontier even before the barbed wire was set up (he sent Eritrean motorized battalions and aircraft to the frontier zone and established a border garrison at Wadi Mra), and by the continuous pressure brought to bear by the English and Egyptian authorities ever since I arrived here. During this period Cyrenaica has seen the Egyptian contraband trade reduced to a trickle and almost wholly eliminated. Any other assertion flies in the face of facts. Not only that, but in my opinion it not only underrates Italian diplomatic action but also that of Graziani himself, who won thanks to an outstanding and complex political and military effort, and not as a result of the creation of . . . a network of barbed wire.' Cantalupo made it clear that Italian diplomacy in Egypt had contributed directly to the victory: 'General Graziani's statement that the greater part of the rebels' weapons consisted of rifles and muskets '91 and that arms reinforcements were carried out by the *sottomessi* themselves, who bought them from Libyan units and from bands of irregulars, *is thoroughly and genuinely true*. This assertion merely confirms the crucial effectiveness of the essential measures of general disarmament, transfer and concentration of the tribes along the coast, for which you rightly claim responsibility. The rebels who have crossed into Egypt are the best judges of the real causes that led to the end of the *duar*, and they fully agree that the Senusi warriors of Omar al-Mukhtar recognized that their existence was precarious *as soon as they found themselves completely isolated on the tableland without any room for manoeuvre or chance of support from the tribes of pseudo-sottomessi with whom they had found food and shelter.* Omar al-Mukhtar thus fell into a trap, and after him the revolt struggled on for a few months and then died out, because it now lacked not *foreign bases* but *home bases*.

'I cannot overlook in silence statements that do not conform to actual facts, which are clear when examined calmly. Appearing as they do in publications which cannot fail to be noticed abroad as well, they are not only likely to have unfavourable repercussions in our relations with a country which, though in the past may have shown sympathy for the Senusi Moslems, now tends more decisively to court our friendship, but also involves the prestige of our diplomatic operations. The determined efforts made by the Fascist government in the last two years to wipe out the last centres of rebellion in Cyrenaica have been accompanied by other measures equally determined and equally effective: an all-out military campaign and radical political measures in the colony itself, and continuous, energetic diplomatic activity here. As the representative of my country and executor in Egypt of the orders of the Foreign Ministry in this operation, which from the very start has proved an effective support to General Graziani's resolute campaign, I have the duty and the right to beg the Colonial Ministry not to underestimate the efforts that have been made and not to make inaccurate judgments that may diminish the prestige of our diplomacy. . . '

The argument is not without significance: it demonstrates how the elimination of Omar al-Mukhtar had failed to solve the political problems of the colonial government, just as the concentration camps did not solve the problem of getting the local people to accept the Italian presence.

International repercussions following the Soluk execution, though numerous, were certainly not of a nature to intimidate colonial Fascism nor to force it to call off its campaign of self-righteous justification for having eliminated the 'bandit Omar al-Mukhtar'. The defamatory version was widely circulated, and the foreign press, with the exception of the Arabic, gave the whole episode little space: the general crisis in international relations during those months diverted the attention of the various political observers elsewhere. Furthermore, the wish of the two major colonial powers in North Africa, France and Great Britain, not to intensify a crisis which could, in the last resort, prove a serious threat to their own rule, helped to explain why there was little talk of Cyrenaica and, after a minimum of comment, just as little mention of Omar al-Mukhtar. This combination of circumstances and general silence encouraged the Fascist authorities to display even more arrogance in handling the problem, and gave Colonial Minister De Bono the chance to react to the press campaign in certain Arab countries by declaring, among other things: 'It's time now to end it all: the Moslem world must no longer be tricked by a handful of intriguers. The name of Italy, with a civilization going back thousands of years, recognized by all the nations, blessed in mosques and schools, in *mahcamah* (courts of the Cadi) and hospitals by more than a million Moslems who for years have benefited from generous government and wise justice as embodied in laws and decrees, known and available to all—the name of Italy cannot be defamed by a group of a few hundred marauders, rebels against all forms of order, against every human and divine law, who, in the name of God, are trying to prolong indefinitely an uncertain situation merely for their own selfish purpose of plundering, exploiting others and committing all manner of violent actions and crimes. . . ' As for the specific episode of the capture and death of Omar al-Mukhtar, De Bono's text repeated that of the public announcement already proclaimed in other places: 'Omar al-Mukhtar was captured *with weapons in hand* on 11 September last month, near Cyrene, by troops of the Italian government, while he was leading a few followers in an attempt at an ambush to attack a supply caravan.

'Omar al-Mukhtar was sent for regular trial before the Benghazi Special Tribunal, which is the court competent to judge the kinds of crimes of which he was charged.

'Among these, the main ones were high treason and armed rebellion against the powers of the state; the *killing* of the Italian officers Beati and Hubner, whom he had captured; *massacre* of a group of Italian carabinieri at Gasr

Benigdem in November 1929, while they were quietly waiting for a telephone line to be repaired, relying on the solemn submission that Omar al-Mukhtar had made shortly beforehand to the Italian government; *a number of killings*, ordered by him, of local people guilty of not following his instructions, as well as innumerable *acts of plunder* and *raids* against the tribes who had offered submission.

'Omar al-Mukhtar admitted all the charges made against him. The death penalty was the inevitable consequence of such a grave series of crimes.

'Nobody, except someone ill-disposed, can argue that there is any country in the world, whether Christian or Moslem, whose government, faced by such a grave phenomenon of social disruption and of stubborn rebellion against law as occurred in Cyrenaica, thanks to Omar al-Mukhtar, could have acted and behaved in any other way than the Italian government did. Law is the same law for everyone, and Omar al-Mukhtar, by the will of God, followed his destiny'[39].

In the same way the entire Moslem religious establishment of Tripoli was mobilized to sanction the Fascist policy and to stress that all the charges levelled against Fascism were unfounded, and that the regime created by the Italian authorities in Libya had the highest esteem for Islam and its adherents[40].

From the local point of view, the elimination of the most important resistance leader, whose successors were in no way equipped to don his mantle, made further guerilla action meaningless. Exile was the only resort for all those who refused to accept the Italian military presence pending the expected wave of Italian immigration into the Gebel. The activities abroad of the Libyan emigrants were not confined to neighbouring Egypt, but were carried on as well by groups of exiles in Tunisia, Syria, Lebanon, Turkey, Iraq and Transjordan. . . . Their story is still to be written, but it could well be that the flames of the nationalist revival that occurred after 10 June 1940 were sparked off among these groups. Their most significant political message, before silence veiled their further activities, was unquestionably in the commemoration of the first anniversary of the death of Omar al-Mukhtar, 'martyr of the Arab nation', which was circulated on 16 September 1932 in a manifesto (a photographic copy of which is illustrated here); in it the main motives of the resistance were recorded virtually as a political testament of the leader and his movement: 'The Fascists believed that the condemnation of Omar al-Mukhtar to death would make it easier for them to occupy the country, but unfortunately for them the souls of the martyrs are an eternal

---

[39] Communiqué from colonial minister De Bono, 20 October 1931, pp. 1 and 3, 4.
[40] Signed by the Cadi of Tripoli, Mahmud Burkis, the statement of the Moslem leaders of Libya was given a lot of space in Italian newspapers of 29 and 30 October 1931.

flame which inspires the national spirit in the hearts of the people still living.

'The martyr of the Tripoli-Barce nation is not dead, for he has left his people with an immortal monument of heroism which will be inherited by future generations.

'This sad monument, built by the Fascist assassins' hands, will remain for ever and will never be forgotten because it has left mortal wounds in our hearts.

'Woe to those oppressors who do not respect the age, the courage and the incomparable heroism of Omar al-Mukhtar: but they cannot understand the significance of this quality.

'The years cannot wipe out the horror of this crime, which struck at the heart of all Arabs, and which will always remain as a stain on their history, washed as it is in the blood of innocents, of women, of men, of the aged and of children.

'People of Tripoli and Barce!

'Always remember that day when the greatest of misfortunes occurred.

'You must always retain this memory so as to learn a lesson that will serve in future to tell you how to avenge yourselves for your martyrs...

'...Omar al-Mukhtar was not only the martyr of the Tripoli-Barce people, but he was the martyr of the whole Arab nation... This must not be forgotten, it must be kept in your hearts until the day when the Fascists have to account to the Arab nation for this assassination.

'Arabs! Always remember our martyr who was condemned to death after being taken prisoner and who had renewed the glory of your glorious fathers.

'Remember and always celebrate this day so as to let the Fascists know that you are not asleep and that you are a unified nation which rejects the scorn of the colonizers.

'And you Fascists, Black Shirts!

'We await a day when you have to render account, and that day we see to be close, whereas you believe it to be far-off; on that day we shall ask the price of the blood of Omar al-Mukhtar and of our noble heroes'[41].

Nevertheless the Fascist government continued a policy of severity to those people as well. No acceptable way of return was envisaged for the Libyan exiles, so fulfilling the hope of the Fascist authorities that repatriation would be minimal. In December 1932, just before the commencement of the European land-division programme in the Gebel Akhdar by the Fascist authorities, the Colonial Ministry reduced the possibility of such re-entry to

---

[41] Free translation of the publication *La commemorazione di Omar el-Mukhtar, il martire della nazione araba*, s.d. nor place, but 16 September 1932, by the Syrian Associazione di difesa Tripolina-Barcina.

a bare minimum by stipulating: 'The basis, the condition for any submission by exiles can only be as follows:

(a) *Direct, individual, unconditional* submissions;

(b) Nobody must consider acting for others and even less of *entering into negotiations.* The slightest hint that might allow the Arabs to suppose there could be any authority apart from the Italian government could be extremely harmful, even lethal, for us. . .

'. . .It would be as well for our consular and diplomatic agents to be given categorical and formal instructions on this point.

'The re-entry of our subjects into Libya is undoubtedly a fact of capital importance; but this ministry, like the government of Tripolitania and also that of Cyrenaica, must give thought as to how these people will be able to live, because there is no question of any talk about restoring confiscated possessions'[42].

The silence of many and the violence of a few, however, did not guarantee the Italian government more security to their colonial triumph, which was not even to last a decade, despite the later phase of exceptional imperial glory in Ethiopia. The impact of these victories, particularly of those in Cyrenaica, was far from enduring; and the words of Chekib Arslan in his anguished obituary of Omar al-Mukhtar were seized upon as representing hope and truth for the many vanquished: '. . . The blood of Omar al-Mukhtar will remain for ever an infamy that will lie heavily on the Italian leader. . . The day will come when he will see the fruit of his arrogance and know that the Moslems are not dead and their rights are not lost'[43].

---

[42] Highly confidential express telegram no. 238006 of 22 December 1932 sent by the Ministry for Foreign Affairs on instructions of the Colonial Ministry to chief residences of Libyan exiles: Damascus, Gedda, Beirut, Aleppo, Jerusalem, Tunis, Algiers, Smyrna and Ankara.

[43] C. ARSLAN, *Omar al-Mukhtar* (in Arabic), in 'el Djihad', 10 October 1931.

I. The secret proceedings
in the trial at Benghazi,
15 September 1931.

1. *Special tribunal in Benghazi: interrogation of the prisoner*

The fifteenth day of the month of September of the year nineteen hundred and thirty-one in Benghazi in the Investigating Office of the Regional Prison. Before us, Dr Giuseppe G. Franceschino, Investigator, with the Public Prosecutor in the person of Military Lawyer cav. off. Giuseppe Bedendo, Investigating Judge, assisted by the undermentioned Clerk, appeared the detainee

OMAR EL MUCTAR

who was questioned as to his personal particulars through the interpreter Mr Giovanni Valenza.

He replied: My name is Omar El Muctar, son of Aescia ben Mahareb, 73 years old, born at Defna, kabyla Menefa, ailet Brahidan, beit Farhat, married with children, literate, no criminal record, leader of the Senusi zavia at Gsur.

Notified of the offences charged, he replied: I take note that proceedings have been taken against me with the warrant of capture for offences according to art. 284-285 of the Penal Code.

Accused: I never submitted to the Italian government: I only had conversations with it. If Hassen Redà had backed me in my demands I would have been with the government.

Accused: There were two leaders: after the break-up of Hassen's 'dor' I was the only one left. The rebels obeyed me blindly, so that all the actions taken by them were ordered by me.

Charged with carrying out torture on our prisoners, he replied:
'War is war.'

Accused: I never gave orders that prisoners should be mutilated: I always saw them dead on the battlefield but I never saw that the bodies had been subjected to outrage.

Accused: It was not I who gave the order to resume hostilities after the pact with the regime, because I was far away. In my opinion it was the Italians who resumed hostilities because they put Saleh El Auami in gaol, and shot our men at Zuetina, who by order of Idris had gone out to collect provisions.

Accused: In my view, too, the breaking off of negotiations was the fault of the Italian government because it made me fall out with Hassen, who then went to Benghazi: I also wrote to Marshal Badoglio, and having received no answer I went away and resumed guerilla warfare.

Accused: I was present at a number of battles and cannot therefore specify them.

Accused: The people of the cities hated me because I brought them bad luck, and I hated them in return because they did not help the cause of their religion, for which alone I fought.

Accused: I did not give the order to kill the Gubba manager: the Mohafdia, driven by hunger, looted and assassinated with and without my orders.

Accused: Major Bassi was killed in battle: war is war: all who were in it, since it was permissible, we killed.

Accused: I admit having given commissions to officers and to chiefs, but only to my subordinates.

Accused: Because Fadil bu Omar had earlier been in the Gbail territory and was therefore able to recognize everything, maybe he persuaded me of the need to name the *sottomesso* Omar Bubaker Gbail leader of the ailet Musa.

Accused: Earlier there were continual contacts between the *sottomessi* and the rebels: It might also have been that Omar himself put his name forward as leader.

Accused: Besides Iorio Carmine (Iusuf el Musulmani), condemned by the Military Court at Gialo in December 28 there were no other Italian deserters in the 'duar': there was a certain Omar el Musulmani, also at Gialo, but I do not know whether he was the deserter mentioned to me as being corporal of artillery. There was also a third, whose name I do not know, but likewise I do not know what happened to them.

Accused: I repeat, I took part in all battles. If sometimes I was not there, the operation was likewise carried out under my orders.

Accused: As for Lieutenant Aviere Beati, I had given orders that he should be held by Abdulamid el Akbar because he had money: when the Italian government came out with large forces, I do not know what the Mohafdia did to him, for they did not even bother burying their dead, especially in a big battle.

Accused: Approximately, there were under a thousand men in the 'duar': of these four hundred were mounted.

Accused: Lieutenant Beati was killed in the wadi, but I do not know whether he was buried.

Accused: It may be that some Italians at Porto Bardia paid tithes, as happened at Barce, but I could not say who they were. But I was told that the Italian citizens of Barce had paid tithes for having their livestock looked after, though I could not say who they were. Aissa el Aquach is a racketeer and I do not know what he received in payment.

Accused: The collectors of tithes are commanded by the 'Caimacan' and not by me, and are responsible for their actions to him.

Accused: I heard of the raid carried out against the Fattoria Iung: however, I was not there at the time because I was in the Abeidat territory. I do not know who led that raid.

Accused: I also took part in raids and cannot remember which.

Accused: We do not have fixed places where we can seek refuge, always keeping on the move by necessity because of the situations in the Brasa and Abid territories.

Accused: In order to live, apart from raids, we make a profit from camels, which we send to Egypt, where they are sold, and from the proceeds we buy provisions.

Accused: The most influential leaders below me are: Abdulamid al Akbar—caimacan of the Auaghir dor; there is also commander Osman Sciamo, caimacan and commander of the Brahasa-Dorsa dor; Ahmed Musa is caimacan and commander of the Ahasa-Abeidat: chief of my tabur is Bubaker Zigri.

Accused: I admit having been taken with weapons in hand on 8 September last at Zavia Beda on a plan called Got-Illfú, near Slonta; I had still not fired a rifle shot because we were surrounded by government troops.

Accused: On other occasions I did shoot: does it seem likely to you that I could be in battle without shooting?

Accused: About two years ago I was wounded in the right shoulder by an air force bomb—I should say rather the left shoulder. It was a bomb splinter.

Accused: We had neither cannons nor machine-guns; those we managed to capture were on my orders buried by persons familiar with such places, and not even I know where they are.

Accused: Abd-el-Gader, from Misurata, whose father's name I do not know, was good with cannons, but I do not know what he is doing in Egypt.

Accused: My son Mohamed Sahle is thirteen years old: he is in Egypt with the family.

Accused: I do not know now what will happen to the 'duar', and thus if they will name a successor to me, whose name I cannot foretell or whether they will cross into Egypt.

Accused: It was not my idea, given Governor Graziani's measures, to cross the frontier: 'I and my men had decided rather to die for our religion.'

Accused: I absolutely deny that there was any intention of surrendering among the rebels.

Accused: It is true that at other times I prepared a *masbhata* against those who were intending to leave me, *masbhata*, which also carried the signature of other leaders. Today it is not like that: we are in the open and anyone who wants to leave us cannot be stopped, and so goes off with his rifle.

Accused: We do not have any cartridges in store: the Mohafdia sell them and exchange them among themselves. Those who were clever, at the appropriate time, made their arrangements.

Accused: We do not have stores of provisions in caves.

Accused: I deny that we got fresh supplies from the sea: they came only from Sollum.

Accused: When the encampments were in their territory we were assisted in every possible way by the *sottomessi* and thus with payment of tithes, with shelter in tents and with information about troop movements.

Accused: I am not sorry for what I did because it was God's will.

Accused: I am not in correspondence with Idris.

L.T.C. and S.

    (F. to) Omar el Muctar (in Arabic)

    Valenza

    Franceschino

    Bedendo

    De Cristofano Edoardo Cane. Mre ff.

2. Typewritten account of the hearing against Omar al-Mukhtar

Opening the hearing, Public Prosecutor Bedendo asked for mention to be made that today was the birthday of His Royal Highness the Prince of Piedmont, and in the certainty that he was the loyal spokesman for the feeling of the people, he called for the most heartfelt alalà.

Italians and local people rose to their feet applauding at length. When silence was restored and the oath administered to the interpreter, Mr. . . ., the President, Colonel Marinoni, asked the accused for his particulars, and he said his name was OMAR EL MUCHTAR, 74 years old, born at Giarabub, head of the Door; asked if he had any convictions, he replied negatively, as he denied being aware that there were warrants of capture out against him.

After this the Clerk Lieutenant De Cristofano read out the bill of indictment.

Proceedings then continued.

Pres.: You fought against whom?

Omar: I fought against the Italian government.

Pres.: In how many battles did you take part?

Omar: In many, I cannot count them exactly. Also those in which I did not take part were carried out under my orders.

Pres.: Did you also open fire?

Omar: Yes, several times.

Pres.: Did you give the order to kill Lieutenant Beati?

Omar: He had been captured and for some time lived with the *dor*. One day while I was absent troops of the Italian government came near to the *dor* and then the mehafdia killed him. War is war, and I do not know whether he was buried.

Pres.: Did you issue orders for all prisoners to be killed?

Omar: I did not give orders for that.

Pres.: Was it you who gave the orders to kill the men who had gone out to repair the telephone line at Gasr Benighden, thus marking the resumption of hostilities?

Omar: Yes, I gave the order to kill these and others.

Pres.: As well as the escorting carabinieri?

Omar: War is war.

Pres.: Why did you resume hostilities?

Omar: The cause of the breakdown was the friction that arose between me and Sidi Redà, in which various people intervened in order to accentuate it.

At this point Prosecuting Counsel thanked the interpreter for the work he had done: but finding that his voice was too weak and therefore could not be heard by the chiefs and the Arabs who were sitting in the court, whereas it was the characteristic of military trials that the public should follow the proceedings of the case in order to decide for themselves whether the accused was guilty or otherwise, he requested the President to replace him with Col. Cav. Lumbroso.

The President called upon Col. Lumbroso and administered the oath.

Pres.: The court wishes to know for what reasons hostilities were resumed.

Omar: Because the government came between me and Sidi Redà.

Pres.: Were you obliged to await the reply to the letter you sent to H. E. Badoglio?

Omar: The reply came, but it was without meaning.

Pres.: And who are you?

Omar: I am the representative of Sidi Ahmed esc Scerif: but the documents which prove this statement of mine have been dispersed.

Pres.: Did you hand out officers' commissions to your mehafdia?

Omar: Yes.

Pres.: Was it you who always gave the battle orders?

Omar: As far as the earliest battles were concerned, there were others in command. I gave the orders for those just before the agreement and for those after the agreement. I have been leader for ten years.

Pres.: How were you captured?

Omar: The battle began around Zuuia Beda. I was wounded and fell under my horse which was killed. Government soldiers then captured me.

Pres.: Did you give your name?

Omar: I did, right away.

Pres.: Did you have your rifle?

Omar: I had a rifle and six cartridges.

Pres.: Did you carry out lootings and raids?

Omar: Yes.

Pres.: Did you order the *sottomessi* to pay tithes?

Omar: At first yes, later no, that is when the people were far away.

P.C.: The other day the extraordinary war tribunal was summoned at Marsa Brega to try the *sottomesso* Omar Bubacher Sabail ailet Musa for having been found in possession of certain documents. I have the honour of showing one of these to you, Mr President. From the document it is clear that the afore-mentioned Omar Bubacher was named head of the ailet by Omar el Muchtar and authorized to collect tithes, as appeared in the accounts, and to make propaganda for Senusiya.

The document bears the date of 17 April 1930 and was subsequent to the resumption of hostilities: it bears the signature and the seal of Omar Muchtar. The document was handed to the President who made the accused examine it, asking him if he recognized it as his.

Omar: At one time the tribe paid tithes...

P.C.: Don't digress—The date is after things got back to normal?

Omar: The Gaoail tribe were placed under Saif ef Fadil and depended on him.

P.C.: But the signature and the seal are yours? What does the document say?

Omar: States that he cannot read but recognizes his signature.

P.C.: He cannot read. And perhaps the document is written in Italian instead of in Arabic, or you do not have the spectacles you lost in a recent battle while running away, and which you had the nerve to ask back from the Governor.

After the President had asked the judges, the Prosecuting Counsel and the Defence Counsel if they had any questions for the accused, Captain Lontano asked: 'Have you ever received payment from the Italian government?'

Omar: No, never.

Defence: Did you ever fight against the Turks prior to our occupation?

Omar: Sometimes.

Defence: Were you educated by the Senusi?

Omar: Since the age of sixteen.

Having completed his questioning of the accused, the President called upon the Prosecuting Counsel Colonel Bedendo, who, amid a respectful silence, began his speech:

With that precise perception that so distinguishes H.E., General Graziani, in the preface of his superb little book, in which are reported the meetings held during the stay of H.E. Lesson and journalists in Benghazi, a book, which, being freely distributed, I hope all have read, writes:

'... So we see increasingly every day how the fame of this legendary hero, who always takes flight in times of danger, is on the wane.' If on this occasion Omar Muchtar was captured, it was due to the fact that he was surrounded by our brave troops and that the horse which was attempting to carry him away from the battle was killed.

It is not by chance that this trial is being held in the former Arab Parliament, now the Palazzo del Littorio! His Excellency wanted this done so as to demonstrate clearly to everyone how the policy of former times has been superseded.

He wished it so that as many Italians and native people as possible could be here to hear the charges levelled against Omar, so that they can honestly and in all conscience judge him, as the court will do.

We could say many things here about Omar el Muchtar, but we wish to limit ourselves and proceed according to the dictates of justice and not according to those based on curiosity and revenge.

This does not mean that the Italian government has abandoned these people to their fate: several times it has chosen the right moment to try for agreements, but your bad faith has always broken such pacts. El Beiada and Gasr Benigdem are shining examples of this, and it is useless today for Omar to excuse himself by saying that he wrote to His Excellency Badoglio and that he did not receive a proper reply.

The powerful Italian government does not traffic its own sovereignty; it makes as many concessions as possible. So much the worse for those who do not appreciate such a gesture.

You have said that you wished to live honestly in this land. But you did not wish it; because you rebelled against the sovereignty of the Italian government. You gave the order at Gasr Benigdem for the carabinieri supervising the repair work on the telephone line to be killed and tortured, while there was peace between us.

You took advantage of small garrisons to surprise and kill them. You are not a soldier but a bandit who has always lived underground. The true soldier kills his adversary in war, but does not torture him, while you have violated the corpses of our officers and our soldiers. You have killed our wounded. Not one of them has returned to us. You have boasted in a public hearing of having taken part in all battles: even if not present yourself, you gave the orders.

Your men attacked our troops whenever they were in greater numbers, but you always ran away, just as at other times our demagogues incited our workers and kept themselves in hiding so as to escape their just punishment.

And that you always ran away is proved by the statement you made that on another occasion you had also been wounded in the shoulder, whilst escaping, by a bomb splinter dropped by our glorious air force, that air force, which, according to your own words, flushed you out from your caves, from your wadis and followed you in your flights. You have always run away; it is proved by your spectacles, your seal which in other battles stayed in place: those spectacles which during your questioning this morning you had the temerity to ask back.

I do not, however, believe that you had much time left to devote to reading. You gave orders to kill prisoners: you have to answer for these killings. You set your followers against the armed forces of the Italian government, which alone rules this colony, in order to wrench the colony away from the motherland; for this crime you have to answer. You have carried out lootings and raids: you will still have to account for these.

El Beida—Gasr Benigdem, the Giona redoubt, Notary Rognoni, Major Bassi, Lieutenant Beati, Marshal Hubner and dozens and dozens of other crimes: these are your glories. For them you shall soon answer.

You have said God has this time abandoned you: if he has failed you, human justice has caught up with you.

You have no remorse for what you have done, for the conditions in which you have placed the people of this country. So be it: you are responsible.

I ask that the court, having decided that the accused is responsible for the crimes of which he is charged, should condemn him for the most serious crime of all, namely that of having taken up arms to wrench this colony from the motherland, pronouncing the death penalty which will take in the other sentences imposed for the lesser crimes.

The Public Prosecutor's demand was received with a general murmur of approval, which was immediately suppressed by the President.

The Defence Counsel, being called upon, asked that the court should take into account the age of the defendant and his religious fanaticism, and that it should give him the benefit of general mitigating circumstances.

Having asked the defendant if he had anything else to say in his defence, and obtained a negative reply, the court retired to the council chamber. After half an hour it returned to the courtroom, where, in a respectful silence, the President read the sentence whereby Omar el Muchtar was found guilty of the crimes charged against him and condemned him to death.

After the interpreter had translated the sentence to the defendant, the latter said: 'From God we have come and to God we must return'; to which the public Prosecutor added: 'Very well, carabinieri, take him out.'

The public files out slowly, commenting favourably on the sentence.

3. *Record of the hearing*

The year one thousand nine hundred and thirty-one on the fifteenth day of the ninth month of September in Benghazi at 17.00 hours and in the Palazzo del Littorio summoned to the Special Tribunal for the Defence of the State

Constituted of Messrs:

Lt. Col. Fanteri Marinoni Cav. Umberto (Presidente f.f.) in substitution for the official legitimately prevented Avv. Romano Dott. Francesco (Rapporteur of the Bench), Maj. Comm. M. Delitala Cav. Gonario (Regular Judge), Seniore M.V.S.N. Manzoni Cav. Giovanni (Regular Judge), Seniore M.V.S.N. Mendolia Cav. Michele (Regular Judge).

The temporary replacements of the regular official legitimately prevented, to plead the case, assisted by Sig. Lt. of Inf. in S.P.E. De Cristofano Edoardo (Military Clerk f.f.)

AGAINST

OMAR EL MUCTAR son of Aescia ben Mahareb, 73 years old, born at Defna, Kabyle Mnefa, ailet Brahidan, beit Farhatn, married with children, literate, no previous convictions, leader of the Senusi zavia at Gsur. Arrested 12/9/1931. IX

CHARGED

of the crimes provided for and set down in Art. 284–285–286–575–576 n. 3–62 n. 2–4–6–10 for having from 1911 up to the date of his capture which occurred on the day of 11 September 1931 south of Slonta, organized and directed the rebellion against the forces of the Italian state in the territory of this colony, participating in ambushes against isolated units of our troops, in numerous battles, in looting and raids, committing murder under the sole impulse of evil brutality, carrying out torture and acting cruelly against various persons, with the purpose of bringing about devastation and havoc, and detaching the colony from the motherland.

The public having been given free access to the court of hearing, the accused stands in the dock, guarded by the military, but free and unshackled.

Also present are the Public Prosecutor in the person of Sig. Bedendo Cav. Uff. Dr. Giuseppe regio. V. Avvocato Militare, and the Defence, in the person of Cap. of Artillery Lontano sig. Roberto.

The President pronounces the hearing open.

The interpreter Signor Nasri Hermes is present.

The President questions him on his private particulars, and he replies:

I am Nasri Hermes, formerly Michele, 53 years old, born at Diar bekir (Mesopotamia), head of the translation office of the government of Cyrenaica.

The President administers the oath to him, issues the required warning, making him repeat the following statement aloud:

'I swear to translate faithfully the questions asked through me and to report the answers faithfully.'

The President questions the accused through the interpreter as to his particulars and the latter gives them as mentioned above; he then warns him to make sure he can be properly heard.

It is noted at this point, that at the request of the Public Prosecutor, since the interpreter Nasri is indisposed, he should be replaced by Cav. Lumbroso di Aronne and Maria Gandus, born in Tunis on 27/2/1891, industrialist.

The President administers the oath to him, issues the required warning, making him repeat the following statement aloud:

'I swear to translate faithfully the questions asked through me and to report the answers faithfully.'

The Clerk reads the bill of indictment which is translated to the defendant by the interpreter.

The Clerk reads the trial documents relating to the case, included in the records on page 2.

After these are read the President has the documents translated by the interpreter since the accused does not understand the Italian language, then questions the accused about the facts contained in them; the accused replies in explanation and the interpreter translates.

It is noted that the accused replies in accordance with the written interrogation, stating that he is the leader of the Cyrenaican rebellion and, as such, author and instigator of all the crimes committed in the colony in the past ten years, the period during which he was the effective leader of the rebellion.

Accused: I have been the leader of the rebellion for about ten years.

It is noted that to each specific charge the accused answers:

'It is useless for you to ask me single facts: Whatever has been committed against Italy and the Italians for the past ten years was willed and permitted by me, whenever I did not personally take part in the acts themselves.

Accused: The raids, too, were ordered by me and some of them carried out by me.

The President calls upon the Public Prosecutor.

The Public Prosecutor, being called upon, concludes by appealing to the Tribunal, having found the accused guilty of the crimes as charged, to condemn him to death, with due consequences.

The Defence, in its turn, concludes by asking the Tribunal to exercise clemency to the accused.

Having called upon the accused for the last time, the President declares the hearing closed, and the Tribunal withdraws to the Council Chamber to consider the verdict.

When the Tribunal returns shortly afterwards to the court, the President reads aloud the judgment in front of all those in the case. The sentence is translated by the interpreter.

From which these minutes are drawn up and signed as follows:
THE MILITARY CLERK
signed. Edoardo De Cristofano
      THE PRESIDENT
      (Lt. Col. Marinoni Cav. Umberto)
      signed. Umberto Marinoni
      P.C.C.
      Military Clerk f.f.
      signed.

4. *List of charges against the prisoner*

OMAR EL MUCHTAR, for having since 1912 up to the date of his capture (11 September 1931) directed in Cyrenaica the rebellion against the forces of the Italian state, and having taken part additionally in ambushes against our troops, in battles, in lootings, in murders, is accused of the following crimes, provided for and punished by articles 284–285–286–575–576–62 C.P., committed at the time and in the place and manner specified below:

(1) Clash between a squad of soldiers of the R.R. force of carabinieri and a band of rebels on 20 February 1914 at Bu Sceriba (Ghemines) in which a non-commissioned officer and five zaptie were killed.

(2) Clash between troops of the Cyrene garrison and a strong group of rebels on 25 March 1914 in a place called Redeima (Cyrene), in which one zaptie was killed and one carabiniere and another zaptie wounded.

(3) Clash between a column of the command of Major cav. Roberto Ponte and a large group of rebels on 5 October 1914 near Mustina, in which Carabiniere R.R. Brigadier Filippo Marri was killed.

(4) Attack on the Slonta redoubt by a rebel formation of 400 soldiers, which took place on 6 November 1914 and in which Second Lieutenant Chiappini and one zaptie met glorious death.

(5) Ambush laid by a rebel band for the post coach which on 21 September 1922 was travelling from Merg to Cyrene by way of Beida; two carabinieri were killed, and also two Italian civilians, including a postal official, a soldier

165

and a native civilian. The cruelty of the assailants was manifested in their mutilation of the victims.

(6) Attack on a patrol of carabinieri and zaptie who were protecting the Cyrene-Marsa Susa road on 29 April 1924; killed in the performance of their duties were four soldiers, one of whom was a non-commissioned officer, while three were wounded.

(7) Raid on 1800 sheep owned by *sottomessi*, carried out on 25 June 1924 near Sidi Mulifa by a rebel group, or recovered from the troops during a violent clash occurring on the same day in Wadi Auenst, in the course of which four *sottomessi* were killed and two zaptie, one private and two *sottomessi* wounded.

(8) Raid for food and money, carried out on 14 August 1924 against local shopkeepers of Msrtuba by 50 rebels, and resultant attack by national and native soldiers of that CC.RR post, in which one native non-commissioned officer was killed and two zaptie were wounded.

(9) Attack on a motorized column of five vehicles, including one military vehicle, which on 30 June 1925 was travelling from Apollonia to Cyrene by way of the 'Siena' redoubt, carried out by a strong rebel force. Twenty-eight soldiers and civilians, both nationals and natives, were killed, and all the vehicles destroyed.

(10) Attack carried out by a strong rebel unit against a patrol of carabinieri and zaptie in Wadi el Hescia (Derna) on 16 June 1928, in which six soldiers, including one Italian, died gloriously.

(11) Raid on 4000 sheep owned by *sottomessi*, carried out on 8 December 1928 at El Abiar by about 3000 rebels, with an ensuing violent battle with troops of that garrison; 24 Dauria privates and one zaptie were killed, and five Eritrean *ascari* and seven Dauria privates were wounded.

(12) Attack on a patrol of soldiers of the R.R. force of carabinieri and zaptie on service along the Ghegab-Gubba road, carried out on 15 May 1930 near Sauia Tert by a hundred or so rebels, who succeeded in killing six native soldiers and wounding another two.

(13) Attack by the *dor* on the caravan of Abeidat *sottomessi* which was travelling from Marmarica to Sirtica, on 9 January 1931 at Abisr Bu Sfeia (Cyrene). Among the convoy escort troops one native soldier was killed, while seven were wounded, including an officer.

(14) Raid on various livestock owned by *sottomessi*, carried out on 27 February 1931 by some 300 rebels at Apollonia. A violent engagement followed, during which two shepherds were killed and three privates from Bande and other *sottomessi* were wounded.

(15) Clash between the whole *dor* and various units of troops, which took place on 30 March 1931 at Wadi Ramle (Derna), in which three Eritrean *ascari* were wounded.

II. The clandestine manifesto of the Cyrenaican resistance celebrating the first anniversary of the execution of Omar al-Mukhtar (September 1932).

While official Fascist propaganda continued to exalt the *pax romana* established in Libya after the 'liquidation' of the rebellion, a noteworthy event was the silent reply of the Cyrenaican resistance movement in circulating, clandestinely, its manifesto on the occasion of the first anniversary of the death of the man now recognized as a Libyan national hero. This secret manifesto is reproduced in the present book for the first time from the original version luckily found in the colonial archives; as translated here, it strikes us as being an important political message in memory of the hero of the Green Mountain.

The commemoration of Omar al-Mukhtar, martyr of the Arab nation

On this day in the year 1931 (16 September) the brave warrior and hero Omar al-Muktar was condemned to death.

On that day the tyrannical Fascist power struck down that eminent old man, that great fighter, and condemned him to death, without any consideration for his age or for his reputation in the hearts of Moslems.

On that day the Fascists added to their history, full of abuse and injustice, a black page to cover this their greatest victory.

Neither history nor the writings of the ancients tell us that a prisoner captured on the field of battle, over eighty years old, has ever been condemned to death. This could only happen in Fascist times, to make the world forget the injustices of even darker ages.

We celebrate the memory of that man on this day, with great sorrow yet with love for that hero who with his sword wrote verses of courage and self-denial in the history of the Arab nation, that man who fought magnificently for the defence of his country.

Omar al-Mukhtar fought for twenty years against the armies of colonization, without ever fearing death and without any fear of the infernal instruments of the enemy, up to the time when, after his horse fell on the field of battle, he was taken prisoner by his oppressors.

How shameful is that crime which makes anyone blush, that crime repudiated even by the most ferocious animals.

History and humanity are innocent of that bestial deed committed by the Fascists who even say they are civilized people.

We shall never forget that brutal and atrocious deed which makes our hearts bleed and pierces our breasts.

The Fascists believed that the condemnation of Omar al-Mukhtar to death would make it easier for them to occupy the country, but unfortunately for them the souls of the martyrs are an eternal flame which inspires the national spirit in the hearts of the people still living.

The martyr of the Tripoli–Barce nation is not dead, for he has left his people with an immortal monument of heroism which will be inherited by future generations.

This sad monument, built by the Fascist assassins' hands, will remain for ever and will never be forgotten because it has left mortal wounds in our hearts.

Woe to those oppressors who do not respect the age, the courage and the incomparable heroism of Omar al-Mukhtar: but they cannot understand the significance of this quality.

The years cannot wipe out the horror of this crime, which struck the heart of all Arabs, and which will always remain as a stain on their history, washed as it is in the blood of innocents, of women, of men, of the aged and of children.

People of Tripoli and Barce!

Always remember that day when that greatest of misfortunes occurred.

You must always retain this memory so as to learn a lesson that will serve in future to tell you how to avenge yourselves for your martyrs.

In that memory there is a lesson that will encourage and bring about the vengeance on those who have colonized your country and who deprived you of your rights and who have killed and driven far away many of your men.

On this day we ask the Arab nation and its patriots to join with us in grief and sadness for the misfortune that we commemorate today.

Omar al-Mukhtar was not only the martyr of the Tripoli–Barce people, but he was the martyr of the whole Arab nation. The lessons of heroism and courage that he gave the Fascist armies do honour to all Arabs, because the Arab people are like one body united in their griefs and joys, and this truth should be known to westerners, who should know that we are united. This memory must not be forgotten, it must be kept in your hearts until the day when the Fascists have to account to the Arab nation for this assassination, unheard of in the history of the world.

Arabs!

Always remember our martyr who was condemned to death after being taken prisoner. Remember that hero who raised the banner of Arabism and who renewed the glory of your glorious fathers.

Remember and always celebrate this day so as to let the Fascists know that your are not asleep and that you are a unified nation which rejects the scorn of the colonizers.

And you Fascists, Blackshirts!

We await a day when you have to render account, and that day we see to be close, whereas you believe it to be far-off; on that day we shall ask the price of the blood of Omar al-Mukhtar and of our noble heroes.

Injustice is short-lived, whereas reason is strong, and the oppressors will not escape their destiny.

Luigi Goglia

The capture, trial and death of
Omar al-Mukhtar in the Italian press

The figure of Omar al-Mukhtar is known in our country to the very rare students of colonial history, to the veterans of the Libyan 'pacification' campaigns and to a handful of elderly colonial officials.

The daily and weekly Italian press displayed a renewal of interest during the latter half of 1979 in the old Cyrenaican partisan leader when a film company put out publicity material for a mammoth film based, apparently, upon Omar's fight against Italian domination. But, with a few exceptions, the tone of this journalistic revival appeared strongly conformist, this time pervaded by a superficial anti-colonialism, with comments and judgments derived more from the chance afforded by the occasion than from documented inquiry, whether historical or political, which by this time could have been considered, balanced and truthful: all the more so because if in the past there had been those who, out of a deeply mistaken and reprehensible sense of patriotism, had stubbornly kept silent and manipulated the truth of the facts, these same documents from the past can today bear witness to what was often a stark reality of oppression and repression.

In this work we are concerned with the days of September 1931, in which Omar al-Mukhtar featured in the pages of the Italian press by reason of the events connected with his capture, his trial (which did not differ substantially from the type experienced by many Italian anti-Fascists) and his execution.

Omar al-Mukhtar was the Libyan resistance fighter who most thoroughly epitomized the struggle against Italian domination, both by reason of his military talents, already tested at the beginning of the century in the fight against French colonial penetration of the regions to the south of Libya, and because of his political ability and loyalty and devotion to the Senusi brotherhood, of which he was the leading exponent and representative of the

173

Emir Idris in Cyrenaica during the latter's exile in Egypt. His stature as a man of religion gave him a very considerable moral ascendancy which, together with his military and political qualities, made him by far the most prestigious and authoritative exponent of the whole resistance movement of the Libyan people between 1911 and 1932. Others might possess his courage and self-denial, but not the combination of those elements determining the personality of the fighter and the charisma of the leader who, during his entire career, played a dominant role whenever the interests of the Senusi brotherhood and his people were threatened, culminating in the calm and conscious sacrifice of his own life. He was known by the inhabitants of Cyrenaica as the 'lord of the night', implying that Italian sovereignty during the years of revolt was restricted to the daylight hours, whereas the resistance enjoyed maximum freedom of movement and action in the evening and during the night[1].

This was the man whom the Governor General of Libya, Marshal Badoglio, and the Colonial Minister and quadrumvir of Fascism, De Bono, had no hesitation in sentencing to death even before setting up the Special Tribunal for the defence of the state, which was to judge him.

We have not managed to find any documentation that might indicate Mussolini's position in this respect. But it is unthinkable that there should have been any contradiction or divergence between the head of government, his minister and his governor. Mussolini never displayed much interest in the internal affairs of the colonial possessions. His tendency, however, when confronted by conflicts with the native populations was always to choose the harshest and most drastic solution; so we can safely assume that as far as the death sentence on Omar was concerned, the decision adopted must have been in keeping with his own ideas as to how the native rebels should be treated[2]. Graziani, then vice-governor of Cyrenaica and commander of the troops of that colony, was, as always, the eager executant of Badoglio's orders; and in his version of the event he exhibited such dishonesty and vulgarity of mind as to create a false image of the imprisoned leader[3], notably boasting of how he had refused to shake the hand that the shackled Omar generously extended

---

[1] Evidence of the father of the author, Rodolfo, who served from 1935–7 as a lieutenant in Cyrenaica before becoming company commander of the Ninth Libyan battalion stationed at Agedabia and then of the Seventh meharist group stationed in the archipelago of Cufra oases. He had repeatedly mentioned that Omar was very clearly remembered, not only by the Arab people but also by the majority of Italian soldiers who served in Cyrenaica and who, for the most part, felt respect and admiration for him.

[2] Renzo de Felice, to whom I turned to find out whether in the vast body of documentation consulted by him for his biography of Mussolini he had ever come across references to Omar al-Mukhtar, replied negatively; as far as the Fascist leader's general attitude to native policy was concerned, he agreed fully with our assessment.

[3] Rodolfo GRAZIANI, *Cyrenaica pacificata*, Milan 1932, pp. 269–72.

to him: 'He tried to give me his hand, manacled, but could not because it would not reach. Anyway, I wouldn't have touched it'[4].

It is not our intention here to examine the behaviour of the colonial authorities towards Omar, but we think it is worth emphasizing that they did not so much lack humanitarianism and magnanimity (virtues, it is true, even in politics, though not binding upon those who exercise power) as intelligence, a sense of opportunity and far-sightedness.

Omar's life could have been spared, for he could have been shipped over to Italy and kept under house arrest or, at worst, in prison. The colonial government's reaction was, nevertheless, brutal: the physical elimination of the defeated enemy. Omar al-Mukhtar's capture and execution marked the virtual end of the revolt and guerilla war in Cyrenaica (during the next few months even the last guerillas who had not found refuge across the border in Egypt were caught and killed); yet they also constituted the finest moment of moral affirmation in the struggle against Italian domination. This again was due to the proud and composed bearing, the strong, serene attitude of the aged Senusi chief who faced the gallows with the same loftiness of spirit as was displayed by patriots of our own risorgimento and with the resigned religious dignity of the mujahid.

The Italian press of the time, completely controlled by the Fascist regime, did not, by and large, assign great importance to the event. Most papers published the information sheets of the Stefani agency; and some of the provincial papers printed slightly shorter, edited articles based on those of the leading dailies. It is evident from the articles of 15–16 September, that is prior to the execution, that there was no discernible censorship or restriction from higher quarters. But the tone was different after the execution.

The news of Omar's capture should logically have been fully reported and commented upon in the interests of Fascist propaganda itself. Yet there were no great repercussions whatsoever. All the dailies certainly carried the news, but only a modest amount of space was devoted to analyzing an event whose importance was played down. The death sentence and the execution of the prisoner signalled the end of all interest in that specific event and, more generally, in the victory over the guerillas and the Cyrenaican-Senusi rebellion.

In our opinion this proves, for one thing, the embarrassment over the execution, but also the scarce interest shown by the national press in our colonies. In fact, even during the Fascist period, when imperial colonialism was a notorious highlight of government propaganda, most of the articles and letters that appeared were more concerned with projections of the regime in the colony than with providing information about the problems and aspects

[4] *Ibid.*, p. 272.

of life in the colonies, either from the viewpoint of the colonizers or the colonized. This is, of course, the general tendency of the press attitude as revealed by our research, but obviously there are exceptions. By and large, the press directed most of its attention to the visits paid to Libya by Mussolini, the colonial ministers, the king and the princes of the House of Savoy, and to the large-scale public works (apart, of course, from the wars themselves which understandably formed separate issues).

Before going on to analyze the matter further, it is necessary to underline a very important fact which determined or greatly influenced the journalistic handling of events around the time it happened. This is that the clash with the small group of warriors accompanying Omar in the neighbourhood of Slonta and the subsequent capture of the rebel leader occurred on 11 September, yet the official acknowledgment of the event dates from the following days and the first news in the press was only given on 15 September. That was the very day when the trial took place in Benghazi before the Special Tribunal for the Defence of the State, and when the death sentence was pronounced on Omar, this being carried out the next morning at 8.30 in the square at Soluk.

News of the capture thus appeared in the national papers on 16 September and of the hanging[5] on 17 September. The short span of time between the official acknowledgment and the publication of the news of the capture and the execution helped to play down and dispose of the matter, as may be deduced from the tone of the articles following the execution. At the time the news of the capture came through, there was, for the most part, and in varying measures, a clear tendency to appreciate the personality of the defeated enemy. In the journalistic comments following Omar's execution there was a brisk change of tone towards vulgar condemnation and even downright insult. Thus we can see how, in the short space of 2–3 days, the figure of Omar al-Mukhtar was partially stripped of those features of admiration and esteem which many journalists had, perhaps, grudgingly, attributed to him, and replaced by a new image of the Senusi leader, portrayed to Italian readers as that of a commonplace criminal who tortured Italian soldiers.

The day of 16 September 1931

The Stefani communiqué, released on the night of 15 September and published the next day in the daily papers, gave succinct news of the capture, but nothing to hint at what was actually happening in the Cyrenaican colony.

---

[5] Inexplicably, the communiqué from the Agenzia Stefani mentions shooting, as a result of which even today, at the historic meeting on Omar al-Mukhtar held at the Gariunis University of Benghazi on 10–16 November 1979, one delegate asked whether it was true that Omar had first been shot and then hanged.

'Rome, night of 15th. On the night of the 11th of this month, following a brilliant encircling action, in the Slonta zone, our Seventh Savari squadron, having been sent in pursuit of the marauders and rebels, succeeded in capturing the leader of the Cyrenaican rebellion and representative of Senusiya, Omar El-Muktar. During the action 12 soldiers and 14 horses were killed, and we took 7 horses with their trappings and a dozen or so muskets. The capture of the active and daring delegated Senusi leader is a new, authentic and positive step forward in our politico-military policing action, which will continue firmly and decisively until the complete pacification of the whole Cyrenaican territory' (Stefani).

La Stampa of the 16th, in addition to the Stefani communiqué, printed twenty-seven lines of comment in which the figure of Omar was highlighted; they recognized, furthermore, that the elderly chief did possess certain qualities.

'Omar El Muktar has all the gifts of a commander and an Arab chief: bravery, leadership ability, prestige and a sense of justice. A good soldier and an excellent leader, the Cyrenaican rebellion survived until yesterday because of his authority and personal merit. An elderly man of over 70, his many experiences on the battlefield gave him the reputation among his followers of being invulnerable. The myth has collapsed: and with it falls the man, Omar El Muktar, principal sustainer of the rebellion in the Cyrenaican Gebel. The disarming of the people and their concentration in compulsory camps near the coast, with the attendant closure of the Egyptian border, plus the policing of the Gebel and the desert zones by highly experienced and expert colonial personnel, placed the rebellion at the government's mercy. The actual capture of a leader of Omar El Muktar's prestige and courage by a few Savari displays our military organization in Cyrenaica to perfection.'

Il Giornale d'Italia published the Stefani communiqué and a longer commentary than the Turin newspaper, but the content, partly overlapping, was almost identical. Here, however, are the more significant passages.

'The capture of Omar-el-Muktar by our magnificent Savari strikes a mortal blow at the already weakened Cyrenaican rebellion. Omar-el-Muktar has all the gifts of a commander and an Arab chief: venerable age, personal courage, leadership ability and prestige in the Arab world. A good soldier and an excellent leader, he is therefore a daunting enemy. One could say that the Cyrenaican rebellion survived until yesterday because of his authority and bravery: in short, his personal merit. An elderly man of over 70, his many experiences on the battlefield gave him the reputation among his followers of being invulnerable. When Graziani clamped down so firmly on semi-nomadism by settling the Gebel peoples in compulsory camps down near the coast, he, with fine political sense, cut all links with the encampments so as not to expose them to reprisal actions and thus to retain his position with them as a prestigious and courageous leader. Yet this myth, too, like so many myths fostered by the ministry about the mysteries and traditions of colonial Africa, has now collapsed; and with it falls Omar el Muktar, principal sustainer of the rebellion in the Cyrenaican Gebel.'

Il Resto del Carlino likewise reproduced in part the same article as the other two, and added:

'When Graziani clamped down so firmly on semi-nomadism by settling the Gebel peoples in compulsory camps down near the coast, he, with fine political sense, cut all links with the tribes, so as not to expose them to repressive measures and to retain his position with them as a prestigious and courageous leader.'

Il Telegrafo, of Leghorn, adopted the same tone:

'. . . The rebels lose with him a spirit of the first rank, a leader of undisputed authority. In fact, he did not lack bravery, leadership ability, personal prestige and a sense of justice. He was a proud enemy, despite his 70 years. . . It will be difficult for the rebels to find another leader with the authority and prestige that Omar el Muktar enjoyed.'

Il Secolo XIX, of Genoa, wrote:

'. . . this audacious chief. . . the fact that a few Saharans[6] managed to surprise a leader of the prestige and courage of Omar el Muktar shows to perfection the level reached by our troops in Africa and by our military organization within the colony.'

Il Gazzettino, of Venice, repeated what had already appeared in the *Giornale d'Italia* and in the other papers quoted, and so did *La Nazione*, of Florence, *La Gazzetta del popolo*, of Turin, *Il Giornale di Genova*, *Il nuovo cittadino*, also of Genoa, *La Gazzetta*, of Messina, *Il popolo Toscano*, of Lucca, and *Il piccolo*, of Trieste. All these papers adopted an attitude of considerable respect for the captured enemy and all made use, apart from the Stefani communiqué of 15 September, of a common source (which we have not managed to identify but which must have been an agency or a ministerial communiqué).

Il Messaggero, of Rome, distanced itself from the leading national newspapers and the majority of provincial papers as well by ridiculing the figure of the warrior chief. It did this by printing a comic but petty anecdote to prove that Omar, 'a crafty, faithless and cruel old man', guilty of 'perfidy and duplicity', was not, after all, that great warrior as depicted in legend; his real

---

[6] Not actually Saharans but Savari.

good fortune, observed the Roman daily, was his horse, a truly intelligent animal which saved him in many a battle by galloping away at speed. On 11 September fortune abandoned the rebel when the 'intelligent' horse was hit, and his master, as a result, was captured.

La Sera, of Milan, wrote of him as a 'proud and extremely stubborn leader of the Senusi rebellion', and went on to describe the actions of the Senusi brotherhood as follows:

'Once the unrelenting operations of our troops had reduced the arrogance of the Senusi leaders to shreds, with the treacherous and evil Idriss fleeing to Cairo to enjoy his ill-gotten cash, and others surrendering, the only man left fighting, with a few desperate followers, was the old Senusi lieutenant, Omar el Muktar.'

Yet after that the writer went on to call Omar 'the Bedouin brigand'. The same contrasting attitude was adopted by Como's *La Provincia*, which, after writing:

'. . . the proud and extremely stubborn leader of the Senusi rebellion, the only man who for twenty years had maintained an attitude of unrelenting hostility towards us',

ended in the same way as the Milanese newspaper.

The dailies of 17 September 1931 and following days

While Italians read the news of the capture and the initial comments by journalists, some of whom expressed respect for, and recognition of, Omar's qualities, the latter was mounting the scaffold at Soluk to be hanged. This drastic, swift solution of events impelled the press to adopt a more uniform tone, clearly under official guidance, in describing the behaviour and personality of the Cyrenaican leader.

Only two dailies stood out from the chorus, namely the *Secolo XIX*, of Genoa (17 September) and the *Roma*, of Naples, on the same day. The former wrote:

'Omar el Muktar was the recognized leader of the Cyrenaican rebels, a chief of undisputed authority and exceptional bravery. He had fought against the Italians with unflagging tenacity and incredible shrewdness. . . . A warrior of exceptional strength in spite of his 70 years, he had to be regarded as a terrible and fierce enemy.'

The *Roma* put it in this way:

'. . . Omar el Muktar, at the age of 70, fought against the Italians with a stubbornness and valour that had to be recognized . . . extremely mobile and shrewd . . . Omar el Muktar never yielded.'

In another group of papers, Omar el Muktar, 'traitor' and 'bandit' was nevertheless acknowledged to be a brave man. Thus *Il Popolo toscano*, of 17

179

September, ran an article headed 'Omar el Muktar treacherous rebel leader executed in front of 30,000 Arab *sottomessi*'. Signed by the correspondent Gabriele Scrimali, it described in a generally sober and serious manner the events in which Omar featured, and a sense of respect was clearly evident in terming him the 'unyielding' rebel. *Il Popolo di Trieste*, on the 18th, wrote:

'When the Senusi had by now abandoned direct struggle, only the elderly Omar was left to nourish the revolt . . . and only the elderly Omar continued to see himself as the last representative of the Islamic sect. The old brigand was isolated. . . .'

Il Popolo di Brescia, of 19 September, wrote:

'. . . perhaps they deluded themselves into supposing that the straight Roman sword would waver when confronted by the personality of Omar el Muktar. . . . Had it not been for the mystique of Omar el Muktar's presence in the Cyrenaican rebel ranks, would his lieutenants have dared carry on the fight?'

The question was a clear recognition of the powerful personality of the Senusi chief. *La Sentinella d'Italia*, of Cuneo, on 19 September, likewise acknowledged this, calling him a 'scoundrel' and writing in these terms of his death:

'. . . Thus vanished not only a bandit chief of exceptional strength and boldness, but also an extremely energetic and shrewd Senusi leader . . . Head of the rebellion and of brigandry . . . considered by the people to be invulnerable.'

And speaking of the succession:

'. . . the four lieutenants who in any event do not enjoy his prestige and do not possess his moral strength . . .'

Finally, there was the group of dailies which treated the facts in a decidedly arrogant and scornful tone, often echoing the phrases of the Fascist action squads, conceding little or nothing to the personality of the defeated, dead enemy. *Il Popolo d'Italia*, of 17 September, in an article headed 'Omar el Muktar executed', wrote of his 'perfidy and duplicity', describing him as a 'crafty bandit', and attributing all the merit of the Cyrenaican leader's reputation for invincibility (as had *Il Messaggero* of the previous day) to his 'very swift, amazingly agile and intelligent horse'.

Il Telegrafo, of Leghorn, wrote on the 17th:

' . . . The legend, so ridiculous in Cyrenaica, of Omar el Muktar's invincibility, a legend which made this crafty, faithless and cruel old man seem like a supernatural hero who would never be caught, has finally disappeared.'

Omar was also described as a 'sad old rebel', reference was made to his 'perfidy and duplicity', and once again the tale of his intelligent horse was included.

Il Resto del Carlino, of the 17th, carried an article headed 'Omar el Muctar executed': '. . . Omar el Muctar was not only a rebel but also a traitor . . . an old, wily Bedouin chief. . . . The death penalty which befell Omar el Muctar so implacably and swiftly should and will be a salutory example for those remaining rebels who are holed up here and there in the hinterland. . . .'

La Provincia di Padova, on the same day, entitled its article 'The figure of a traitor', denouncing him as a 'wily bandit' animated by 'perfidy and duplicity'.

Il Giornale d'Italia, on the 18th, in an article devoted to Omar and signed O. F., wrote of him thus: '. . . he was a traitor, a classic traitor . . . like a petty thief hiding in the bushes. . . .'

Il Popolo d'Italia of 19 September gave space to a report from Sandro Sandri in Benghazi. The article appeared under the heading: 'The rebellion in Cyrenaica energetically crushed. How Omar-el-Muktar, torturer of our soldiers, was captured and executed.' Here for the first time was that new note aiming to discredit the Cyrenaican leader morally, accusing him of cowardly behaviour during the trial and on the gallows.

'. . . His behaviour up to and during the trial, which was held at the Palazzo Littorio in Benghazi, certainly did not befit the reputation of the legendary leader which had surrounded him for so many years. He acknowledged his crimes, stating that he had fought for the glory of Senusiya, and received the pronouncement of the sentence with manifest emotion.'

Yet what Sandri and others considered to be an admission of guilt was, in fact, the very opposite: it was a strong affirmation by Omar that he alone was responsible for the charges brought against him by the enemy, just as he was for the events in the battles that he had directed. That there was no hint of repentance or of weakness in this is clear from the way in which Omar declared he was fighting for Senusiya and for God.

Il Piccolo, of 20 September, in a report from Tripoli returned to the theme of the imprisoned Omar's behaviour, but gave a different version of the condemned man's reactions:

'Omar el Muktar, who had kept himself under control during the trial and the reading of the sentence, could not manage to conceal his deep emotion on the execution scaffold. . . .'

Il Giornale di Genova of 20th printed an article headed 'The inglorious death of Omar el Muctar', and went further than all the other papers in denigrating his behaviour during the trial and on the point of death:

'. . . When he learned of the death sentence, Omar el Muctar collapsed and did not live up to his reputation for courage. . . . Omar el Muctar mounted the scaffold with evident signs of weakness, supported by our *zaptie*, and died complaining and weeping. . . .'

Gerarchia, the monthly review of the Fascist revolution, founded by Mussolini, in its column *Cronache di politica coloniale* in issue 9 of September

181

1931, tackled the subject in a vulgar, broadly insulting and ridiculously propagandistic manner:

'Omar El Muktar. The capture of Omar El Muktar, which took place on 11 September in the Slonta zone, was one of the many brilliant colonial policing operations carried out by Italian troops in Libya. There is no need to dwell on the murky figure of the Cyrenaican bandit, because readers are familiar with it. We will merely remark that Omar's end was predictable. He was unable to escape our encircling manoeuvres, that colonial strategy which has amazed the outside world and which has made it possible to conquer the two Mediterranean colonies, spiritually and materially. Now that the fierce exponent of the final desperate stage of Cyrenaican rebel resistance has been captured, Senusism is now no more than a sorry reminder of the craven colonial policies of the past. Omar attempted—with his criminal activities—to arouse large-scale anti-Italian feeling and to frighten the Italian command. All he managed to do was to prove his ever-increasing isolation and to stir up hatred and ill-feeling among his few followers, who were tired of being subjected to his tyranny. The thieving bandit was a dispossessed king. More recently he had devoted himself to plunder, not being able to count on his friends of the religious brotherhood. The conquest of Cufra, which dealt a mortal blow to Senusiya, forced Omar to lead a nomadic life. Since the Egyptian frontier area was unsafe, the mercenary roamed the Slonta zone, trusting in the bravery of his people. Familiar with the terrain, he certainly could not have imagined such an inglorious end! Omar had forgotten that *all difficulties* can be overcome by our troops. The harsh lessons of the very recent past ought to have reminded him that he could not challenge with impunity a leader such as Graziani.'

The Italian colonial press

L'azione coloniale, in an article on 20 September by Mario Pigli, carried the news that Omar had been shot. This was obviously a piece written after the Stefani communiqué which went into print without subsequent corrections.

The following, which appeared in the same newspaper on 1 October, is of interest both for its ideological content and for its editorial postscript to the article by Sandro Sandri headed 'The barbed wire crushed the Cyrenaican rebellion':

'We leave the analysis of the technical side of the operation to Comrade Sandri, who is well acquainted with people and events and who is well versed in the thinking of the commanders. But there are other aspects of this new Cyrenaican history that deserve to be underlined. Above all, the style, that unmistakable style, so simple and so strongly and clearly Tacitan, which General Graziani exhibits in initiating action, carrying it through to completion and announcing it to the masses in Italy and abroad. An axiomatic

182

principle is his will to win, using sufficient and energetic methods as have never been seen throughout our colonial history, and a determination to achieve complete and total success, without any omissions and regrets. That is why—to mention nothing else—in speaking of this operation we emphasize this characteristic of style, which both at home and overseas carries the resolute hallmark of a single Leader—the Duce—victorious because the commanders of Fascist Italy have no other goal, and that they should have no other goals is the wish of all those who have the honour of serving their country.'

L'Italia coloniale, no. 10, October, devoted several pages to a report, illustrated by photographs and maps, entitled 'The end of Omar el Muctar'. Apart from the photographic interest, however, it contained nothing original, but was rather a hotchpotch of press communiqués and articles that had appeared the previous month in the dailies.

The October issue of the *Rivista delle colonie italiane* devoted several lines, under the 'Cyrenaica' heading in the *Cronache coloniali* column on pp. 804–5, to the affair, stating among other things: 'The bandits of the Gebel have lost a leader who will be very difficult to replace.'

L'Oltremare, on p. 403 of its December issue, published a short article entitled 'The end of Omar el Muctar in the foreign press'.

'The capture and execution of Omar el-Muctàr, the notorious traitor and stubborn leader of the last rebel hordes in Cyrenaica, aroused considerable interest even outside Italy. As we write, few foreign commentaries have so far reached us, but all are full of admiration for the resolute way in which the regime has waged victorious battle against Senusiya and especially for the energy and shrewdness so magnificently displayed by General Graziani, who now appears to everyone as one of the finest colonial soldiers, of the stamp of Bugeaud and Kitchener.

'In its editorial the day after the capture of Omar el-Muctàr, *The Times* warmly hailed the important Italian success, which deservedly crowned a whole series of anti-guerilla actions, carried out with incomparable mastery. After describing the activities of the rebel leader in his fight against Italy, the great City newspaper asserted that the twenty-year war which, with occasional pauses, had been going on since the autumn of 1911, when the Italians took Tripoli, Benghazi and Derna from the Turks, was now at an end. "It has been," wrote *The Times*, "a long and bloody struggle, a war of skirmishes, ambushes and surprises of doubtful outcome, so long as the inflexible will of the Fascist government did not grant the invaders moral ascendancy over their enemies."

'*Le Temps*, for its part, commented in a long article on the capture of the leader of Senusi dissidents in Cyrenaica, thus:

"...The last movement of resistance to the Italians in Libya thereby suffered one of its severest blows. The rebellion in Cyrenaica, in fact, depended entirely upon the courage, the daring and the personal renown of Omar el-Muctàr, who may, in some respects, be compared to Abd el-Gader. He was in any event a leader of special stature and proven ability. Several times previously he had been on the point of falling into Italian hands but on each occasion had escaped almost miraculously. His numerous exploits, what is more, had earned him the reputation of invulnerability. He posed, too, as the true inheritor of Senusi tradition. His war was a holy war, and thus he personified Islamic resistance to Italian conquest. This is why his capture is so important. One could even take the point of view that with the disappearance of Omar el-Muctàr, Senusism, representing the last resistance in North Africa to European penetration, is finally destroyed. The capture of the old Bedouin chief is due to the many measures shrewdly conceived and methodically applied by General Graziani, Libya's Bugeaud."

'After making particular mention of the complex and vigorous action against the rebels undertaken by General Graziani, *Le Temps* continued and concluded:

"The efforts of Omar and of his partisans seemed increasingly desperate, and to tell the truth they were the final spasms. Omar's capture therefore appears to be the very end. With this event, which exhibits a clear improvement of Italian military organization in Libya, and especially in Cyrenaica, the two former Turkish provinces can be regarded as having been pacified, and this fact will certainly have important consequences, since until now the rebellion was concentrated in the heart of the country, affecting the richest lands that were most coveted by the Italian colonists. Now colonization can develop in Cyrenaica in conditions of full security, and nothing can prevent Italy carrying out in this land its noble and fruitful civilizing mission."'

The author of the article appears almost to be seeking a kind of international approval, tantamount to a diploma awarded by the most prestigious newspapers of Great Britain and France, the two great colonial powers.

The colonial press in Cyrenaica

The whole affair was given the greatest prominence in the local press of the colony where Omar had been born and where he lived and worked. It was clearly recognized that Cyrenaica—from the colonial point of view—would obviously be first to benefit from the execution of Omar and the crushing of the rebellion.

La Cirenaica of 16 September carried a definition of Graziani which, though immediately effective in terms of propaganda, was quite stupid. The vice-governor, in fact, described Omar as 'a legendary hero always on the run'.

The article by Sandro Sandri, who was very close to Graziani[7], is important because it typefies the shoddiest kind of Fascist colonial mentality. A number of characteristic elements can be identified in it, notably a form of unfulfilled, substandard romanticism in which sentiments are expressed concerning the attributes of the foe, only to be even more forcefully refuted. Then, too, there is the more or less explicit celebration of strong-arm methods for resolving native problems. Finally, there is the falsification or perhaps genuine incomprehension of native culture, which is exemplified in this instance by Sandri's treatment of the Senusi brotherhood. The overblown style of writing is also very commonplace, the highly colourful and inflated language simply concealing the often banal and sometimes deeply offensive nature of the content.

The article, which appeared in *La Cirenaica* of 23 September, is entitled 'Omar el Muctar Hound of the Lord'. We reproduce it in its entirety in the Appendix. There is, too, an interesting last word by Sandri in the issue of 16 December 1931, headed 'The agony of the rebellion in Cyrenaica'. At the very end, when it has become obvious that the anti-Italian guerilla war is really over, Sandri writes as follows, perhaps showing a hint of appreciation, a touch of remorse stifled maybe by a sense of shame:

'... Basically, old Omar el Muktar did not act in bad faith. His master (Mohammed Idris) had ordered him to play the hero, and this tough and sad old man believed it.'

The anti-Fascist press

Apart from a few emigrant papers, mainly the Communist ones, which adopted a very generalized position, appealing to principle and calling for freedom and independence for colonial peoples, militant anti-Fascists did not devote much time or effort to fighting colonialism as such. The major exception, of course, was the attack on Ethiopia, which, by virtue of its extreme gravity in national and, even more, international terms, transcended mere colonial interest to become, in those years, an event that was crucial to the world's political situation.

The death of Omar and the harsh repression of the rebellion and of the anti-Italian guerilla activities in Libya did not arouse much interest in the ranks of anti-Fascism, or at any rate not sufficiently to be exploited as anti-colonial propaganda (which was, as already mentioned, very scarce and full of gaps) or even as a weapon against the Fascists.

It is clear that militant anti-Fascism was confronted by far more serious problems, partly because of the way the regime had consolidated power at

---

[7] Sandri sang the praises of the Fascist Scipio in a profile, *Il generale Graziani*, Edizione Azione coloniale, Rome, 1932, and in his book on the Ethiopian campaign *Sei mesi di guerra sul fronte somalo*, Arti Grafiche Bertarelli, Milan-Rome, 1936.

home, managing to reflect a generally acceptable image abroad, and partly because of difficulties in recruitment and effective action; for these reasons it did not dwell long on colonial issues. But in our opinion there were other reasons for the anti-Fascist lack of interest in colonial affairs, in large measure reflecting the unpopularity and scant interest in such matters on the part of the Italian public as a whole.

While the tragedy of Cyrenaican resistance was being enacted, the 1931 issue of *L'Unità*, published in Paris, was exclusively devoted to the most detailed information about the Fascist party organization in Italy and, for the rest, to proclaiming the existence of imperialist plots against the Soviet Union and China, which it was seeking to unmask. In July 1929 the Parisian *L'Unità* had published an appeal by the Italian Communist party 'Against Fascist brigandry in the colonies'. It is one of the rare communist documents on the Libyan question, although there are factual errors (it mentions armed operations in Tripolitania, which had ceased some years previously, whilst continuing in Fezzan and Cyrenaica) with much reliance on generalizations and old drafts, giving the impression of having been compiled in an office by someone who knew little if anything about the real situation. A note that appeared in the December 1929 issue of the same journal shows the superficiality and slipshod methods adopted by the contributors. It mentions the truce of Tarhuna and names Omar al-Mukhtar as the leader who surrendered while the people carried on the fight. As we know, Tarhuna was a truce and not a surrender, and during the entire period when Omar took care to observe it, not judging it opportune to break it, there were no guerilla operations against the Italian soldiers[8]. The short article ended with the catch-phrase 'Libya for the Libyan people'.

The only news of Omar that we can find in *Le correspondence internationale*, organ in the French language of the Third Communist International, is contained in a report of 14 November 1931 by one J.B., from Jerusalem, entitled 'The Congress of Islam and its political lessons', with the following reference:

'At the same time one can detect a tendency to strengthen solidarity, to create a general anti-imperialist united front whenever any type of imperialism attempts to strangle a weaker Arab or Mohammedan country. Thus we have seen a veritable storm of demonstrations against France as soon as news

---

[8] For more detailed information, see the essay by Giorgio Rochat in this book. Luigi Longo also deals with the Libyan problem in an article signed with the pseudonym L. Gallo which appeared in *Stato operaio* a. III, no. 8, November 1929, pp. 678–83, entitled 'Due anni di guerra coloniale fascista'. Longo, although he very probably based his information mainly on the Italian journals of the regime, correctly picked out Badoglio as the brain and heart of Italian military repression. But he too saw the truce of 1929 as a capitulation and on three occasions cited Omar al-Mukhtar as the man who had surrendered and offered submission.

was received of her acts of violence in Morocco and in Syria; against Italy who is systematically exterminating the Arab population of Tripolitania and has recently executed Omar el Muchtar, leader of the insurgents; and against the regime of imperial oppression set up by Holland in Indonesia, etc.'

L'*Avanti!* of Paris, on 27 September 1931, carried a short article, unsigned, on page three, entitled 'From the Fascist gaol', with the subtitle 'Another martyr'. The piece was highly coloured and deliberately sensational, referring to Libyan children deported to Italy 'to make them slaves and Catholics' and to deportees left on beaches to die of hunger. As for the claims of 'Arab chiefs being thrown out of aeroplanes for the amusement of the blackshirts', there was nothing to prove it true although there were many rumours in the contemporary Arabic press and even in colonial military circles.

'Like Gortan[9], like the four martyrs of Pola, Omar al Muctar has fallen, a New Martyr, for a cause that was not ours. But he died a victim of our common enemy, for the liberation of his country from the assassin ranks of Fascism. The frightful horrors perpetrated by Fascism in Libya, ranging from the systematic massacre of people to the deportation to Italy of children to make them slaves and Catholics, to leaving thousands of Arabs on the beaches to let them die slowly of hunger, and to Arab chiefs being thrown out of aeroplanes for the amusement of the blackshirts, are known all over the world. Against these nameless infamies Omar al Muctar ventured heroically on to the battlefield, at the head of a group of brave young men. Defeated by the enemy's superior numbers, the power of their weapons and their facilities, he was taken prisoner and dragged before a caricature of a tribunal of blackshirts. There, head held high, he shouted, in the face of all the foul devices of Fascism, his implacable and indomitable hatred. He died a hero. Glory to the New Martyr. And let us also remember him for the Day of Judgment.'

The article by the socialist journal has objective historical interest not only because, as in the references by the communist press, it represents a rare document, but, above all, because it restores for us the truer image of the fighter, Omar al-Mukhtar, at the head of his people, wise, courageous, tough, proud and never giving in.

[9] Wladimir Gortan, Croat farmer shot, after being sentenced to death by the Special Tribunal for State Defence in 1929, for having offered armed resistance to the Fascist militia.
Source: La Stampa, 19 September 1931.
Source: La Cirenaica, Benghazi, 23 September 1931.
Source: G. BEDENDO, La pulitica dde Grazziani 1930–1934, Benghazi, 1934, pp. 16–18.

In the Appendix to this book I have decided to include a group of documents which I consider to be of interest to the reader but which would have weighed down the text if given space in the main sections. This is also the place to provide some additional information about them.

The first item is the article by Dante Maria Tuninetti, which is of interest principally because at that time the author was commissioner of the Fascist Federation in Cyrenaica.

The second piece has already received sufficient attention in the main body of the book.

The third Appendix is a list of newspapers consulted, which carried news reports of the capture, trial and execution of Omar. I am indebted to Professor Francesco Castro for having placed most of this material at my disposal. This research has not been exhaustive but is broadly representative, furnishing a critical panorama of the Italian press in its coverage of the final events in Omar's life.

I. After the execution of Omar al Mukhtar.

The surviving rebels in Cyrenaica called on to surrender by H. E. Graziani

Benghazi, night of the 18th

Continuing with the realization of the political and military programme announced on his arrival in the colony—in agreement with the Colonial Minister H. E. De Bono and with the Governor of Libya Marshal Badoglio— H. E. Rodolfo Graziani had recently been forcing the surviving rebels to lead a hard life, keeping them on the move like gypsies as our mobile groups harried and hunted them constantly. They were starved of reinforcements, provisions and weapons because of their isolation from the people of the Cyrenaican Gebel, the closing of the Egyptian frontier with a barbed wire network 320 kilometres in length, and increased surveillance of the coast.

It was thus inevitable that the rebellion should die of exhaustion. The capture and execution of Omar el Muctar, leader of the Senusi rebels and delegate of Senusiya, are therefore properly part and parcel of the general rebel-war scenario, constituting the most significant episode of that revolt and at the same time its logical and grim consequence.

The capture

We can now provide more details about the dramatic capture of the elderly Akhuan, for nine years supreme head of the rebellion. At dawn on the 11th, following a signal from our aircraft, which on the previous day had carried out a raid on the zone, and as a result of reports from our informers which indicated the certain presence of a large rebel *door* in the Slonta Beda zone, the Gebel military command planned an encircling movement, entrusting the operation to the Ragazzi, Piatti and Marone groups, with tank squadrons, and concentrating several fresh native cavalry units, recently selected and improved by General Rodolfo Graziani, at the probable rebel exit points. These

189

units had the job of pursuing the rebels so as to wear out their horses and eventually to capture the soldiers themselves.

Things went exactly according to plan. Omar el Muctar's *door*, pursued by the Ragazzi group, tried to flee westward, where it ran into the Piatti group. Thrown back as well by this group, the rebel *door* tried to escape again but came up against the armoured cars which had spread out, in anticipation of such a manoeuvre, along the line of the Scenescen wood. The group of rebels, thrown back on three sides and having by now decided that it was impossible to avoid encirclement, made off headlong for Got Gilmana, where, as mentioned, the Seventh Savari squadron was in position. The latter immediately launched itself at the rebel horsemen.

During the encounter, Omar el Muctar, who commanded the *door*, in an attempt to avoid death in battle—as had befallen the *caimacan* Fadil bu Omar the year before—in keeping with his old system of leaving behind a light covering formation to protect the withdrawal, tried to escape by hiding in a nearby region of bushland. The manoeuvre of the faithless rebel chief—who had so often used all his guile to set traps for our forces—did not go unnoticed by the Savari.

One of our native horsemen immediately caught up with him. The horse of the rebel leader had been injured, and Omar el Muctar no longer had any way out. He then tried desperately to play his last card, relying on his renown as an invincible commander—a reputation created over many years of ambushes and treacherous acts committed against Italy. Confronted by the Savari, he shouted out his name, in the unthinkable hope of avoiding his just punishment. Meanwhile, the violent and bloody encounter ended with our men victorious. Omar el Muctar, the unyielding traitor, last leader of the rebel brigands, who had assassinated our patrols and carried out raids on the *sottomessi*, was beaten.

The execution

Taken to Apollonia and from there to Benghazi, he was tried by Special Tribunal, convened in the hall of the Palazzo del Littorio, which had already accommodated—during the sorry times of weakness and bargaining—the famous Cyrenaican parliament, conceded by the Rome government prior to the arrival of Fascism.

The trial was swift but very clear and thorough. The old rebel chief admitted all the crimes with which he was charged: armed insurrection, treason, leading rebels, and innumerable others; and he stated that he fought for the glory of Senusiya—the xenophobic sect now driven from its last refuges in Cyrenaica—adding that in his actions he had followed the will of Allah.

The massacre of our soldiers and of natives loyal to Italy was unable to sustain his cynical behaviour throughout the trial. During the final speech of the public prosecutor and the reading of the sentence, he often displayed visible emotion, nor was this concealed on the execution scaffold. Condemned to death by hanging, he was executed the other day at Soluk, as already reported in yesterday's official communiqué.

Present at the hanging of Omar el Muctar were some 20,000 Bedouins and all the colony's political prisoners, who expressed their delight in the passing of the indomitable rebel, prime and sole cause of the present situation in Cyrenaica.

In order to let Italians understand and appreciate the difficulties of the guerilla war that we had to fight so as to crush the rebellion, and in order that they may properly evaluate the episode that has taken place, we now give briefly the relative facts concerning the repression of the rebel brigandry and the pacification of Cyrenaica after General Graziani became vice-governor of the colony.

Here is a list which says more than any assessment or comment: 17 battles, 151 clashes, 23 encounters from which the rebels sought immediate flight, with a total loss to them of 1411 men, 803 rifles, 6 pistols, 3 cannons and 3 machine-guns, plus 74 rifles surrendered. Losses of livestock 28,606 head, of which there were 21,459 sheep, 6399 camels, 673 horses and the rest cattle.

Here is the list of our own losses: 3 officers dead and 6 wounded, 121 ordinary soldiers killed and 228 wounded, 29 rifles lost, as well as about 3000 animals lost by the native population submitted to Italy as a result of rebel raids.

These cold figures give a general idea of the determination, the enthusiasm and the dedication shown by all our officers and troops in their tireless conduct of the struggle.

The proclamation to the rebels

After the execution of the condemned Omar el Muctar, H. E. Graziani, loyal representative of traditional Roman and Italian justice, issued the following proclamation which has today been scattered all over the Cyrenaican Gebel by aeroplanes:

'To the *duar* of Omar el Muctar! The lawless rebel chief Omar el Muctar, who for twenty years has brought us ruin and destruction, has been captured by the glorious troops of the Italian government and condemned to death by the Special Tribunal. This is God's punishment and the will of those poor people who thanks to him had to abandon their lands of origin.

'People of the *door*, I now warn you again, after the passing of this leader, that the powerful and generous Italian government will grant pardon to all

191

those who surrender immediately and give up their weapons. If you do not carry out the act of surrender, the government, as it has defeated Omar al Muctar, will sooner or later defeat all those who persist in the rebellion. Hear my words and submit to us.'

Now that the main protagonist of the Cyrenaican rebellion has disappeared from the scene, and the call has gone out to the surviving rebels for pacification and disarming of the region so as to pave the way for an era that is rich in toil and culture, the Fascist government is pursuing its calm and dignified policy, avoiding any return to the past and stating clearly its future will and responsibility.

D. M. Tuninetti.

II. Omar el Muktar, Hound of the Lord.

For many of us who cannot fail to admire the heroism even of our enemies, and who frequently give vent to such feelings even when pure logic tends to lead us to quite different conclusions, the figure of Omar el Muktar seems to us to be enveloped in a glow of legend, daring and epic achievement.

Omar el Muktar was always our enemy: an evil, mean, stubborn, implacable enemy.

Between our millenary civilization and all the human values that nourish our romantic sensibilities, between the beauty of our feelings directed as they are towards the most sublime goals, and this solitary highlander, sick with ferocious xenophobia, there was a deep, unbridgeable abyss; and whereas we, civilized people of our time, looked on him with the simple generosity of the brave, he nurtured his scornful ferocity.

Thus it was during his entire life, for he was born a slave, and acted as such throughout the best years of his youth; and he died a slave, having reduced to brutality those Senusi to whom he owed everything and to whom he devoted his whole adventurous life.

I do not think there can be any comparison in history between this fanatical chief and any other leader of men, not even if we go back to our own medieval period. Our captains of fortune were political men and, above all, logical men; and apart from the looting and ransacking, their followers were motivated by a mixture of impulses that were very much issues in their historical context and represented ideals totally in keeping with the times in which they lived.

Omar el Muktar was illogical and is thus far removed, very far removed from the historical climate of the modern era.

One realizes that there is no more negative example of isolation than his. He thrust away civilization and kept it at a distance, considering it dangerous, denying its adavantage for those of his race and religion, regarding any form of contact with us as unclean, whereas the entire Moslem world trades and lives with Europeans; even his masters, the Senusi, derived considerable benefit, in his time, from acceptance of the fact of our occupation of Libya.

The great nomadic chiefs of Tripolitania, including Ramadan Scetemi and Sef en Nasser, to mention no others with whom comparison is pointless, had earlier accepted our rule as an accomplished fact, taking it in their stride for as long as they could, whereas Omar el Muktar was savagely and determinedly against us from the day we set foot there until the end of his life as a dangling corpse on the gallows at Soluk.

He was therefore not a martyr to any cause because martyrs do not serve a master. By aiming too high, after doing immense harm to his people, he undoubtedly rendered very bad service to Senusiya and the Senusi.

If we calmly examine the life of this strangely ambitious individual and endeavour to trace the idealistic or mystical motives that presumably animated him, making him the absurd and inhuman Dominican that he was, we find in him the most salient qualities of the Bedouin highlander who was obstinate and fanatical to the point of self-destruction.

In fact, he chose as his kingdom the Gebel, driven by the same spirit as the great nomadic chiefs of Tripolitania who, having found refuge in the desert, considered they had solved the problem of their existence and their liberty because, in their view, the desert was beyond the bounds of the Europeans.

Omar el Muktar controlled the rugged, difficult, inaccessible mountain region, the terrible Cyrenaican Gebel, with its yawning ravines, its woods and tangled thickets, dense and dangerous, confident that we would never be able to quench the dazzling flames of the rebellion to which he had forced all the tribes to subscribe, by means of a system that could be described as 'industrialized guerilla warfare'. But whereas the great Tripolitanian nomad chiefs defended their rights of dominion over their people just as the ancient lords had defended their castles from the attacks of invaders, and proudly boasted themselves thieves, robbers and plunderers by reason of the age-old rights exercised by their ancestors to raid and rob and despoil the weak and the wretched, Omar el Muktar, poor as St Francis, despatched tithes to Saied Idris in Cairo, and waged war to enrich his old benefactors and masters.

The former deserve a certain degree of respect, while the old 'akuan' merits our scorn.

'I disdain and hate,' he once said to me at the time of the famous settlement in 1929, 'the people of Benghazi who, for their part, disdain and hate me.'

It is easy now, as it was easy for me then, to understand why the inhabitants of the coastal towns were lost to their master while the mountain Bedouins remained staunchly loyal vassals of Senusiya and paid both in money and kind.

The glib censors and glib critics, especially those versed in Oriental studies, protest to me that Senusiya offered the Bedouin tribes a body of religious ideals sufficient to justify the spirit of the rebellion.

This absurd notion has to be refuted immediately, and old Omar el Muktar was intelligent enough to recognize the absurdity, knowing his own people too well not to be amused at such westernized imbecilities.

The cowardly pack of Senusi found fertile ground in Cyrenaica, where they bred, lived and prospered, thanks to the miserably brutish conditions in which the tribes existed; the latter passively aquiesced to the bullying methods of the Senusi with their false religious trappings and all the familiar histrionics in which the Bedouins professed to believe for as long as it suited them.

It is worth pointing out, once and for all, that from 1922 onwards Senusiya was the focal point for all manner of malcontents and folk engaged in the shadiest of practices; it should be added, too, that the Senusi always exploited the tribes, and that the so-called 'night government' of Omar el Muktar existed solely for the collection of levies and tribute, and for the continual imposition of taxes by forcible blackmail and the cruel destruction of those camps where the 'cabile' had failed to comply with the orders of the taxmen and the agents responsible for recruiting men for the 'duar'.

In addition to all this there were intriguers at work, especially among the Zavia chiefs, and harsh financial exactions made all the easier by the characteristic conditions of the land, with no built-up areas, where the tribes could not protect themselves from the sun and had to submit to all the indecencies of the soldiers; whereas we, for many long years, had to accept a situation of compromise, always hoping that the light of reason would prevent the Senusi from totally exterminating the people, caught as they were between the anvil of obedience to our laws and the hammer of rebellion.

All Omar el Muktar's mysticism collapses before these clear considerations, and the aura of heroism that surrounded this 'fighter for the faith' is transformed into something quite wretched, especially bearing in mind the fact that the Senusi family was not a distant myth for the old 'akuan' (who was a part of it) but a shameful, everyday reality.

'I die for the faith,' he said as he climbed the scaffold and doubtless he said it in the hope that his voice would reach the tribes and that the most ambitious of his dreams would be realized, namely, in dying, to be worshipped as a saint.

Too late: the tribes remained impassive and indifferent to the man who had betrayed his own mission for good, bringing it to ruins in a furious and futile war.

He had gone beyond all bounds. Had we hanged him in 1923 we would have created a martyr: today we have eliminated a madman more dangerous to others than to himself.

Allah is just.

He fought against us for almost ten years and the only miracle he was able to achieve was to hold together the crafty organization of the rebellion, the strength of which was represented by the armed 'duar'.

The tiny army, which seldom amounted to more than a thousand men, was sufficiently powerful to exercise complete domination over the mountain tribes; and to be part of it conferred enormous prestige, no matter how cruel the discipline it imposed on its men.

This iron discipline was all the more easily applied inasmuch as the 'mohafdia'—or so-called soldiers of the faith—were regarded by us as outlaws to be executed if taken with weapons in hand, and thus had a special incentive to serve in the 'duar', where the extremely harsh life supplemented the natural marauding instinct that animates all Bedouins.

With his perfect understanding of the psychology and mentality of his followers, he never sought anything for himself and lived humbly and in great poverty, bequeathing the fruits of his raiding and plundering to his officers and men.

In happier times, at the beginning of every battle, when the first shots of our *ascari* broke the silence of the mountains, he would appear on his white horse among his men, letting the most fanatical of them risk their lives, pretending to lead them.

The fifty horsemen of his guard would then prevent him advancing and would eventually hand over their loot to him. This incident is typically Moslem: face was saved, and so too was skin.

Those who knew him well described him as arrogant and endowed with cold, sinister cynicism: he expressed himself in monosyllables and his very curt orders brooked no kind of argument. Some of his writings, relating to 'duties', which happened to fall into our hands, give us some idea of the man: 'In the name of merciful and compassionate God,' he wrote in 1928, 'I order you to visit Chief Salah el Tobgi and to bring me back his head.' The bearer, shot by us at Gialo, stated during his trial that he had carried out the order.

We know little of his early life, except that after his father had died during the pilgrimage to Mecca in the year 1224 of the Hegira (1877–8) he was commended, on the wish of his dying parent, to El Gariani, a prominent citizen of Benghazi, father of the elderly Sciaref El Gariani, who still lives in that city.

'My father and his sister,' says Sciaref, 'performed the duty of pilgrimage and returned with the mother of the dead man's children.'

He was thus sent to Giarabub, the Koranic school, by the El Gariani family, who belonged to the Senusi brotherhood, and although he himself came from a slave tribe—the Mnefa of eastern Marmarica—he was able to derive immense advantage from pursuing these Koranic studies.

According to Sciaref El Gariani: '. . . . he was not very intelligent and therefore did not manage to learn.' However, this statement contradicts the choice made by the 'akuan' of Giarabub, who sent him to Cufra after the Madhi, so that he could serve him.

During the three years that he stayed in the remote Sahara oasis, the death occurred of the Zavia chief of Gsur, a place in the Cyrenaican Gebel, in Abid territory, and Saied el Madhi appointed Omar el Muktar in his place. His career had started. The Senusi El Madhi had recognized the exceptional qualities of his servant, so much so that a few years afterwards, when he was due to leave for the Sudan, he recalled him so that he could take command of the tribes of the Wadi sent out to fight the French as a result of Senusi incitement. Omar el Muktar obeyed, fighting in southern Libya and then taking over the leadership of the Zavia of Ain Galacca, replacing their chief who had fallen in battle against the French.

After peace returned to the southern oases, he requested and was permitted to go back to Abid territory, and to his old Zavia at Gsur.

He fiercely opposed the Turks at the time they were occupying Libya, and it is recorded that the Ottoman officials had their work cut out to obtain, through him, payment of the taxes owed by the tribes under his jurisdiction.

By 1920 he was definitely against us, and from then on he commenced his pig-headed anti-Italian activity which he was to pursue to the bitter end.

At the time of our agreements with Senusiya, he maintained a contempt-uous attitude, although complying with the acrobatic policies of his lord, the Grand Senusi Idris, and in 1922, after pacts with Senusiya had been broken and the Grand Senusi had fled to Egypt, he was appointed leader of all the 'duar', a command he held until 11 September of last year, the day when he fell into our hands.

As soon as General Graziani landed in Benghazi, he issued a kind of challenge, openly declaring that the roads through the Gebel would never be built and involving his marauders in exploits that had never previously occurred, such as the destruction of telegraph and telephone lines. Empty boast. The first signs of the 'Graziani method' terrified him to such an extent that he was forced to admit, as he well knew, that it would have been better to have accepted Marshal Badoglio's open offer of loyalty than to have reverted to rebellion.

By now, however, it was too late. The Badoglio proclamation was perfectly clear and he had found an admirable interpreter in General Graziani, who immediately came to grips with the matter.

Nevertheless he waited and still hoped, for a whole year.

When the amazing migration began of the peoples of the Gebel towards the pasture zones of southern Benghazi, where our control was total, the old man was compelled to recognize that this was the beginning of the end.

The mountain region was depopulated. Where only a few days ago his tribes had been camping, there was now empty desert. He was quite powerless to halt the descent of the nomads towards the sea; down from the mountains and the vast woodlands came his Abid, the Abeidat from Dernino, the Dorsa, the Orfa, the loyal Brasa, the Hasa of Cyrene and even his own race from Marmarica, trekking in long enormous columns through the Gebel and towards the west in biblical disarray, taking with them their flocks and herds, their household goods and their tents.

The day came when he found himself alone on the deserted mountain. The shock must have been tremendous.

Here was the master of the Gebel, lord of the wilderness, king of the desert: his black banner might still flutter over the cemeteries that remained up there, but the measured song of the shepherds and rejoicing trills of the Bedouin women no longer greeted him as he passed by, only the harsh, strident howl of hyenas and the sinister barking of jackals.

But that was not enough: Graziani gave him no respite.

Each day, whatever the weather, under the dazzling heat of the August sun, in the teeth of the blinding, suffocating southern winds, and battered by the strong winter rains which transformed the clearings into slimy swamps and the 'uidian' into terrifying torrents, our troops dogged his heels implacably.

The legendary hero became a poor old fugitive, terrified by the roar of the engines of the aircraft that cruised over the barren Gebel, hunted like a wild beast from gorge to gorge, from wood to wood, from ravine to ravine.

He gave orders for the 'duar' to scatter in expectation of better times and let out an alarm cry to his lord; but the latter could not send any more cash because that damned Graziani had locked up the Zavia chiefs, put to death anyone paying a single coin in tithe and, terrible to relate, taken away the chiefs' salaries.

Saied Idris, his religious principles offended by this money business, the source of which was now dried up thanks to the fearful Graziani, mobilized the whole of Islam, the trumpets of the press blasting out from Cairo to Jerusalem, Beirut and Damascus, the alarm ringing loudly through all Islam, as far as the Dutch East Indies.

How vain and useless was this stupid hubbub.

Graziani responded with the barbed wire which, by closing the Egyptian frontier, removed Omar el Muktar's last hope of aid from Egyptian smugglers fleeing English rule.

The dark lie concerning Italian atrocities in Cyrenaica remained just that, and the drama of the rebellion rushed headlong into dark tragedy.

One fine day Fadil Bu Omar, administrator of the 'duar' and Omar el Muktar's second-in-command, was killed in battle; soon afterwards the old chief himself miraculously escaped from us and lost his spectacles, which were taken to Benghazi. On that same evening—I remember it well—H. E. Graziani showed them to me, saying: 'They are a foretaste; soon we will have the head.'

And he proved prophetic.

Dawn of 11 September, clear and luminous in the sky which the sun will later turn to mother-of-pearl.

Old Omar el Muktar, thin, haggard, aged, short-sighted and sad, heads for Apollonia to carry out a raid. Even he, general of the Gebel, lieutenant to the Grand Senusi Saied Idris, the 'Lord's Anointed', exhausted by hunger, has to get himself a sheep, at risk to his life. Sad fate. There are fifty horsemen with him, his most loyal men, his private escort.

The cavalcade proceeds slowly towards the tents of the Hasa: the lure.

Curse it! Is Allah now on Graziani's side? Suddenly there is shooting, cracking out in flashes of dazzling light from every bush: the *ascari*.

The old man makes a run for it, galloping as swiftly as the wind towards the wood while the plane quickly dives low, spots him, veers away and then comes back, as the shots are now aimed at the horses, crazed with terror.

The tragic old man is still trying to escape, this time towards Scenescen, to the tangled woodland of dwarf junipers and crowded, blackish mastics; but now the terrible armoured cars hem him in and drive him in the direction of our last position, the 'savari' of the Seventh Squadron.

They lie in wait at the gap for the tiny band, reduced now to some fifteen horsemen on steeds covered in sweat, panting and exhausted; and as soon as they are in range they are mown down by a terrible, precise and deadly fusillade.

Omar el Muktar's horse, fatally hit, stumbles and falls to its knees, throwing the old 'akuan' to the ground.

He gets up, starts to run and reaches a bush; but by now the 'savari' attack has hit home, and he watches motionless as his men are killed, having been stopped dead in their tracks, aghast at the end of their leader.

One of the 'savari', a Libyan, of the same race and religion, points the rifle at his chest, ready to finish him off in a flash.

'I am Omar el Muktar,' he shouts. It is all over!

Sandro Sandri

LIST OF NEWSPAPERS AND REVIEWS CARRYING NEWS OF THE CAPTURE, TRIAL AND EXECUTION OF OMAR EL MUKHTAR

"L'Arena", Verona, 16 September 1931, *Brillanti azioni d'armi in Cirenaica*.

"L'Arena", Verona, 17 September 1931, *Il traditore Omar el Muktar giustiziato a Bengasi*.

"L'Avanti!", Paris, a. XXXVI, n, 34, 27 September 1931, *Dalla galera fascista. Un altro martire*.

"L'Avvenire d'Italia", Bologna, 16 September 1931, *La cattura del capo dei ribelli cirenaici*.

"L'Avvenire d'Italia", Bologna, 18 September 1931, *La fine dell'ultimo capo dei ribelli cirenaici*.

"L'Azione coloniale", 20 September 1931, *La cattura e la fucilazione del ribelle Omar el Muctar*.

"L'Azione coloniale", 1 October 1931, *Il reticolato ha vinto la ribellione in Cirenaica*.

"La Cirenaica", Benghazi, 12 September 1931, *La politica coloniale italiana nel giudizio degli stranieri*.

"La Cirenaica", Benghazi, 16 September 1931, *Omar el Muctar, il capo della ribellione senussita in Cirenaica catturato*.

"La Cirenaica", Benghazi, 17 September 1931, *La condanna a morte di Omar el Muctar*.

"La Cirenaica", Benghazi, 18 September 1931, *Per la pacificazione definitiva della Cirenaica*.

"La Cirenaica", Benghazi, 23 September 1931, *Omar el Muchtar, cane del Signore*.

"La Cirenaica", Benghazi, 10 October, *La funzione del reticolato nello stroncamento della ribellione cirenaica*.

"La Cirenaica", Benghazi, 16 December 1931, *L'agonia della ribellione cirenaica*.

"La Cirenaica", Benghazi, 27 December 1931, *Agonia della ribellione cirenaica*.

"La Correspondance Internationale", 14 November 1931.

"Corriere della Sera", Milan, 16 September 1931, *La cattura di Omar el Muktar il capo dei ribelli della Cirenaica*.

"Corriere della Sera", Milan, 17 September 1931, *Omar el Muktar giustiziato. Come avvenna la cattura*.

"Corriere della Sera", Milan, 17 September 1931, *Omar el Muktar giustiziato . . . Un commento britannico*.

"Corriere del Tirreno", Leghorn, 15 September 1931, *Il capo dei ribelli della Cirenaica catturato dopo una brillante azione notturna*.

"Corriere del Tirreno", Leghorn, 19 September 1931, *Come è caduto nella rete di Graziani il capo dei ribelli della Senussia*.

"Corriere Emiliano", Parma, 16 September 1931, *Il capo della ribellione senussita catturato*.

"Corriere Emiliano", Parma, 17 September 1931, *Il traditore Omar el Muctar giustiziato*.

"Corriere Mercantile", Genoa, 15 September 1931, *La cattura del capo delegato della Senussia (sic)*.

"Cronaco Prealpina", Varese, 16 September 1931, *Il capo dei ribelli cirenaici è stato arrestato*.

"Cronaca Prealpina", Varese, 24 September 1931, *Scech Omar el Muktar.*
"L'Eco di Bergamo" Bergamo, 18 September 1931, *Omar el Muctar è stato fucilato.*
"La Gazzetta", Messina, 16 September 1931, *Omar el Muktar capo della Senussia catturato da uno squadrone di Savari cirenaici.*
"La Gazzetta", Messina, 17 September 1931, *Omar el Muctar giustiziato.*
"La Gazzetta", Messina, 18 September 1931, *Pronta inesorabile giustizia contro il traditore Omar el Muctar.*
"La Gazzetta", Messina, 29 September 1931, *Con la morte di Muctar la Cirenaica è pacificata.*
"La Gazzetta del Popolo", Turin, 16 September 1931, *Il capo della ribellione senussita catturato dai savari.*
"La Gazzetta del Popolo", Turin, 17 September 1931, *Omar el Muctar è stato giustiziato.*
"La Gazzetta del Popolo", Turin, 18 September 1931, *Il cerchio di ferro di Graziani si stringe attorno agli ultimi ribelli.*
"La Gazzetta del Mezzogiorno", Bari, 16 September 1931, *Il capo dei ribelli cirenaici catturato dalle nostre truppe.*
"La Gazzetta del Mezzogiorno", Bari, 18 September 1931, *Il passato di Omar el Muctar.*
"Gazzetta di Venezia", Venice, 16 September 1931, *La cattura di Omar el Muctar capo dei ribelli del Gebel cirenaico.*
"Gazzetta di Venezia", Venice, 17 September 1931, *La condanna a morte e l'esecuzione di Omar el Muctar.*
"Il Gazzettino", Venice, 16 September 1931, *Vittoriosa azione in Cirenaica contro bande di predoni: il capo della ribellione catturato.*
"Il Gazzettino", Venice, 17 September 1931, *Traditore giustiziato.*
"Gerarchia", a. IX, n. 9, September 1931.
"Giornale di Genova" Genoa, 16 September 1931, *Il capo della ribellione senussita catturato.*
"Il Giornale di Genova", Genoa, 17 September 1931, *Omar el Muctar condannato a morte.*
"Il Giornale di Genova" Genoa, 20 September 1931, *La morte senza gloria di Omar el Muctar.*
"Il Giornale di Sicilia", 16 September 1931, *La cattura di El Muctar.*
"Il Giornale di Sicilia", 17 September 1931, *El Muctar impiccato a Soluk.*
"Il Giornale d'Italia", Rome, 16 September 1931, *Il capo della ribellione in Cirenaica catturato da un nostro squadrone di savari.*
"Il Giornale d'Italia", Rome, 18 September 1931, *Il capo dei ribelli della Cirenaica è stato giustiziato presso Bengasi.*
"L'Italia", Milan, 16 September 1931, *Brillanti azioni militari: il capo dei ribelli catturato.*
"L'Italia", Milan, 17 September 1931, *Omar el Muctar è stato giustiziato.*
"L'Italia coloniale", n. 10, October 1931, *La fine di Omar el Muktar.*
"L'italie", Rome, 15 September 1931, *Une brillante action de nos troupes en Cyrénaïque.*
"L'Italie", Rome, 18 September 1931, *Omar el Muctar condamné à la peine capitale. L'execution de la sentence.*
"Il Lavoro" Genoa, 16 September 1931, *La cattura di Omar el Muctar il vecchio capo di tutte le ribellioni della colonia.*
"Il Lavoro", Genoa, 17 September 1931, *Il Senusso Omar el Muktar condannato alla pena capitale.*
"Il Lavoro fascista", Rome, 16 September 1931, *La cattura in Cirenaica del delegato della Senussia.*

"Il Lavoro fascista", Rome, 18 September 1931, *Il ribelle e traditore Omar el Muctar è stato processato e fucilato ieri.*

"Il Mattino", Naples, 16–17 September 1931, *Il capo dei ribelli in Cirenaica catturato.*

"Il Messaggero" Rome, 16 September 1931, *La cattura di Omar el Muktar, capo dei ribelli della Cirenaica.*

"Il Messaggero", Rome, 17 September 1931, *Omar el Muktar è stato giustiziato.*

"La Nazione", Florence, 16 September 1931, *Il cap dei ribelli in Cirenaica catturato dalle nostre truppe.*

"La Nazione", Florence, 17 September 1931, *Omar el Muctar il senusso traditore è stato condannato a morte e giustiziato.*

"La Nazione", Florence, 19 September 1931, *Il proclama di Graziani agli ultimi ribelli.*

"Il Nuovo cittadino" Genoa, 16 September 1931, *Il capo della ribellione senussita catturato in Cirenaica dalle nostre truppe.*

"Il Nuovo cittadino". Genoa, 17 September 1931, *Omar el Muctar è stato fucilato ieri.*

"Il Nuovo Giornale", Florence, 16 September 1931, *Il capo dei ribelli della Cirenaica catturato dopo una brillante offensiva.*

"Il Nuovo Giornale", Florence, 18 September 1931, *La pacificazione della Cirenaica dopo la scomparsa di Omar el Muctar.*

"L'Oltremare", n. 10, October 1931, *La fine di Omar el Muktar nei commenti stranieri.*

"L'Ora", Palermo, 17 September 1931, *Omar el Muctar capo dei ribelli cirenaici catturato dopo brillante combattimento.*

"L'Ora", Palermo, 17–18 September 1931, *Omar el Muctar giustiziato a Soluch.*

"L'Ordine", Como, 16 September 1931, *Brillante operazione in Cirenaica.*

"L'Ordine", Como, 17 September 1931, *Il capo dei ribelli cirenaici catturato dalle nostre truppe.*

"Il Piccolo", Rome, 17–18 September 1931, *Il capo dei ribelli senussiti condannato a morte.*

"Il Piccolo" Trieste, 16 September 1931, *La cattura di Omar el Muctar capo della Senussia in Cirenaica.*

"Il Piccolo", Trieste, 17 September 1931, *Omar el Muctar giustiziato.*

"Il Piccolo", Trieste, 20 September 1931, *Un proclama del gen. Graziani dopo l'esecuzione di Omar el Muctar.*

"Il Popolo di Brescia", Brescia, 16 September 1931, *Il capo della ribellione Omar el Muctar catturato dalle nostre truppe.*

"Il Popolo di Brescia", Brescia, 17 September 1931, *Omar el Muctar giustiziato a Soluch.*

"Il Popolo di Brescia", Brescia, 19 September 1931, *Il cerchio di ferro si stringe intorno ai ribelli.*

"Il Popolo d'Italia", Milan, 16 September 1931, *Omar el Muctar, capo dei ribelli, fatto prigioniero.*

"Il Popolo d'Italia", Milan, 17 September 1931, *Omar el Muctar giustiziato.*

"Il Popolo d'Italia", Milan, 19 September 1931, *La ribellione in Cirenaica energicamente stroncata. Come Omar el Muctar torturatore dei nostri soldati, è stato catturato e giustiziato.*

"Il Popolo di Roma", Rome, 16 September 1931, *La cattura di Omar el Muktar. Dodici armati ribelli rimasti sul terreno.*

"Il Popolo di Roma", Rome, 17 September 1931, *Il ribelle e traditore Omar el Muktar condannato a morte: la sentenza è stata eseguita.*

"Il Popolo di Sicilia", Catania, 16 September 1931, *Il capo dei ribelli catturato dalle nostre truppe in Cirenaica, la caduta di un mito.*

"Il Popolo di Sicilia", Catania, 17 September 1931, *Omar el Muctar condannato a morte e giustiziato.*

"Il Popolo Toscano", Lucca, 16 September 1931, *Omar el Muctar ultimo ed andace ribelle della Cirenaica catturato dai nostri savari in una brillante azione verso Slonta.*

"Il Popolo Toscano", Lucca, 17 September 1931, *Omar el Muctar giustiziato a Soluch.*

"Il Popolo di Trieste", Trieste, 16 September 1931, *Un terribile a fiero nemico catturato nella trappola del gen. Graziani.*

"Il Popolo di Trieste", Trieste, 17 September 1931, *Omar el Muctar il traditore capo ribelle è stato giustiziato alla presenza di trentamila arabi sottomessi.*

"Il Popolo di Trieste", Trieste, 18 September 1931, *Pacificazione fascista della Cirenaica.*

"La Provincia di Bolzano", Bolzano, 16 September 1931, *Il capo della ribellione senussita catturato.*

"La Provincia di Bolzano", Bolzano, 17 September 1931, *Omar el Muctar fucilato.*

"La provincia di Bolzano", Bolzano, 19 September 1931, *La pacificazione della Cirenaica dopo la scomparsa di Omar el Muctar.*

"La Provincia di Como", Como, 16 September 1931, *Il capo della ribellione cirenaica catturato dai 'savari'.*

"La Provincia di Como" Como, 17 September 1931, *Omar el Muctar è stato giustiziato ieri.*

"La Provincia di Padova", Padua, 15 September 1931, *Brillante azione di polizia in Cirenaica.*

"La Provincia di Padova", Padua, 17 September 1931, *La condanna a morte e l'esecuzione di Omar el Muctar.*

"La provincia di Padova", Padua, 19–20 September 1931, *Come fu catturato Omar el Muctar.*

"Il Regime fascista", Cremona, 16 September 1931, *Il capo dei ribelli catturato.*

"Il Regime fascista", Cremona, 17 September 1931, *Omar el Muctar condannato a morte.*

"Il Regime fascista", Cremona, 20 September 1931, *Come Omar el Muctar ha espiato. Un proclama lanciato sul Gebel.*

"Il Resto del Carlino--, Bologna, 16 September 1931, *Il capo dei ribelli cirenaici catturato dalle nostre truppe.*

"Il Resto del Carlino". Bologna, 17 September 1931, *Omar el Muctar giustiziato.*

"Il Resto del Carlino" Bologna, 18 September 1931, *La pacificazione della Cirenaica dopo la scomparsa di Omar el Muctar.*

"Ribista delle colonie italiane", a. V, n. 10, October 1931 (voce Cirenaica della rubrica Cronache coloniali, *La cattura di Omar el Muktar*).

"Il Roma", Naples, 16 September 1931, *Il capo dei ribelli e delegato della Senussia catturato dalle nostre truppe in Cirenaica.*

"Il Roma", Naples, 17 September 1931, *Omar el Muctar il capo dei ribelli della Cirenaica è stato giustiziato ieri a Soluch.*

"Il Secolo XIX", Genoa, 16 September 1931, *Il capo della ribellione cirenaica catturato dopo brillante azione.*

"Il Secolo XIX", Genoa, 17 September 1931, *Omar el Muctar condannato a morte: la sentenza è stata eseguita.*

"Sentinella d'Italia", Cuneo, 16–17 September 1931, *La cattura di Omar el Muktar capo dei ribelli senussit.*

"Sentienilla d'Italia", Cuneo, 17–18 September 1931, *Omar el Muktar è stato fucilato.*

"Sentinella d'Italia", Cuneo, 19 September 1931, *La fine di un mito.*

"La Sera", Milan, 16 September 1931, *Il capo della ribellione senussita catturato.*

"Il Solco Fascista", Reggio Emilia, 16 September 1931, *Il capo dei ribelli catturato a Slonta.*

"Il Solco Fascista", Reggio Emilia, 17 September 1931, *Omar el Muctar è stato giustiziato.*

"La Stampa", Turin, 16 September 1931, *Omar el Muctar catturato da un reparto di savari cirenaici.*

"La Stampa", Turin, 17 September 1931, *Omar el Muctar è stato fucilato.*

"La Stampa", Turin, 19 September 1931, *I superstiti ribelli della Cirenaica invitati alla sottomissione da S.E. Graziani.*

"Il Telegrafo", Leghorn, 16 September 1931, *Il capo dei ribelli della Cirenaica catturato dopo brillante azione notturna.*

"Il Telegrafo", Leghorn, 17 September 1931, *Il capo ribelle Omar el Muktar giustiziato davanti a 30.000 indigeni.*

"Il Tevere", Rome, 16–17 September 1931, *La cattura di Omar el Muctar capo dei ribelli in Cirenaica.*

"Il Tevere", Rome, 17 September 1931, *Omar el Muctar è stato giustiziato ieri mattina.*

"La Tribuna", Rome, 17 September 1931, *Il capo della Ribellione senussita catturato dalle nostre truppe.*

"La Tribuna", Rome, 19 September 1931, *Come fu catturato Omar el Muctar.*

"L'Unione Sarda", Cagliari, 16 September 1931, *Il capo della ribellione cirenaica catturato dalle nostre truppe.*

"L'Unione Sarda", Cagliari, 17 September 1931, Il ribelle cirenaico condannato a morte.

"L'Unione Sarda", Cagliari, 25 September 1931, *Dopa la caduta di Omar el Muctar in vibrante ordine del giorno di S.E. Graziani alle truppe.*

"La Vendetta fascista", Vicenza, 16 September 1931, *Il capo senussita Omar el Muctar catturato in Cirenaica.*

"La Vendetta fascista", Vicenza, 17 September 1931, *Il capo senussita Omar el Muctar fucilato a Soluch.*

"Il Veneto", Padua, 16–17 September 1931, *La cattura del capo dei ribelli del Gebel cirenaico.*

"Il Veneto", Padua, 17–18 September 1931, *Omar el Muctar giustiziato.*

"La Voce di Bergamo", Bergamo, 17 September 1931, *Il capo senusso traditore e ribelle è stato fucilato.*

"La Voce di Mantova", Mantua, 16 September 1931, *Brillante azione bellica dei savari in Cirenaica.*

"La Voce di Mantova", Mantua, 17 September 1931, *Il capo della ribellione senussita condannato e ginstiziato.*

INDEX